BIOGRAPHY OF WORLD GREAT POLITICAL SCIENTISTS

BIOGRAPHY OF WORLD GREAT POLITICAL SCIENTISTS

G.K..Pagare

CYBER TECH PUBLICATIONS
4264/3, Ansari Road, Daryaganj, New Delhi-110002 (India)
Ph.: 011-23244078, 011-43559448 Fax: 011-23280028
E-Mail: cyberpublicationsdelhi@yahoo.com
Website: www.cybertechpublications.com

BIOGRAPHY OF WORLD GREAT POLITICAL SCIENTISTS

G.K. Pagare

First Edition 2010

Published by :

G.S. Rawat for **Cyber Tech Publications**
4264/3, Ansari Road, Daryaganj, New Delhi-110002 (India)
Ph.: 011-23244078, 011-43559448 Fax: 011-23280028
E-Mail: cyberpublicationsdelhi@yahoo.com
Website: www.cybertechpublications.com

Printed at: Asian Offset Printers, Delhi-53

Preface

Over the centuries, scientists made great discoveries that impacted on our daily lives. Many of their efforts however were in areas we don't recognise as touching us, but which actually do. Often their struggles went unsung. The author has selected the men and women he considers have had the greatest impact on us, based on their ability to come up with new theories and the significance of their discoveries. His jargon-free biographies introduce the characters and controversies behind the scenes in a refreshing manner that is certain to appeal.

This book contains biographies of people who, the author believes had an impact on us. This book introduces the characters and controversies behind the scenes.

— *Author*

CONTENTS

Biography of World Great Political Scientists

ANTONINO ZICHICHI

Antonino Zichichi (born October 15, 1929) is an Italian physicist who has worked in the field of nuclear physics.

Biography

Zichichi was born in Trapani, Sicily, in 1929. He has collaborated to several important discoveries in the field of subnuclear physics and has worked in some of the most important research laboratories in the world (Fermilab in Chicago, CERN in Geneva, etc.). He is known to the Italian public, above all, for his popularizations of scientific ideas, both as the author of numerous books and essays and because of his appearances on television programmes of RAI television. In this work of popularization, the Sicilian scientist places great emphasis, above all, on trying to demonstrate that there is no contrast between science and the Catholic faith in which he strongly believes. In 1963 he founded the *Centro Ettore Majorana* of Erice, dedicated to scientific culture.

He has been president of the Istituto Nazionale di Fisica Nucleare from 1977 up to 1982 and in 1980 he strongly backed the creation of the Laboratori Nazionali del Gran Sasso. Currently, he is an emeritus professor of physics at the University of Bologna. He is president of the World Federation of Scientists, an organization concerned with the fight against planetary emergencies.

Zichichi was at the centre of a diplomatic incident during the elections for director of CERN: a letter from the Ministry of

Research nominated him for the post, since there was an informal rotation of seats taking place. But the pressure brought to bear on the part of Italy in favour of Zichichi caused a sharp break at CERN between Italy and the supporters of other candidates. The candidacy of Zichichi was rejected by 12 votes and a German, Herwig F. Schopper, was elected in his place. The Italian government threatened to retaliate by cutting its funding of CERN, passing to the status of non-contributing observer nation.

Another controversial incident involving Zichichi concerned a Eucharistic pantomime which took place at Aquila, where a chorus of students begged Zichichi to explain the mysteries of the atom, after which there followed a conference. The episode caused another rupture: he was sharply criticized by one large section of the University heads, and appreciated by another, with the particular support of the leaders of the Christian Democrats, the party to which Zichichi was always tied.

In his essay *L'irresistibile fascino del tempo* ("The Irresistible Fascination of Time") he cites the rule of the "Perfect Calendar" in an attempt to improve on the Gregorian Calendar by eliminating three days every 10,000 years. In this system, the days of the year are 365, plus one every four years, minus three every four centuries, and minus three every 10,000 years. Zichichi therefore accepts the idea of not considering as leap years the years 4,000, 8,000 and 12,000 which, according to the Gregorian calendar, would be. It should be recalled that the definition of a high-precision calendar (superior to the Gregorian) has been studied at various times and places: in particular, the Persian calendar defined in the 11th century is very precise.

ALVIN M. WEINBERG

Alvin Martin Weinberg (April 20, 1915-October 18, 2006) was a nuclear physicist and administrator at Oak Ridge National Laboratory (ORNL). He came to Oak Ridge, Tennessee in 1945 and remained there until his death in 2006.

Early Years in Chicago

Alvin Weinberg was born April 20th, 1915 in Chicago, Illinois. He received his Ph.D. from the University of Chicago in mathematical biophysics in 1939. He then worked at the Metallurgical Laboratory at the University of Chicago until the war intervened. He then went to work at a newly formed laboratory in Oak Ridge, Tennessee.

Work at Oak Ridge

He served as director of Oak Ridge National Laboratory's Physics Division from 1945 until 1948, when he became Research Director for the laboratory. He was named director of the laboratory in 1955. Weinberg often sat in the front row at ORNL division information meetings and ask the first, often a very penetrating, question after each scientific talk. For young scientists giving their first presentation, the experience could be frightening but was also exciting and stimulating. When asked how he found the time to attend every meeting, Weinberg replied jokingly, "We didn't have a DOE in those days." Weinberg had the Materials Testing Reactor converted into a mock-up of a real reactor called the Low Intensity Test Reactor (LITR), or the "Poor Man's Pile." Experiments at the LITR led to the design of both pressurized-water and boiling-water nuclear reactors, which have since become the dominant reactor types in commercial nuclear power plants.

In the late 1940s Weinberg asked ORNL's reactor engineers to design a reactor using fluid fuel instead of solid fuel. This Homogeneous Reactor Experiment (HRE) was affectionately dubbed "Alvin's 3P reactor" because it required a pot, a pipe, and a pump. The HRE went into operation in 1950 and at the criticality party Weinberg brought the appropriate spirits: "When piles go critical in Chicago, we celebrate with wine. When piles go critical in Tennessee, we celebrate with Jack Daniel's." The HRE operated for 105 days before it was closed down. Weinberg even invited Senator Jack Kennedy and Senator Albert Gore, Sr. to visit the reactor, but to no avail. Nevertheless, information was still gained from operation of the HRE.

Weinberg's next project, the Molten Salt Reactor Experiment, set a record for continuous operation and was the first to use uranium-233 as fuel. It was known as the "chemist's reactor" because so many of the problems which cropped up were chemical ones.

Under Weinberg's tenure as director, ORNL's Biology Division grew to five times the size of the next largest division. This division was charged with understanding how ionizing radiation interacts with living things and to try and find ways to help them survive radiation damage, such as bone marrow transplants. In the 1960s Weinberg He also pursued new missions for ORNL, such as using nuclear energy to desalinate seawater. He recruited Philip Hammond from Los Alamos to further this mission and in 1970 started the first big ecology project in the United States: the National Science Foundation-Research Applied to National Needs Environmental Programme.

In 1958 Weinberg published *The Physical Theory of Neutron Chain Reactors* with Nobel Laureate Eugene Wigner. It was destined to become a classic in the field. He was elected president of the American Nuclear Society in 1959 and began service on President's Science Advisory Committee the following year. In 1965 he was appointed vice president of the Union Carbide Corporation's Nuclear Division. Weinberg retired from ORNL in 1973 after 18 years as the lab's director.

Washington and ORAU

Weinberg was named director of the U.S. Office of Energy Research and Development in Washington, D.C. in 1974. The following year he founded and became the first director of Institute for Energy Analysis at Oak Ridge Associated Universities (ORAU). This institute focused on evaluating alternatives for meeting future energy requirements. From 1976 to 1984, the Institute for Energy Analysis was a centre for study of diverse issues related to carbon dioxide and global climate. Weinberg worked at ORAU until retiring to become an ORAU distinguished fellow in 1985.

Retirement

Weinberg remained active in retirement. In 1992 he was named chairman of the International Friendship Bell Committee, which arranged for the installation of a Japanese bell in Oak Ridge. He also called for strengthening of the International Atomic Energy Agency and systems to defend against nuclear weapons.

ARNOLD SOMMERFELD

Arnold Johannes Wilhelm Sommerfeld (December 5, 1868 – April 26, 1951) was a German theoretical physicist who pioneered developments in atomic and quantum physics, and also educated and groomed a large number of students for the new era of theoretical physics. He introduced the fine-structure constant into quantum mechanics.

Education

Sommerfeld studied mathematics and physical sciences at the Albertina University of his native city, Konigsberg, East Prussia. His dissertation advisor was the mathematician Ferdinand von Lindemann, and he also benefited from classes with mathematicians Adolph Hurwitz and David Hilbert, and physicist Emil Wiechert. His participation in the student fraternity Deutsche Burschenschaft resulted in a fencing scar on his face. He received his Ph.D. in 1891. After receiving his doctorate, Sommerfeld remained at Konigsberg to work on his teaching diploma. He passed the national exam in 1892 and then began a year of military service, which was done with the reserve regiment in Konigsberg. He completed his obligatory military service in September 1893, and for the next eight years continued voluntary eight-week military service. With his turned up moustache, his physical build, his Prussian bearing, and the fencing scar on his face, he gave the impression of being a colonel in the hussars.

Career

In October, Sommerfeld went to the University of Gottingen, which was the centre of mathematics in Germany. There, he became assistant to Theodor Liebisch, at the Mineralogical Institute, through a fortunate personal contact-Liebisch had been a professor at the University of Konigsberg and a friend of the Sommerfeld family.

In September 1894, Sommerfeld became Felix Klein's assistant, which included taking comprehensive notes during Klein's lectures and writing them up for the Mathematics Reading Room, as well as managing the reading room. Sommerfeld's Habilitationsschrift was completed under Klein, in 1895, which allowed Sommerfeld to become a Privatdozent at Gottingen. As a Privatdozent, Sommerfeld lectured on a wide range of mathematical and mathematical physics topics. His lectures on partial differential equations were first offered at Gottingen, and they evolved over his teaching career to become Volume VI of his textbook series *Lectures on Theoretical Physics*, under the title *Partial Differential Equations in Physics.*

Lectures by Klein in 1895 and 1896 on rotating bodies led Klein and Sommerfeld to write a four-volume text *Die Theorie des Kreisels* – a 13-year collaboration, 1897-1910. The first two volumes were on theory, and the latter two were on applications in geophysics, astronomy, and technology. The association Sommerfeld had with Klein influenced Sommerfeld's turn of mind to applied mathematics and in the art of lecturing.

While at Gottingen, Sommerfeld met Johanna Hopfner, daughter of Ernst Hopfner, curator at Gottingen. In October, 1897 Sommerfeld began the appointment to the Chair of Mathematics at the Bergakademie in Clausthal-Zellerfeld; he was successor to Wilhelm Wien. This appointment provided enough income to eventually marry Johanna. At Klein's request, Sommerfeld took on the position of editor of Volume V of *Encyklopadie der mathematischen Wissenschaften*; it was a major undertaking which lasted from 1898 to 1926.

ALEXEI SMIRNOV

Alexei Yu Smirnov is one of the world's leading researchers in the Neutrino Physics (as one of the founders of the MSW Effect).

Education

Alexei Smirnov graduated from Moscow State University in 1974. In 1977 he began working at the Institute for Nuclear Research (INR) of the Academy of Sciences of the USSR where he received his Ph.D. in 1979. In 1989 he received a degree of Doctor of Physical and Mathematical sciences. He also taught at the physics department of Moscow State University from 1982 to 1990.

Smirnov joined the International Centre for Theoretical Physics, ICTP (Trieste, Italy) in 1992 as a staff-associate while continuing his affiliation with INR (Moscow) as a leading research scientist. He became a staff member with ICTP in 1997 and presently holds the position of principal research scientist.

Research and Achievements

The main area of Smirnov's research is neutrino physics and astrophysics. In 1984-1985, following earlier work by Lincoln Wolfenstein, Smirnov, together with Stanislav Mikheyev, uncovered effects of resonance enhancement of neutrino oscillations in matter and the adiabatic conversion in non-uniform media (the MSW-effect). Solutions to the solar neutrino problem based on the MSW effect have been proposed. The effects were also applied to supernova neutrinos and neutrinos of various origins propagating in the Earth.

In the following years Smirnov and his colleagues developed a number of aspects of theory and phenomenology of neutrino conversion in various media. Currently Smirnov is working on implications of the obtained neutrino results for fundamental physics (quark-lepton complementarity, unification, etc.) as well as on future programmes of studies in neutrino physics.

Alexei Smirnov is a co-recipient of the 2006 Bruno Pontecorvo Prize. He was being honoured "for his prediction and study of the influence of matter on neutrino oscillations", which is known as the MSW effect. He has been named a Humboldt Research Fellow, one of Germany's most prestigious awards in science. Smirnov was honoured for his lifetime achievements in physics. The award enables outstanding scientists and scholars from abroad to spend up to six months at the Humboldt Institute to carry out research on projects of their own choosing. Recently Alexei Smirnov with Stanislav Mikheyev have been awarded the 2008 J. J. Sakurai Prize "for pioneering and influential work on the enhancement of neutrino oscillations in matter, which is essential to a quantitative understanding of the solar neutrino flux".

Smirnov is an editor of journals JHEP and JCAP and a divisional associate editor for Physical Review Letters. His awards and honours include the Biedenharn endowed chair in physics (University of Texas, Austin, 2002), the award of the Japanese Society for promotion of science (2004), the Alexander von Humboldt research award (2004), the Bruno Pontecorvo prize (2005), and the Schroedinger guest professorship (Vienna, 2007).

ARTHUR LEONARD SCHAWLOW

Arthur Leonard Schawlow (May 5, 1921 – April 28, 1999) was an American physicist. He is best remembered for his work on lasers, for which he was awarded a 1981 Nobel Prize.

Biography

His mother, Helen Mason, was from Canada and his father, Arthur Schawlow, was an immigrant from Latvia. When Arthur was three years old, they moved to Toronto, Canada. At the age of 16 he completed high school and received a scholarship in science at the University of Toronto. After earning his undergraduate degree Schawlow continued in graduate school at the University of Toronto which was interrupted due to World War II. At the end of the war he began work on his Ph.D at U of T with Professor Malcolm Crawford. He then took a postdoctoral position with Charles Townes at the physics department of Columbia University in the fall of 1949.

In 1951 he married Aurelia Townes, younger sister to Charles Townes, and together they had three children; Arthur Jr., Helen, and Edith. Arthur Jr. was autistic, with very little speech ability. He considered himself to be an orthodox Protestant Christian and attended a Methodist Church. He went on to accepted a position at Bell Labs in late 1951. He left in 1961 to join the faculty at Stanford University as a professor. He remained until he retired to emeritus status in 1996.

Schawlow and Professor Robert Hofstadter at Stanford, who also had an autistic child, teamed up to help each other find solutions to the condition. Arthur Jr. was put in a special centre for autistic individuals, and later Schawlow put together an institution to care for people with autism in Paradise, California. It was later named the Arthur Schawlow Centre in 1999, shortly before his death.

Schawlow was a promoter of the controversial method of facilitated communication with patients of autism.

Although his research focused on optics, in particular, lasers and their use in spectroscopy, he also pursued investigations in the areas of superconductivity and nuclear resonance. Schawlow shared the 1981 Nobel Prize in Physics with Nicolaas Bloembergen and Kai Siegbahn for their contributions to the development of laser spectroscopy.

Schawlow coauthored *Microwave Spectroscopy* (1955) with Charles Townes. Also with Townes, they prepared a much disputed, by Gordon Gould, laser patent filed by Bell Labs in 1958. In 1991 the NEC Corporation and the American Physical Society established a prize: the Arthur L. Schawlow Prize in Laser Science. The prize is awarded annually to "candidates who have made outstanding contributions to basic research using lasers."

Schawlow was born in Mount Vernon, New York and died of leukemia in Palo Alto, California. He is survived by Cleo and Thomasina Johnson and Andy, Rachel, and Colin Dwan.

ABDUS SALAM

Abdus Salam (January 29, 1926; Jhang Punjab – November 21, 1996; Oxford, England) was a Pakistani theoretical physicist and Nobel laureate in Physics for his work in Electro-Weak Theory.

Salam, Sheldon Glashow and Steven Weinberg shared the prize for this discovery. Salam holds the distinction of being the first Pakistani Nobel Laureate, and was the first Muslim Nobel Laureate in science. The validity of the theory was ascertained through experiments carried out at the Super Proton Synchrotron facility at CERN in Geneva, particularly, through the discovery of the W and Z Bosons.

Biography

Salam's father was an official in the Department of Education in a poor farming district. His family has a long tradition of piety and learning. At the age of just fourteen, Salam scored the highest marks ever recorded for the Matriculation Examination at the University of the Punjab. He won a scholarship to the Government College, University of the Punjab, in Lahore. As a fourth-year student there, he published his work on Srinivasa Ramanujan.. He took his master's degree at the Government College in 1946. That same year, he was awarded a scholarship to St. John's College, Cambridge University, where he took a BA degree with Double First-Class Honours in Mathematics and Physics in 1949. In 1950, he received the Smith's Prize from Cambridge University for the most outstanding pre-doctoral contribution to Physics.

He obtained a PhD degree in Theoretical Physics at Cambridge. His doctoral thesis contained fundamental work in Quantum Electrodynamics. By the time it was published in 1951, it had already gained him an international reputation and the Adams Prize.

ARNO ALLAN PENZIAS

Arno Allan Penzias (born April 26, 1933) is an American physicist and Nobel laureate in physics.

Penzias was born in Munich, Germany. At age six he was among the Jewish children evacuated to Britain as part of the Kindertransport rescue operation. Six months later his parents also fled Nazi Germany for the U.S., and the family settled in the garment district of New York City in 1940. In 1946, Penzias became a naturalized citizen of the United States. He graduated Brooklyn

Technical High School in 1951 and received a bachelor's degree from the City College of New York in 1954. From Columbia University, he received his Master's degree in 1958 and his Ph.D. in 1962.

He went on to work at Bell Labs in Holmdel, New Jersey where, with Robert Woodrow Wilson, he worked on ultra-sensitive cryogenic microwave receivers intended for radio astronomy observations. In 1964, on building their most sensitive antenna/ receiver system, the pair encountered radio noise which they could not explain. It was far less energetic than the radiation given off by the Milky Way, and it was isotropic, so they assumed their instrument was subject to interference by terrestrial sources. They tried, and then rejected, the hypothesis that the radio noise emanated from New York City. An examination of the microwave horn antenna showed it was full of pigeon droppings (which Penzias described as "white dielectric material"). After the pair removed the guano buildup, and the pigeons were shot (each physicist says the other ordered the deed), the noise remained. Having rejected all sources of interference, the pair published a paper announcing their findings. This was later identified as the cosmic microwave background radiation (CMB), the radio remnant of the Big Bang. This allowed astronomers to confirm the Big Bang, and to correct many of their previous assumptions about it.

Penzias and Wilson received the 1978 Nobel Prize, sharing it with Pyotr Leonidovich Kapitsa (Kapitsa's work was unrelated to Penzias and Wilson's). The two had received the Henry Draper Medal the previous year. Penzias is also the recipient of The International Centre in New York's Award of Excellence. Penzias has been a resident of Highland Park, New Jersey. He currently serves as a venture partner at New Enterprise Associates.

ABRAHAM PAIS

Abraham (Bram) Pais (May 19, 1918, Amsterdam, The Netherlands — July 28, 2000, Copenhagen, Denmark) was a Dutch-born American physicist and science historian. Pais earned his Ph.D. from University of Utrecht just prior to a Nazi ban on Jewish participation in Dutch universities during World War II. When the Nazis began the forced relocation of Dutch Jews, he went into hiding, but was later arrested and saved only by the end of the war. He then served as an assistant to Niels Bohr in Denmark and was later a colleague of Albert Einstein at the Princeton Institute for Advanced Study. Pais wrote books documenting the lives of these two great physicists and the contributions they and others made to modern physics. He was a physics professor at Rockefeller University until his retirement.

Early Life

Pais was born in Amsterdam, the first child of middle-class Dutch Jewish parents. His father, Isaiah "Jacques" Pais, was the descendant of Sephardic Jews who migrated from Portugal to the Low Countries around the beginning of the 17th century. His mother, Kaatje "Cato" van Kleeff, was the daughter of an Ashkenazi diamond cutter. His parents met while studying to become elementary-school teachers. They both taught school until his mother quit when they married on December 2, 1916. His only sibling, Annie, was born on November 1, 1920. During Pais's childhood his father was an elementary schoolmaster, headmaster, and later the headmaster of the Sephardic Hebrew school.

Pais was a bright student and a voracious reader during his early education and said he had a happy childhood and felt integrated in Dutch society. At age twelve he passed examinations to enter a higher burgher school and attended a school in Amsterdam with a five-year curriculum of basic subjects. He passed his final examinations as number one in his class. He was graduated with a working knowledge of English, French, and German.

AMEDEE MOUCHEZ

Amedee Ernest Barthelemy Mouchez (August 24, 1821 – June 29, 1892) was a French naval officer who became director of the Paris Observatory and launched the ill-fated *Carte du Ciel* project in 1887.

Life

Born in Madrid, Spain, Mouchez embarked on a career in the French Navy as an ensign in 1843. This was a period of relative international maritime peace and much of the navy's activities were dedicated to exploration and discovery. Mouchez was initially occupied on hydrographic studies along the coasts of Korea, China and South America, penetrating 320 km up the Paraguay River and exploring the Abrolhos Islands. He improved the practice of surveying at sea, adapting terrestrial instruments for naval use, and was especially concerned with the problems of determining longitude. He developed the use of the theodolite and meridian telescope to improve the error in establishing longitude from around 303 to 3-43.

Attaining the rank of post captain in 1868, he embarked on a series of expeditions to chart the coast of Algeria. However, in 1870, during the Franco-Prussian War, he was called upon to make an heroic defence of the port of Le Havre.

Returning to his Algerian survey, he brought it to a conclusion in 1873, when he was elected to the Bureau des Longitudes and, in the following year, was sponsored by the *Academie des sciences* to observe the transit of Venus from St. Paul Island in the Indian Ocean. On December 9, he made a sequence of superb photographic plates of the event.

In 1875, the *Academie* elected him a member of the astronomy section and in 1878 he was promoted to rear admiral and awarded the role of director of the Paris Observatory. The observatory had fallen into disrepair and disrepute since the chaos of the 1870 war and the Paris Commune of 1871. Mouchez set about a programme of reconstruction but failed to persuade the government to fund a new observatory outside the centre of Paris.

In 1887, he collaborated with Sir David Gill to host an international astronomical conference in Paris. The principal outcome of the conference was a multi-national project to compile and index a photographic atlas of the heavens, the *Carte du Ciel.* The project consumed massive effort over several decades before it was rendered obsolete by modern astronomical methods. Mouchez died in Wissous, Seine-et-Oise.

ALBERT ABRAHAM MICHELSON

Albert Abraham Michelson (December 19, 1852 – May 9, 1931) was a Prussian-born American physicist known for his work on the measurement of the speed of light and especially for the Michelson-Morley experiment. In 1907 he received the Nobel Prize in Physics. He became the first American to receive the Nobel Prize in sciences.

Biography

Michelson, the son of a Jewish merchant, was born to a Jewish family in what is today Strzelno, Poland (then Strelno, Provinz Posen in the Kingdom of Prussia). He moved to the United States with his parents in 1855, when he was two years old. He grew up in the rough mining towns of Murphy's Camp, California and Virginia City, Nevada, where his father was a merchant. He spent his high school years in San Francisco in the home of his aunt, Henriette Levy (nee Michelson), who was the mother of author Harriet Lane Levy.

President Ulysses S. Grant awarded Michelson a special appointment to the U.S. Naval Academy in 1869. During his four years as a midshipman at the Academy, Michelson excelled in optics, heat and climatology as well as drawing. After his graduation in 1873 and two years at sea, he returned to the Academy in 1875 to become an instructor in physics and chemistry until 1879. From 1880 to 1882, Michelson undertook postgraduate study at Berlin under Hermann Helmholtz and at Paris.

Michelson was fascinated with the sciences and the problem of measuring the speed of light in particular. While at Annapolis, he conducted his first experiments of the speed of light, as part of a class demonstration in 1877. After two years of studies in Europe, he resigned from the Navy in 1881. In 1883 he accepted a position as professor of physics at the Case School of Applied Science in Cleveland, Ohio and concentrated on developing an improved interferometer. In 1887 he and Edward Morley carried out the famous Michelson-Morley experiment which seemed to rule out the existence of the aether. He later moved on to use astronomical interferometers in the measurement of stellar diameters and in measuring the separations of binary stars.

In 1889 Michelson became a professor at Clark University at Worcester, Massachusetts and in 1892 was appointed professor and the first head of the department of physics at the newly organized University of Chicago.

In 1899, he married Edna Stanton and they raised one son and three daughters.

In 1907, Michelson had the honour of being the first American to receive a Nobel Prize in Physics "for his optical precision instruments and the spectroscopic and metrological investigations carried out with their aid". He also won the Copley Medal in 1907, the Henry Draper Medal in 1916 and the Gold Medal of the Royal Astronomical Society in 1923. A crater on the Moon is named after him.

Michelson died in Pasadena, California at the age of 78. The University of Chicago Residence Halls remembered Michelson and his achievements by dedicating Michelson House in his honour. Case Western Reserve has also dedicated a Michelson House to him, and an academic building at the United States Naval Academy also bears his name. Michelson Laboratory at Naval Air Weapons Station China Lake in Ridgecrest, California is named after him. There is an interesting display in the publicly accessible area of the Lab of Michelson's Nobel Prize medal, the actual prize document, and examples of his diffraction gratings.

ALEKSANDR LYAPUNOV

Aleksandr Mikhailovich Lyapunov (June 6, 1857 – November 3, 1918, all new style) was a Russian mathematician, mechanician and physicist. Sometimes his name is also written as Ljapunov, Liapunov or Ljapunow, and often improperly pronounced 'la-yapunov'.

Biography

Lyapunov was born in Yaroslavl, Imperial Russia. His father Mikhail Vasilyevich Lyapunov (1820-1868) was a well known astronomer and a head of the Demidovski lyceum. Because of the reaction of the university administration, after the departure of Lobachevsky, he gave up his work entirely in 1864 at the observatory of the University of Kazan. He moved with his family on his wife's estate in Simbirsk province (now Ulyanovsk Oblast), where he devoted his time to the education of his oldest sons, Aleksandr and Sergei (1859-1924). During long winter nights he stayed with his sons and he taught them assiduously with the aid of games on maps of the world. He possessed a lot of books in Russian, German and French on subjects as varied as mathematics, astronomy, philosophy, history, ethnography, political economy and literature. After the sudden death of his father Aleksandr was educated by his uncle R. M. Sechenov, brother of the famous physiologist Ivan Mikhailovich Sechenov. At his uncle's Lyapunov learned with his cousin, his intended Nataliya Rafailovna. In 1870 his mother moved with her sons to Nizhny Novgorod, where he started to attend the third class of the gymnasium. He passed gymnasium in 1876 with distinction.

Education

He studied at the Physico-Mathematical department of the University of Saint Petersburg, where he was a schoolfellow of Markov. In the beginning he listened to Mendeleyev's lectures on chemistry. After a month he transferred to the mathematics department of the university, but he continued attending the chemistry lectures. Mathematics was taught at that time by Chebyshev and his students Aleksandr Nikolaevich Korkin and Yegor Ivanovich Zolotarev. Lyapunov wrote his first independent scientific works under the guidance of professor of mechanics, D. K. Bobylev. In his fourth year he received the gold medal for a work on hydrostatics, which had been suggested by the faculty. This was the basis for his first published scientific work *About the equilibrium of solid bodies in vessels with arbitrary forms, filled with dense fluids* and *About the potential of hydrostatic pressure.* In both works he used many new approaches and developed new rigorous proofs of a few earlier incomplete theorems from hydrostatics. With the first work he gained the title of candidate in mathematical sciences. Now he was able to leave the university to prepare for a professorial calling.

He graduated in 1880. He received a Master's degree in applied mathematics in 1884 with the thesis *About the stability of elliptic forms in the equilibrium of turbulent fluid.* This work treated an important and difficult task about understanding the shapes of celestial bodies. This task was offered by Chebyshev to Zolotarev and to Sofia Vasilyevna Kovalevskaya and Chebyshev was aware of the difficulty. As was said by Vladimir Andreevich Steklov, "Chebyshev saw in the young man such an immense research power, that he had dared to lay on him such a toilsome task". Lyapunov had already begun to study this stability in his previous two-years attempts at solving the task. After the public announcement his work instantly attracted the attention of mathematicians, mechanicians, physicists and astronomers all over the world.

ARCHIBALD LOW

Professor **Archibald Montgomery Low** (1888-September 1956) was an English Astronautics engineer, research physicist and inventor, and author of more than 40 books.

Low has been called the ***"father of radio guidance systems"*** due to his pioneering work on guided rockets, planes and torpedoes. He was a pioneer in many fields though, often leading the way for others, but his lack of discipline meant he hardly ever saw a project through, being easily distracted by new ideas. If it weren't for this inability to see things to a conclusion, Low could well have been remembered as one of the great men of science. Many of his scientific contemporaries disliked him, due in part to his using the title *Professor*, which technically he wasn't entitled to do as he didn't occupy an academic chair. His love of the limelight and publicity probably also added to the dislike.

Later Life

Low died in 1956 from a malignant tumour on his lung. He is buried in Brompton Cemetery, London. In 1976 Low was inducted into the International Space Hall of Fame

ALFRED LEE LOOMIS

Alfred Lee Loomis (November 4, 1887-August 11, 1975) was an American attorney, investment banker, physicist, philanthropist, and patron of scientific research. He established the Loomis Laboratory in Tuxedo Park, New York, and his role in the development of radar is considered instrumental in the Allied victory in World War II. In 2002 the book displayed to the right was published about him and his secret research in his private laboratory. He is the inventor of the *Aberdeen Chronograph*, the LORAN navigational system, and the electroencephalograph; participated in the development of a ground controlled approach technology for aircraft, the centrifuge microscope, and the preliminary meetings of the Manhattan Project.

He married Elizabeth Ellen Farnsworth of Dedham, Massachusetts, a member of a prominent Boston society family, on June 22, 1912 and they had three sons, Albert Lee Jr., William Farnsworth, and Henry. In 1945 he married Manette Seeldrayers Hobart.

The theme of the comic books and movie, *Batman*, is based on the life of Alfred Loomis and he is considered the model for Bruce Wayne.

Early Years

Born in Manhattan, Loomis was the son of Julia Stimson and Henry Patterson Loomis. There were distinguished members on both sides of his family, primarily physicians, and they held high positions in society. Loomis' mother and father separated when he was very young and his father died when Alfred was in college. His first cousin was Henry Stimson, secretary of war and secretary of, state in the Taft administration. Stimson became a great influence upon him from an early age.

He completed his undergraduate work at Yale University in mathematics and science, and was graduated, *cum laude*, from Harvard Law School in 1912. Immediately following his graduation, Loomis married and began the practice of corporate law in the law firm of Winthrop and Stimson and achieved great success.

In 1917 he and his brother-in-law, Landon K. Thorne, the wealthy husband of his sister Julia, purchased 17,000 acres of Hilton Head Island and established the property as a private preserve for riding, boating, fishing, and hunting. His hobbies included automobiles and yachting—racing America's Cup yachts against the Vanderbilts and the Astors—and the pursuit of many sciences.

ADOLF KRATZER

B. Adolf Kratzer (October 16, 1893 in Gunzburg, Germany –) was a German theoretical physicist who made contributions to atomic physics and molecular physics, and was an authority on molecular band spectroscopy.

From 1912 to 1914, Kratzer studied physics at the Technische Hochschule Munchen (today, Technische Universitat Munchen), and then he spent two years in the army, after which he began studies at the University of Munich under Arnold Sommerfeld. He was granted his doctor of philosophy in 1920; his thesis was on the band spectra of molecules. While at Munich, he was Sommerfeld's assistant; he had been trained by Sommerfeld's assistant and student Wilhelm Lenz to fill this role. While at Munich, Kratzer extended the theory of diatomic molecular spectroscopy by including anharmonic forces between the nuclei, which changed the oscillation frequencies.

It was Sommerfeld's practice to send some of his assistants to be personal assistants for physics to the mathematician David Hilbert, at the University of Gottingen. Kratzer was sent to Gottingen during the period 1920 to 1921. Upon his return to Munich, he became a Privatdozent, and it was during this time that he became acquainted with Werner Heisenberg, also a student of Sommerfeld. Based on his work at Munich, it was in 1922 that Krazter's detailed analysis on the cyanide spectroscopic bands was published. His analysis resulted in the introduction of half-integral quantum numbers to account for molecular rotation. During 1922, he was also called as an ordinarius professor of theoretical physics to the University of Munster. Here, Kratzer made contributions to quantum mechanics and became a leading authority in the field of molecular band spectroscopy.

At this time, there were three centres of development for quantum mechanics and the interpretation of atomic and molecular structure, based on atomic and molecular spectroscopy, especially the Sommerfeld-Bohr model: the Theoretical Physics Institute at the University of Munich, under Arnold Sommerfeld, the Institute of Theoretical Physics at the University of Gottingen, under Max Born, and the Institute of Theoretical Physics, under Niels Bohr. These three institutes effectively formed a consortium for the exchange of assistants and researchers. Furthermore, with Sommerfeld educating such capable physicists as Kratzer, and others, when they were called to other facilities, they effectively became extensions of Sommerfeld's Institute of Theoretical Physics. This was the case with Kratzer when he went to Munster, as was the case of Sommerfeld's former student Paul Peter Ewald when he went to the Stuttgart Technische Hochschule.

Kratzer published a number of physics books, based on his lectures on electrodynamics, mechanics, optics, relativity, thermodynamics, and quantum mechanics (wave mechanics). A book on transcendental functions was written with Walter Franz, also a student of Sommerfeld. The Kratzer potential, a central force in molecular physics, is named in his honour.

A. Q. KHAN

Abdul Qadeer Khan (born April 1, 1936) in Bhopal, undivided British India, is a Pakistani scientist and metallurgical engineer, widely regarded as the founder of Pakistan's nuclear programme.

His middle name is occasionally rendered as **Quadeer, Qadir** or **Gadeer,** and his given names are usually abbreviated to **A.Q.**

In January 2004, Khan confessed to having been involved in a clandestine international network of nuclear weapons technology proliferation from Pakistan to Libya, Iran and North Korea. On February 5, 2004, the President of Pakistan, General Pervez Musharraf, announced that he had pardoned Khan, who is widely seen as a national hero. Recently Dr. Qadeer cleared the issue of confession which he said was handed to him by authorities.

In an August 23, 2005 interview with Kyodo News General Pervez Musharraf confirmed that Khan had supplied gas centrifuges and gas centrifuge parts to North Korea and, possibly, an amount of uranium hexafluoride.

On May 30th, 2008, ABC News reported that Khan, who previously confessed to his involvement with Iran and North Korea, now denies involvement with the spread of nuclear arms to those countries. He explained in an interview with ABC News that the Pakistani government and President Pervez Musharraf forced him to be a "scapegoat" for the "national interest." He denies ever travelling to Iran or Libya and claims that North Korea's nuclear programme was well advanced before his visit.

Early Life

Khan was born (Bhopal) into a middle-class Muslim-Muhajir family, which migrated from India to Pakistan in 1952. He obtained a B.Sc. degree in 1960 from the University of Karachi, majoring in physical metallurgy. He then obtained an engineer's degree in 1967 from Delft University of Technology, the Netherlands, and a Ph.D. degree in metallurgical engineering from the Catholic University of Leuven in Belgium in 1972.

B. ROY FRIEDEN

B. Roy Frieden is a mathematical physicist living in Tucson, Arizona, in the United States. He is an Emeritus Professor of Optical Sciences at the University of Arizona. His main work is the use of Fisher information for purposes of deriving and developing physical theories. These theories take the form of known differential equations or probability distribution functions. (Examples are the Schrodinger wave equation of quantum mechanics, and the Maxwell-Boltzmann distribution of statistical mechanics.)

The derivations utilize the mathematical principle of extreme physical information (EPI). This principle builds on the well known idea that the observation of a "source" phenomenon is never completely accurate. That is, information is inevitably lost in transit from source to observation. Furthermore, the random errors that creep in are presumed to define the distribution function of the source phenomenon. That is, "the physics lies in the fluctuations." Finally, the information loss may be shown to be an extreme value.

Thus, if the observed level of Fisher information in the data has value *I*, and the level of Fisher information that existed at the source has value *J*, the EPI principle states that *I* " *J* = extremum. The extremum is a minimum in most problems, meaning that there is a tendency for any observation to faithfully match up with its source. The physical and mathematical correctness of Frieden's ideas have been characterized as highly dubious by several knowledgeable observers; see, for example, Raymond F. Streater's Lost Causes in Theoretical Physics: Physics from Fisher Information, and Cosma Shalizi's review of *Physics from Fisher Information.* The EPI principle is a variational principle that has been used to derive most fundamental laws of physics, as well as laws of biology, cancer growth, chemistry, and economics. These include new laws and concepts as well. In this way, Fisher information, and in particular its loss *I* " *J* during observation, provides a bridge for deriving laws of nature in general.

BENJAMIN FRANKLIN

Benjamin Franklin (January 17, 1706 [O.S. January 6, 1705] – April 17, 1790) was one of the Founding Fathers of the United States of America. A noted polymath, Franklin was a leading author and printer, satirist, political theorist politician, scientist, inventor, civic activist, statesman and diplomat. As a scientist he was a major figure in the Enlightenment and the history of physics for his discoveries and theories regarding electricity. He invented the lightning rod, bifocals, the Franklin stove, a carriage odometer, and a musical instrument. He formed both the first public lending library in America and first fire department in Pennsylvania. He was an early proponent of colonial unity and as a political writer and activist he, more than anyone, invented the idea of an American nation and as a diplomat during the American Revolution, he secured the French alliance that helped to make independence possible.

Franklin is credited as being foundational to the roots of American values and character, a marriage of the practical and democratic Puritan values of thrift, hard work, education, community spirit, self-governing institutions, and opposition to authoritarianism both political and religious, with the scientific and tolerant values of the Enlightenment. In the words of Henry Steele Commager, "In Franklin could be merged the virtues of Puritanism without its defects, the illumination of the Enlightenment without its heat." To Walter Isaacson, this makes Franklin, "the most accomplished American of his age and the most influential in inventing the type of society America would become."

Born in Boston, Massachusetts, Franklin learned printing from his older brother and became a newspaper editor, printer, and merchant in Philadelphia, becoming very wealthy, writing and publishing *Poor Richard's Almanack* and the *Pennsylvania Gazette*. Franklin was interested in science and technology, and gained international renown for his famous experiments. He played a major role in establishing the University of Pennsylvania and Franklin & Marshall College and was elected the first president of the American Philosophical Society. Franklin became a national hero in America when he spearheaded the effort to have Parliament repeal the unpopular Stamp Act. An accomplished diplomat, he was widely admired among the French as American minister to Paris and was a major figure in the development of positive Franco-American relations. From 1775 to 1776, Franklin was Postmaster General under the Continental Congress and from 1785 to 1788 was President of the Supreme Executive Council of Pennsylvania. Toward the end of his life, he became one of the most prominent abolitionists.

Franklin's colourful life and legacy of scientific and political achievement, and status as one of America's most influential Founding Fathers, has seen Franklin honoured on coinage and money; warships; the names of many towns, counties, educational institutions, namesakes, and companies; and more than two centuries after his death, countless cultural references.

Early life

Benjamin Franklin was born on Milk Street in Boston on January 17, 1706 and baptized at Old South Meeting House. His father, Josiah Franklin, was a tallow chandler, a maker of candles and soap, whose second wife, Abiah Folger, was Benjamin's mother. Josiah's marriages produced 17 children; Benjamin was the fifteenth child and youngest son. Josiah wanted Ben to attend school with the clergy but only had enough money to send him to school for two years. He attended Boston Latin School but did not graduate; he continued his education through voracious reading. Although "his parents talked of the church as a career" for Franklin, his schooling ended when he was ten. He then worked for his father for a time and at 12 he became an apprentice to his brother James, a printer. When Ben was 15, James created the *New England Courant*, the first truly independent newspaper in the colonies. When denied the option to write to the paper, Franklin invented the pseudonym of **Mrs. Silence Dogood**, who was ostensibly a middle-aged widow. The letters were published in the paper and became a subject of conversation around town. Neither James nor the Courant's readers were aware of the ruse, and James was unhappy with Ben when he discovered the popular correspondent was his younger brother. Franklin left his apprenticeship without permission and in so doing became a fugitive.

At age 17, Franklin ran away to Philadelphia, Pennsylvania, seeking a new start in a new city. When he first arrived he worked in several printer shops around town. However, he was not satisfied by the immediate prospects. After a few months, while working in a printing house, Franklin was convinced by Pennsylvania Governor Sir William Keith to go to London, ostensibly to acquire the equipment necessary for establishing another newspaper in Philadelphia. Finding Keith's promises of backing a newspaper to be empty, Franklin worked as a compositor in a printer's shop in what is now the Church of St. Bartholomew-the-Great in the Smithfield area of London. Following this, he returned to Philadelphia in 1726 with the help of a merchant named Thomas Denham, who gave Franklin a position as clerk, shopkeeper, and bookkeeper in Denham's merchant business.

In 1727, Benjamin Franklin, 21, created the Junto, a group of "like minded aspiring artisans and tradesmen who hoped to improve themselves while they improved their community." The Junto was a discussion group for issues of the day; it subsequently gave rise to many organizations in Philadelphia.

Reading was a great pastime of the Junto, but books were rare and expensive. The members created a library, and initially pooled their own books together. This did not work, however, and Franklin initiated the idea of a subscription library, where the members pooled their monetary resources to buy books. This idea was the birth of the Library Company, with the charter of the Library Company of Philadelphia created in 1731 by Franklin.

Originally, the books were kept in the homes of the first librarians, but in 1739 the collection was moved to the second floor of the State House of Pennsylvania, now known as Independence Hall. In 1791, a new building was built specifically for the library. The Library Company flourished with no competition and gained many priceless collections from bibliophiles such as James Logan and his physician brother William. The Library Company is now a great scholarly and research library with 500,000 rare books, pamphlets, and broadsides, more than 160,000 manuscripts, and 75,000 graphic items.

Upon Denham's death, Franklin returned to his former trade. By 1730, Franklin had set up a printing house of his own and had contrived to become the publisher of a newspaper called *The Pennsylvania Gazette.* The Gazette gave Franklin a forum for agitation about a variety of local reforms and initiatives through printed essays and observations. Over time, his commentary, together with a great deal of savvy about cultivating a positive image of an industrious and intellectual young man, earned him a great deal of social respect; though even after Franklin had achieved fame as a scientist and statesman, he habitually signed his letters with the unpretentious 'B. Franklin, Printer.' In 1731, Franklin was initiated into the local Freemason lodge, becoming a grand master in 1734, indicating his rapid rise to prominence in Pennsylvania. That same year, he edited and published the first Masonic book in the Americas, a reprint of James Anderson's Constitutions of the Free-Masons. Franklin remained a Freemason throughout the rest of his life.

BENOIT PAUL EMILE CLAPEYRON

Benoit Paul Emile Clapeyron (February 26, 1799-January 28, 1864) was a French engineer and physicist, one of the founders of thermodynamics.

Life

Born in Paris, Clapeyron studied at the Ecole polytechnique and the Ecole des Mines, before leaving for Saint Petersburg in 1820 to teach at the *Ecole des Travaux Publics.* He returned to Paris only after the Revolution of July 1830, supervising the construction of the first railway line connecting Paris to Versailles and Saint-Germain.

Work

In 1834, he made his first contribution to the creation of modern thermodynamics by publishing a report entitled the *Driving force of the heat* (*Puissance motrice de la chaleur*), in which it developed the work of the physicist Nicolas Leonard Sadi Carnot, deceased two years before. Though Carnot had developed a compelling analysis of a generalised heat engine, he had employed the clumsy and already unfashionable caloric theory.

Clapeyron, in his memoire, presented Carnot's work in a more accessible and analytic graphical form, showing the Carnot cycle as a closed curve on an indicator diagram, a chart of pressure against volume (named in his honour Clapeyron's graph). In 1843, Clapeyron further developed the idea of a reversible process, already suggested by Carnot and made a definitive statement of *Carnot's principle*, what is now known as the second law of thermodynamics.

These foundations enabled him to make substantive extensions of Clausius' work, including the formula, now known as the Clausius-Clapeyron relation, which characterises the phase transition between two phases of matter. He further considered questions of phase transitions in what later became known as Stefan problems.

BARTHELEMY FAUJAS DE SAINT-FOND

Barthelemy Faujas de Saint-Fond (May 17, 1741–July 18, 1819), French geologist and traveller, was born at Montelimar. He was educated at the Jesuit's College at Lyon; afterwards he went to Grenoble where he studied law and was admitted as an advocate to the parlement.

He rose to be president of the seneschal's court in Montelimar (1765), where he acquitted himself with distinction. However, he became disenchanted with law and wished to pursue his love of nature that had begun earlier in his life. His favourite pastime was visiting the mountain regions in the Alps and Massif Central. There be began to study the forms, structure, composition and superposition of rocks.

In 1775 in the Velay he discovered a rich deposit of pozzuolana, that was eventually mined by the government. In 1776 he established a relationship with Buffon, who recognised the value of his scientific efforts immediately. Invited by Buffon to Paris, Faujas ceased his legal work and was appointed assistant naturalist to the natural history museum by Louis XVI. Later, he was appointed royal commissioner for mines. One of his most important works was *Recherches sur les volcans eteints du Vivarais et du Velay*, which appeared in 1778. This publication documented his astute observations allowing Faujas to develop a theory about the origin of volcanoes. In his capacity of commissioner for mines Faujas travelled to most European countries where he closely observed the natural environment and the rock formations. Faujas was the first to recognize the volcanic nature of the basaltic columns of Fingal's Cave, on Staffa. The island was visited in 1772 by Sir Joseph Banks, who remarked that the stone was a coarse kind of basalt, very much resembling the Giant's Causeway in Ireland as noted in (Pennant's *Tour in Scotland and Voyage to the Hebrides*). Faujas' *Voyage en Angleterre, en Ecosse et aux Iles Hebrides* (1787) contains anecdotes about Sir Joseph Banks and Dr. John Whitehurst, including an amusing account of *The Dinner of an Academic Club* (the Royal Society), which was translated into English (2 vols., 1799).

In 1785, Faujas was named king's commissioner to factories, armories, and royal forests. This brought a salary of 4,000 livres, and 2,000 livres for travelling expenses, in addition to his 6,000 livres for the assistant naturalist post. Faujas was appointed the first professor of geology at the Jardin des Plantes in 1793, a post he held until he was nearly eighty years of age. He retired in 1818 to the estate of Saint-Fond in Dauphine. Faujas had a keen interest in the balloon experiments of the Montgolfier brothers, and published the very complete 2 volume work, *Description des experiences de la machine aerostatique de MM. Montgolfier, &c.* (1783, 1784). He also contributed many scientific memoirs to the *Annales* and the *Memoires* of the museum of natural history. Among his other works are: *Histoire naturelle de la province de Dauphine* (1787, 1782), *Mineralogie des volcans* (1784), and *Essai de geologie* (1803–1809).

BARNUM BROWN

Barnum Brown (February 12, 1873-1963), born February 12, 1873 in Carbondale, Kansas. He was named after the circus showman P.T. Barnum, and was perhaps the most famous fossil hunter of the early twentieth century. Based out of the American Museum of Natural History (AMNH), Brown traversed the country bargaining and trading for fossils. His field was not limited to dinosaurs. He was known to collect or obtain anything of possible scientific value or that could take up space in the museum. Often, he simply sent money to have the fossil shipped to the American Museum, and any new specimen of interest often resulted in a flurry of letters between the discoverer and Brown.

After working a handful of years in Wyoming for the AMNH in the late 1890s, Brown led an expedition to the Hell Creek Formation of Southeastern Montana. There, in 1902, he discovered and excavated the first documented remains of *Tyrannosaurus rex*. The Hell Creek digs were prosperous, and Brown collected enough fossils to fill up whole train cars. As was a more common practice back then Brown's crews used controlled blasts of dynamite to remove the tons of rock covering their fossil discoveries. Everything was moved with horse-drawn carriages and pure man-power. Although the total amount of fossils removed from the badlands was impressive, there was seldomly any site data recorded.

After nearly a straight decade in Montana, Brown headed to Alberta, Canada and the Red Deer River near Drumheller. Here, Brown and his crew spent the middle 1910's floating down the river on a flatboat and stopped along the way to prospect for fossils in promising-looking localities. At this time, the famous Sternberg family floated down the river as well. The two parties, Brown's being American and Sternberg's being Canadian, exhibited a playful but friendly rivalry. The discoveries were all for the good of palaeontology.

One of Brown's most significant finds, made in 1910, were several hind feet from a group of *Albertosaurus* collected in Dry Island Buffalo Jump Provincial Park. His find was largely forgotten in the recesses of the American Museum of Natural History in New York. Dr. Phil Currie, who was the Head of Dinosaur Research at the Royal Tyrrell Museum of Palaeontology at the time, relocated the site of the bones using only an old photograph as a guide, and reopened the site for excavation in the summer of 1998. Excavation of the site under Tyrrell Museum auspices ceased in August, 2005. However, once Dr. Currie took a new job at the University of Alberta, his new crew worked the site in 2006 and will continue for several years to come.

An homage to the paleontologist was made in the 1998 IMAX film *T-Rex: Back to the Cretaceous* in which he was played by actor Laurie Murdoch.

Barnum was quite a colourful character. During World War I and II, he worked as a "intelligence asset". In addition, he picked up some spare cash acting as a corporate spy for oil companies, during his many trips abroad. Durning his time in Canada, Barnum was frequently photographed wearing a large fur coat at dig sites.

Brown's wife, Lilian Brown, wrote a book of memoirs *I Married a Dinosaur* (Dodd Mead, 1950) about her expeditions with Barnum Brown.

BRUCE BOLT

Bruce Bolt (born February 15, 1930 – died July 21, 2005) was a Professor of Earth and Planetary Science at the University of California, Berkeley. Professor Bolt was a seismologist known as pioneer of engineering seismology. He served for 15 years on the California Seismic Safety Committee leading public debate on earthquake safety in that state, and acted as a consultant on major projects throughout the world. As well, Bolt published a number of popular and technical books on seismology.

Early Life and Career

Bolt was born in Largs, New South Wales just north of Maitland in 1930. He studied at the University of Sydney obtaining his Bachelors Degree in 1952, Masters Degree in 1955 and a Doctorate in Applied Mathematics in 1959. He also lectured at Sydney University in Mathematics but developed an interest in mathematical modelling of the earth's interior. He obtained a D. Sc from Sydney University in 1972 while working at Berkeley. After visiting the Lamont Geological Observatory in New York, he visited the Department of Geodesy and Geophysics at Cambridge University where he met Professors Perry Byerly and John Verhoogen of UC Berkeley who invited him there.

Career at Berkeley

Bolt started as Director of the Berkeley Seismological Stations (now the Berkeley Seismological Laboratory in 1963 and served in that position until 1991. In that position, he was at the forefront of seismology especially as a pioneer of engineering seismology. He identified the impact of near-fault effects of earthquakes as well as the "fling" where the fault slips during an earthquake which has a strong impact on structures near the quake. Professor Bolt was elected to the US National Academy of Engineering in 1978 as recognition for his contribution to that profession. As Director of the Berkeley Seismology Centre, Bolt pioneered the use of digital recordings rather than paper readouts to read data.

Bolt identified that the epicenter of the 1906 San Francisco Earthquake was near Daly City, California not near Olema, California in Marin County as had been previously thought. He also helped to design a simulation of the 1906 quake at the California Academy of Sciences museum in Golden Gate Park which has been seen by millions of people. He has written a number of works including *Earthquakes: a Primer* in 1978 and *Inside the Earth: Evidence from Earthquakes* in 1982.

Professor Bolt served on the California Seismic Safety Committee for 15 years including a year as Chairman in 1986. In that position, he had a significant impact on California's earthquake safety legislation and helped to create that states mandatory system of earthquake hazard mapping. He was a consultant for every major engineering project on seismology including on the Diablo Canyon nuclear power plant as well as international projects including the Aswan Dam and the Trans-Alaska Pipeline System. He loved ESS8. Professor Bolt retired in 1993. He died of pancreatic cancer in July 2005 at the Kaiser Permanente Medical Centre in Oakland. He was a citizen of the US at the time of his death.

BERNARD KETTLEWELL

Henry Bernard Davis Kettlewell (24 February 1907-1979) was a British geneticist, lepidopterist and medical doctor, who carried out important research into the influence of industrial melanism on natural selection in moths, showing why moths are darker in polluted areas.

Early Life

Kettlewell was born in Howden, Yorkshire, was educated at Charterhouse School, and from 1926 studied medicine with zoology at Gonville and Caius College, Cambridge. In 1929 he began clinical training at St Bartholomew's Hospital, London, then in 1935 joined a general medical practice in Cranleigh, Surrey. He also worked as an anesthetist at St. Luke's Hospital, Guildford. During World War II, from 1939 to 1945, he worked for the Emergency Medical Service at Woking War Hospital.

He emigrated to South Africa in 1949, and from then until 1954 was a researcher at the International Locust Control Centre at Cape Town University, investigating methods of locust control and going on expeditions to the Kalahari, the Knysna Forest, the Belgian Congo and Mozambique.

In 1952 he was appointed to a Nuffield Research Fellowship in the Department of Genetics of the Department of Zoology at Oxford University. Until 1954 he divided his time between South Africa and Oxford, then he gained the position of Senior Research Officer in the Department of Genetics and spent the rest of his career in Oxford as a genetics researcher. His supervisor was E. B. Ford.

Peppered Moth Investigation and Experiments

His grant was to study industrial melanism in general, and in particular the peppered moth *Biston betularia* which had been studied by William Bateson in the 1890s. Kettlewell's research from three surveys between 1952 and 1972 appeared to show a static pattern with a high frequency of the dark-coloured *carbonaria* phenotype in industrial regions, and the light coloured *typica* moths becoming the most common in more rural areas. In the first of Kettlewell's experiments moths were released into an aviary to observe how insectivorous birds reacted.

He showed that the birds ate the moths, and found that where the camouflage of the moths made them difficult for him to see against a matching background, the birds too had difficulty in finding the moths. Most famously he then carried out experiments involving releasing then recapturing marked moths in polluted woodlands in Birmingham, and in unpolluted rural woods at Deanend Wood, Dorset, England. He demonstrated experimentally the efficiency of natural selection as an evolutionary force: light-coloured moths are more conspicuous than dark-coloured ones in industrial areas, where the vegetation is darkened by pollution, and are therefore easier prey for birds, but are less conspicuous in unpolluted rural areas, where the vegetation is lighter in colour, and therefore survive predation better. His experiment led to better understanding of industrial melanism and its effects on the evolution of species.

In 1979 Kettlewell died from an accidental drug overdose.

BORIS EPHRUSSI

Boris Ephrussi (May 9, 1901–May 2, 1979) was a French geneticist of Russian origin. He was one of the many famous Jewish life scientists. He had published two papers in November 1966 which represented a key step in a decade of research in his laboratory. This research helped transform mammalian, and especially human, genetics. Boris started his scientific training as a Russian emigre in 1920. He studied the initiation and regulation of embryological processes by intracellular and extracellular factors. A major strand of his early research concerned the effect of temperature on the development of fertilized sea urchin eggs. In this work he used a micromanipulator, which was developed by Robert Chambers, an American biologist. During Ephrussi's time, writing a second dissertation was standard practice in France. Ephrussi's involved culturing tissues. Ephrussi ran into difficulties typically associated with early tissue culture techniques, but despite these obstacles Ephrussi managed to conclude from studies of brachyury in mice that intrinsic factors (i.e genes) play a key role in development.

As the next phase of his career, Ephrussi coupled his embryological concerns with a firm conviction that one must understand the role of genes in order to decipher embryological processes. He moved to Caltech in 1934 and stayed until 1935 to learn genetics within the intellectual empire of T.H. Morgan. This move was supported by the Rockefeller Foundation Fellowship. During this period he conducted important work with George Beadle, who joined him in Paris in the autumn of 1935. There they produced results from experiments with Drosophila eye transplants which became integral to the work of Beadle and Tatum, who were working with Neurospora, and from this research developed the 'one gene, one enzyme' hypothesis.

During World War II, Ephrussi spent most of his time as a refugee at Johns Hopkins University. Following this he began work in France on yeast and cytoplasmic genetics. He began working at the Institut de Biologie Physicochimique (the Rothschild Institute) in Paris, and later worked at the CNRS at Gif-sur-Yvette, where he studied the contribution of cytoplasm to the cell phenotype and pursued the interactions between nuclear and cytoplasmic genetic endowments necessary to the yielding of an intact, functioning (albeit single-celled) organism.

BARUJ BENACERRAF

Baruj Benacerraf (born 29 October 1920) is a US immunologist born in Venezuela, son of a Jewish family originating from North Africa, who shared the 1980 Nobel Prize in Physiology or Medicine for the "discovery of the Major histocompatibility complex genes which encode cell surface molecules important for the immune system's distinction between self and non-self". His brother is well-known philosopher Paul Benacerraf. Born in Caracas, his parents were Sephardic Jews: his father was born in the Spanish Morocco and his mother in Algeria. Dr. Benacerraf moved to Paris from

Venezuela with his family in 1925. After having come back to Venezuela, in 1940 he emigrated to the USA and in 1943, he became a naturalized citizen. He earned his B.S. at Columbia University School of General Studies. He then went on to attain the degree of Doctor of Medicine from the Medical College of Virginia, the only school to which he was accepted.

After his medical internship and US Army service (1945–48), and working at he military hospital of Nancy, he became a researcher at Columbia University College of Physicians and Surgeons (1948–50). He performed research in Paris (1950–6), relocated to New York University (1956–68), moved to the National Institutes of Health (1968–70), then joined Harvard University (1970–91), concurrently serving the Dana-Farber Cancer Institute, Boston (1980). He began studies of allergies in 1948, and discovered the Ir (immune response) genes that govern transplant rejection (1960s).

In 1990, Benacerraf also received National Medal of Science for his contributions to the world of medicine.

BARRY WAKEMAN

Barry Noble Wakeman (1939-September 21, 2004) was an American naturalist and educator.

Born in Glenridge, New Jersey, he became interested in nature as a child, having explored the woods near his home. He received a B.S. in biology from Colgate University and a M.S. in botany from Indiana University. He served in the Peace Corps in Uganda.

After working as a curator at the Oklahoma City Zoo he came to the Cincinnati Zoo in 1968. That year he was part of an expedition to Antarctica, where he visited the South Pole and brought penguins to Cincinnati. At the Cincinnati Zoo he worked to teach children about nature, establishing the Junior Zoologist Club for twelve-to-sixteen year olds in 1968. This became a model for other zoos. He became the Cincinnati Zoo's director of education in 1974 and retired in 1995. But after leaving the zoo he was still busy, serving as director of the Nature Academy, another programme for young people, and at the (Highlands Nature Santuary) in Bainbridge, Ohio. Barry also taught (ILR) classes at the University of Cincinnati during his retirement, and shared his insights, writing and reading list with a circle of friends and students who met with him weekly at St. John's Unitarian Universalist Church, in Clifton, Cincinnati, Ohio. Barry continued teaching in that weekly meeting until just a few weeks before his passing.

Barry has four children;Barry, Amy Hunter and Brooke. He has three grandchildren;Gabriel, Morgan, and Orion. He died at his home in Pierce Township, Clermont County, Ohio.

BERNHARD RENSCH

Bernhard Rensch (21 January 1900–4 April 1990) was a German evolutionary biologist, and ornithologist who did field work in Indonesia and India. He is probably best known as one of the architects of the modern evolutionary synthesis, which he popularised in Germany. Besides his work on how environmental factors influenced the evolution of geographically isolated populations and on evolution above the species level, which contributed to the modern synthesis, he also worked extensively in the area animal behavior (ethology). His education and scientific work was interrupted by service in the German military during both World War I and World War II.

Biography

Rensch was born in Thale. He served in the German army from 1917-1920, and then continued his education. He received his PH.D from the university of Halle in 1922. He joined the zoological museum of the University of Berlin as an assistant in 1925. In 1927 he participated in a zoological expedition to the Sunda islands. He studied the geographical distribution of subspecies of polytypic species and of complexes of closely related species with attention to how local environmental factors influenced their evolution. In 1929 he published the book *Das Prinzip Geographischer Rassenkreise und das Problem der Artbildung* that discussed the relationship between geography and speciation. His work in this area would influence Ernst Mayr, who was also an assistant at the Berlin museum from 1927-1930, and contribute to the development of the modern evolutionary synthesis. In 1937 he was forced to leave the Berlin museum because he refused to join the Nazy party and he took a position at a zoological garden in Munster. In 1940 he was recalled for military service, but was discharged for medical reasons in 1942. In 1947 he published a book that would later be translated into English under the title *Evolution Above the Species Level.* The book discussed how the evolutionary mechanisms that drove speciation could also explain the differences between higher taxa and it was considered a major document in the modern synthesis. That same year he became chairman of the zoology department and director of the zoological institute at the University of Munster. In 1953 he would take part in zoological expedition to India. Later in his career he would work extensively in the areas of animal behavior (ethology), learning, and memory. He published an autobiography in 1979 and remained scientifically active until his death in 1990..

BARRY MARSHALL

Barry James Marshall, (born 30 September 1951) is an Australian physician, Nobel Prize laureate in Physiology or Medicine, and Professor of Clinical Microbiology at the University of Western Australia. Marshall is well-known for proving that bacteria *Helicobacter pylori* are the cause of most stomach ulcers, reversing decades of medical doctrine which held that ulcers were caused by stress, spicy foods, and too much acid. He has recently accepted a part-time appointment at the Pennsylvania State University.

Early Years

Marshall was born in Kalgoorlie, Western Australia and lived in Kalgoorlie and Carnarvon until moving to Perth at seven. He attended High School at Newman College and the University of Western Australia, where he received a Bachelor of Medicine, Bachelor of Surgery in 1975. He married his wife Adrienne in 1972.

Life and Research

In 1979 Marshall was appointed as a Registrar in Medicine at the Royal Perth Hospital. He met Robin Warren, a pathologist interested in gastritis, during internal medicine fellowship training at Royal Perth Hospital in 1981. Together, the pair studied the presence of spiral bacteria in association with gastritis. The following year (1982), they performed the initial culture of *H. pylori* and developed their hypothesis related to the bacterial cause of peptic ulcer and gastric cancer. It has been claimed that the *H. pylori* theory was ridiculed by the establishment scientists and doctors, who did not believe that any bacteria could live in the acidic stomach. Marshall has been quoted as saying in 1998 that "Everyone was against me, but I knew I was right". On the other hand, it has also been argued that medical researchers showed a proper degree of skepticism until the *H. pylori* hypothesis could be proved.

After failed attempts to infect piglets in 1984, Marshall drank a petri-dish of the bacteria and soon developed gastritis with achlorhydria. Symptoms included vague stomach discomfort, nausea, vomiting and halitosis. On the 14th day of the infection, biopsies of Marshall's stomach did not reveal any bacteria-so spontaneous eradication may have occurred. However, on the insistence of his wife, he did take antibiotics immediately after that endoscopy so there was no way of double-checking the negative result. Interestingly, he did not develop antibodies to H.pylori, suggesting that innate immunity can sometimes eradicate acute H.pylori infection. His illness and recovery, based on a culture of organisms extracted from a patient, fulfilled Koch's postulates for *H. pylori* and gastritis, but not for peptic ulcer. This experiment was published in 1985 in the Medical Journal of Australia and is among the most cited articles from the journal.

After this work at Fremantle Hospital, Marshall did research at Royal Perth Hospital (1985-86) and at the University of Virginia, USA (1986-1996), before returning to Australia. He held a Burnet Fellowship at the University of Western Australia from 1998-2003 and continues research related to *H. pylori* and runs the H.pylori Research Laboratory at UWA.

BERNARD GERMAIN DE LACEPEDE

Bernard-Germain-Etienne de La Ville-sur-Illon, comte de Lacepede or **La Cepede** (December 26, 1756 – October 6, 1825) was a. French naturalist.

Biography

He was born at Agen in Guienne. His education was carefully conducted by his father, and the early perusal of Buffon's Natural History (*Histoire naturelle, generale et particuliere*) awakened his interest in that branch of study, which absorbed his chief attention. His leisure he devoted to music, in which, besides becoming a good performer on the piano and organ, he acquired considerable mastery of composition, two of his operas (which were never published) meeting with the high approval of Gluck; in 1781–1785 he also brought out in two volumes his *Poetique de la musique.* Meantime he wrote two treatises, *Essai sur l'electricite* (1781) and *Physique generale et particulaire* (1782–1784), which gained him the friendship of Buffon, who in 1785 appointed him subdemonstrator in the Jardin du Roi, and proposed that he continue Buffon's *Histoire naturelle.* This continuation was published under the titles *Histoire des quadrupedes, ovipares et des serpents* (2 vols., 1788–1789) and *Histoire naturelle des reptiles* (1789).

After the French Revolution Lacepede became a member of the Legislative Assembly, but during the Reign of Terror he left Paris, his life having become endangered by his disapproval of the massacres. When the Jardin du Roi was reorganized as the Jardin des Plantes, Lacepede was appointed to the chair allocated to the study of reptiles and fishes. In 1798 he published the first volume of *Histoire naturelle des poissons*, the fifth volume appearing in 1803, and in 1804 appeared his *Histoire des cetaces.* From this period until his death the part he took in politics prevented him making any further contribution of importance to science. In 1799 he became a senator, in 1801 president of the senate (a role he also fulfilled in 1807-08 and 1811-13), in 1803 grand chancellor of the Legion of Honour, in 1804 minister of state, and at the Bourbon Restoration in 1819 he was created a peer of France. He died at Epinay-sur-Seine. During the latter part of his life he wrote *Histoire generale physique et civile de l'Europe*, published posthumously in 18 volumes, 1826.

BERNARD DE JUSSIEU

Bernard de Jussieu (August 17, 1699-November 6, 1777) was a French naturalist, younger brother of Antoine de Jussieu.

Bernard de Jussieu was born in Lyon. He took a medical degree at Montpellier and began practice in 1720, but finding the work uncongenial he gladly accepted his brother's invitation to Paris in 1722, when he succeeded Sebastien Vaillant (1669-1722) as sub-demonstrator of plants in the Jardin des Plantes. In 1725 he brought out a new edition of Joseph Pitton de Tournefort's *Histoire des plantes qui naissent aux environs de Paris*, 2 vols., which was afterwards translated into English by John Martyn, the original work being incomplete. In the same year he was admitted into the French Academy of Sciences, and communicated several papers to that body.

Long before Abraham Trembley (1700-1784) published his *Histoire des polypes d'eau douce*, Jussieu maintained the doctrine that these organisms were animals, and not the flowers of marine plants, then the current notion; and to confirm his views he made three journeys to the coast of Normandy.

Singularly modest and retiring, he published very little, but in 1759 he arranged the plants in the royal garden of the Trianon at Versailles, according to his own scheme of classification. This arrangement is printed in his nephew Antoine Laurent de Jussieu's *Genera plantarum*, and formed the basis of that work. He cared little for the credit of enunciating new discoveries, so long as the facts were made public. On the death of his brother Antoine, he could not be induced to succeed him as professor of botany at the Jardin des Plantes, but prevailed upon L. G. Lemonnier to assume the higher position.

The standard botanical author abbreviation **B.Juss.** is applied to plants described by de Jussieu.

BERNARDO HOUSSAY

Bernardo Alberto Houssay (April 10, 1887 – September 21, 1971) was an Argentine physiologist who in 1947 with Carl Ferdinand Cori and Gerty Cori received Nobel Prize for Physiology or Medicine for their discovery of the role played by pituitary hormones in regulating the amount of blood sugar (glucose) in animals. He is the first Argentine and Latin American Nobel laureate in the Sciences.

Biography

Bernardo Alberto Houssay was born in Buenos Aires, to emigrees from France, Albert and Clara Houssay. A precocious youngster, he was admitted to the Pharmacy School at the University of Buenos Aires at 14 years of age and subsequently to the Medical School of the same University from 1904 to 1910, beginning when he was only 17 years old. While a third year medical student, Houssay took up a post as a research and teaching assistant in the Chair of Physiology.

Career

After graduating, he quickly developed and presented his M.D. thesis on the physiological activities of pituitary extracts, published in 1911, a theme he would pursue for the rest of his scientific career. Since 1908 he was already an assistant lecturer in the same department, and immediately after his doctorate he took up the post of Professor of Physiology in the University's School of Veterinary Medicine. Simultaneously, he started a private practice and as assistant physician at the municipal hospital of Buenos Aires. In 1913 he became Chief Physician at the Alvear Hospital, and, in 1915, Chief of the Section of Experimental Pathology at the National Public Health Laboratories in Buenos Aires.

In 1919 Houssay was appointed to the chair of physiology at the University of Buenos Aires Medicine School, and, until 1943, he transformed and directed it into a highly respected research department in experimental physiology and medicine of international class. In that year, however, the military dictatorship deprived him of his university posts, due to his liberal political ideas and Houssay was forced to re-establish his research lines and staff at a privately funded Instituto de Biologia—Medicina Experimental.

This situation, reinforced by a second dismissal by the Peronista government in 1945, was prolonged until 1955, when Peron was ousted from power and Houssay was reinstated in the University of Buenos Aires, where he remained till he died. His retirement. After this he was also director of the National Scientific and Technical Research Council, from 1957 on.

Houssay's worked in many fields of physiology, such as the nervous, digestive, respiratory and circulatory systems, but his main contribution, which was recognized by the Nobel Prize in Physiology or Medicine of 1947, was on the experimental investigation of the role of the anterior hypophysis gland in the metabolism of carbohydrates, particularly in diabetes mellitus. Houssay demonstrated in the 1930s the diabetogenic effect anterior hypophysis extracts and the decrease in diabetes severity with anterior hypophysectomy. These discoveries stimulated the study of hormonal feedback control mechanisms which are central to all aspects of modern endocrinology.

Houssay's many disciples along his years of activity became also influential by themselves as they spread around the world; such as Eduardo Braun-Menendez, and Miguel Rolando Covian (who went to become the "father" of Brazilian neurophysiology, as chairman of the Department of Physiology of the Medical Faculty of Ribeirao Preto of the University of Sao Paulo).

Houssay wrote with them the most influential textbook of Human Physiology in Latin America, in Spanish and Portuguese (the latter was translated by Covian and collaborators), which, since 1950 has been published in successive editions and used in almost all medical schools of the continent. Houssay published more than 600 scientific papers and several specialized books. Besides the Nobel, Houssay won many distinctions and awards from the Universities of Harvard, Cambridge, Oxford and Paris and 15 other universities, as well as the Dale Medal of the London Society for Endocrinology in 1960. Houssay was also very active as a scientific leader and promoter of the advancement of scientific research and medical education, in Argentina as well as in Latin America.

Personal Life

Houssay died in Buenos Aires at age 84. He is buried in the La Chacarita Cemetery.

BIRUTE GALDIKAS

Birute Marija Filomena Galdikas, OC Ph.D. (born May 10, 1946 (1946-05-10) (age 62), Wiesbaden, Germany), is a primatologist, conservationist, ethologist, and author of several books relating to the endangered species orangutan. Well known in the field of modern primatology, Galdikas is recognized as an authority on orangutans.

Early Life and Education

Galdikas was born in Germany to Lithuanian parents. She later became a naturalized Canadian and grew up in Toronto, Canada.

In college she studied psychology and biology. In 1966, Galdikas earned her bachelor's degrees in psychology and zoology from the University of British Columbia and the University of California, Los Angeles, her master's degree in anthropology from UCLA in 1969 and her doctorate in anthropology, also from UCLA, in 1978. It was there, as a graduate student, she first met famed Kenyan paleontologist Louis Leakey and expressed her desire to study orangutans in their natural habitats.

Leakey's Angels

Determined to study and understand the world of the elusive 'red ape', Galdikas convinced Leakey to help orchestrate her endeavour, despite his initial reservations. Orangutans comprise an exceedingly intelligent great ape genus native to Malaysia and Indonesia, who have long arms and reddish, sometimes brown, hair.

In 1971, Galdikas and her then husband, photographer Rod Brindamour, arrived in one of the world's few remaining wild places, Tanjung Puting Reserve, in Indonesian Borneo. Galdikas thus become the third of a trio of women hand-picked by Leakey to study mankind's nearest relatives, the other great apes, in their natural habitat. Known as 'Leakey's Angels', the other two were Jane Goodall, who studied chimpanzees, and Dian Fossey, who became a martyr in her quest to study and protect mountain gorillas.

Leakey and the National Geographic Society helped Galdikas initially set up her research camp to conduct field study on orangutans in Borneo. Before Leakey's fortuitous decision to anoint Galdikas as the third of his 'Angels', the orangutan was much less well understood than the African great apes. Galdikas went on to further burnish Leakey's legacy by greatly expanding scientific knowledge of orangutan behavior, habitat and diet.

Research and Advocacy

At 25, Galdikas arrived in Borneo to begin her field studies of orangutans in a jungle environment extremely inhospitable to most Westerners. Galdikas proceeded to make many invaluable contributions to the scientific understanding of Indonesia's biodiversity and the rainforest as a whole, while also bringing the orangutan to the attention of the rest of the world.

When she arrived in Borneo, Galdikas settled into a primitive bark and thatch hut, at a site she dubbed 'Camp Leakey', near the edge of the Java Sea. Once there, she encountered numerous poachers, legions of leeches, and swarms of carnivorous insects. Yet she persevered through many travails, remaining there for over 30 years while becoming an outspoken advocate for orangutans and the preservation of their rainforest habitat, which is rapidly being devastated by loggers, gold miners, and unnatural conflagrations.

Galdikas' conservation efforts have extended well beyond advocacy, largely focusing on rehabilitation of the many orphaned orangutans turned over to her for care. Many of these orphans were once pets, before becoming too smart and difficult for their owners to handle. Galdikas' rehabilitation efforts have become the centre of several controversies for Galdikas and the Orangutan Foundation. The effectiveness of her rehabilitation efforts spawned widespread debate in the late 1990s, due in part to articles and books about Galdikas by Canadian Linda Spalding. It was suggested that wild orangutan populations might be harmed as a result of the manner in which rehabilitation was being conducted at the Camp Leakey field station.

BARRY FELL

Barry Fell (born **Howard Barraclough Fell** on June 6, 1917 in Lewes, Sussex, England; died on April 21, 1994, of heart failure in San Diego, California) was a professor of invertebrate zoology at the Harvard Museum of Comparative Zoology. His primary research was on starfish and sea urchins; however, Fell is also widely known for his controversial work in New World epigraphy.

Biography

Fell moved to New Zealand with his mother in the early 1920s, after his father, who was a merchant seaman, died in a shipboard fire. He received his Ph.D. at the University of Edinburgh in 1941, after which he served in the British Army during World War II. In 1946 he returned to New Zealand where he resumed his academic career. In 1964 he joined the Museum of Comparative Zoology at Harvard, where he stayed until retirement in 1979.

Epigraphy

Though Fell was an accomplished marine biologist at Harvard University, he is best known for his work on epigraphy. This interest began early in his career with a study of Polynesian petroglyphs published in 1940. His most famous work came much later, starting in 1976 with the publication of the book *America BC*, in which he proposed translations of alleged inscriptions found on rock surfaces and artifacts in North and South America that he believed to be written in Old World scripts and languages. He followed up this work in 1980 with *Saga America* and in 1982 with *Bronze Age America.* Fell's work led to the establishment of several amateur epigraphic associations such as the "Epigraphic Society" and the "Midwestern Epigraphic Society".

One example of Fell's claims is his contention that Irish monks reached North America centuries before Columbus. This is based on Fell's translation, published in the magazine *Wonderful West Virginia* in 1983, of two rock-cut inscriptions located at archaeological sites in Wyoming County, West Virginia. According to Fell, these inscriptions narrate the story of Christ's nativity and are written in an old Irish script called Celtic Ogham (also referred to as Ogam) dating back to the 6th or 8th century AD. This led to the publication of various articles in the journal *The West Virginia Archeologist* highly critical of Fell's conclusions and methodology, including a 1983 article by archaeologist and historian W. Hunter Lesser describing Fell's claims as pseudoscientific and unreliable, and a 1989 article by lawyers Monroe Oppenheimer and Willard Wirtz that relies on the opinions of academic archaeologists and linguists to dispute that the inscription is written in Ogam script, and which accuses Fell of deliberate fraud.

Fell's epigraphic work has not been well-received in academia. Critics of Fell's work have routinely dismissed him as an amateur, pointing out his lack of formal training in ancient scripts and languages. Criticism of Fell is not limited to academia, as some of Fell's critics themselves lack professional backgrounds in archaeology or linguistics, such as Oppenheimer and Wirtz.

Critics of Dr. Fell have pointed out that he seemed to jump to conclusions, and "to translate ancient languages to English with apparent ease" that was not typical of a critical analysis.

Richard D. Flavin wrote that:

'Fell often worked from material mailed to him, which he reacted to (read: "deciphered") without checking further. This seems to be a general complaint regarding his epigraphic work. He was an accomplished scholastic, well published, who knew the rigors of academic argument and presentation, yet with his epigraphic work Fell seldom stepped away from his desk to research an item or view it in person. Such pervasive carelessness (or, as some say, arrogance) marred his efforts and induced a negative reaction in most professionals. Which is unfortunate, as he had some interesting ideas.

David Kelley, an archaeologist at the University of Calgary who is credited with a major breakthrough in the decipherment of Mayan glyphs, complained about Fell in a 1990 essay:

'Fell's work [contains] major academic sins, the three worst being distortion of data, inadequate acknowledgment of predecessors, and lack of presentation of alternative views."

In the same essay, Kelley went on to acknowledge that, "I have no personal doubts that some of the inscriptions which have been reported [by Fell] are genuine Celtic ogham."

Having acknowledged Fell's shortcomings, Kelley concluded that, "Despite my occasional harsh criticism of Fell's treatment of individual inscriptions, it should be recognized that without Fell's work there would be no [North American] ogham problem to perplex us.

We need to ask not only what Fell has done wrong in his epigraphy, but also where we have gone wrong as archaeologists in not recognizing such an extensive European presence in the New World.

C. V. RAMAN

Chandrasekhara Venkata Raman, (7 November 1888 – 21 November 1970) was an Indian physicist who was awarded the 1930 Nobel Prize in Physics for his work on the molecular scattering of light and for the discovery of the Raman effect, which is named after him.

Biography

Chandrasekhara Venkata Raman was born on November 7, 1888, in an Iyer family in Tiruchirapalli, Tamil Nadu. At an early age Raman moved to the city of Visakhapatnam, Andhra Pradesh. His father was a lecturer in mathematics and physics, so he grew up in an academic atmosphere. His nephew Subramanyan Chandrasekhar also won a Nobel prize in physics in 1983.

Middle Years

Raman entered Presidency College, Madras, in 1902, and in 1904 gained his BA, winning the first place and the gold medal in physics. In 1907 he gained his MA, obtaining the highest distinctions. He joined the Indian Finance Department as an Assistant Accountant General in Calcutta. As the story goes, one evening while returning from work, he spotted the sign of the Indian Association for the Cultivation of Science (IACS). He started visiting the laboratory after office hours and did experiments, which culminated with his Nobel Prize winning work.

In 1917 Raman resigned from his government service and took up the newly created Palit Professorship in Physics at the University of Calcutta. Simultaneously, he continued doing research at the IACS, where he became the Honourary Secretary. Raman used to refer to this period as the golden era of his career. Many talented students gathered around him at the IACS and the University of Calcutta. He was president of the 16th session of the Indian Science Congress in 1929.

Raman won the 1930 Nobel Prize in Physics for his work on the scattering of light and for the discovery of the Raman effect. Raman spectroscopy is based on this phenomenon. He was the first Asian and first non-White to get any Nobel Prize in Science. Before him Sir Rabindranath Tagore (also Indian) had received Nobel Prize for Literature.

Raman also worked on the acoustics of musical instruments. He worked out the theory of transverse vibration of bowed strings, on the basis of superposition velocities. He was also the first to investigate the harmonic nature of the sound of the Indian drums such as the tabla and the mridangam.

In 1934 Raman became the director of the Indian Institute of Science in Bangalore, where two years later he continued as a professor of physics. Other investigations carried out by Raman were: his experimental and theoretical studies on the diffraction of light by acoustic waves of ultrasonic and hypersonic frequencies (published 1934-1942), and those on the effects produced by X-rays on infrared vibrations in crystals exposed to ordinary light.

He also started a company called Travancore Chemical and Manufacturing Co. Ltd. in 1943 along with Dr. Krishnamurthy. The Company during its 60 year history, established 4 factories in Southern India. In 1947, he was appointed as the first National Professor by the new government of Independent India.

In 1948 Raman, through studying the spectroscopic behaviour of crystals, approached in a new manner fundamental problems of crystal dynamics. He dealt with the structure and properties of diamond, the structure and optical behaviour of numerous iridescent substances (labradorite, pearly felspar, agate, opal, and pearls). Among his other interests were the optics of colloids, electrical and magnetic anisotropy, and the physiology of human vision.

Old Age

He retired from the Indian Institute of Science in 1948 and a year later he established the Raman Research Institute in Bangalore Karnataka, serving as its director and remained active there until his death in 1970, in Bangalore, Karnataka, at the age of 82.

CARL HERMANN

Carl Hermann (17 June 1898 – 12 September 1961) was a German professor of crystallography. With Charles-Victor Mauguin, he invented an international standard notation for crystallographic groups known as the Hermann-Mauguin notation or International notation.

Born in the north German port town of Wesermunde to parents both of long-time ministerial families, he got his doctorate from Gottingen in 1923, as a pupil of Max Born and a fellow student with Werner Heisenberg. With Paul P. Ewald at Stuttgart, he nurtured the growing field of crystallography, especially the study of space groups, and began what was later to become *Structure Reports*, a reference series giving every known crystal structure determination.

When the Nazi Party rose to power, he objected to its political restrictions on academic positions, leaving to take a position as a physicist with industrial dye firm I.G. Farbenwerke at Ludwigshafen, where he continued his crystallographic research and studied symmetry in higher-dimensional spaces.

During World War II, he and his wife Eva helped many Jews hide and escape the Holocaust, for which he was imprisoned and sentenced to death. As he was an eminent scientist with influential friends, the sentence was never carried out.

After the war, he lectured briefly at Darmstadt Polytechnic. Then, in 1947, he accepted a newly formed chair in crystallography at the University of Marburg, where he became director of the Crystallographic Institute and remained until his death.

An active Quaker, and having a gift for languages, he devoted much time to promoting international understanding.

In August 1994, the German Crystallographic Society (DGK) established the Carl Hermann Medal, its highest distinction, for outstanding contributions to the science of crystallography.

CHARLES H. HENRY

Charles H. Henry was born in Chicago, Illinois on May 6, 1937. He received an MS. degree in physics in 1959 from the University of Chicago, and a PhD degree in physics in 1965 from the University of Illinois, under the direction of Charles P. Slichter. In March, 2008, he was featured in an article in the Physics Illinois News, a publication of the Physics Department of the University of Illinois.

Henry's entire professional career was spent in the research area of Bell Laboratories in Murray Hill, New Jersey. He joined Bell Laboratories in 1965 as a member of technical staff. From 1971 to 1975, he was head of the Semiconductor Electronics Research Department. He retired from Lucent Technologies Bell Laboratories in 1997 as a Distinguished Member of Technical Staff. He has published 133 technical papers and holds 28 patents, including a 1976 patent covering what is now called the quantum well laser.

Throughout his career, Henry worked at the forefront of semiconductor-based optical technologies and science: light-emitting diodes, semiconductor lasers, and photonic integrated circuits. He was an inventor as well as an experimenter, with a particular interest in understanding the theory underlying semiconductor optical devices.

Quantum Wells

The idea of the quantum well occurred to Henry in late 1972. While thinking about optical waveguides, Henry suddenly realized that a double heterostructure is a waveguide for electrons, and that a heterostructure with a thin central active layer would have discrete electron modes. Such a heterostructure was later named a quantum well, and the modes are the electron states of the quantum well.

Henry further realized that these discrete electron states would greatly alter the optical absorption edge of the semiconductor. Instead of the absorption being a smooth curve steeply rising with optical energy, it would consist of a series of steps.

In early 1973, he proposed to R. Dingle that he look for these steps, and they were observed and reported in 1974 in a paper the pair wrote with W. Wiegmann.

After Dingle's experiment showed the reality of Henry's predicted quantum effects, Henry realized that the quantum well structure would alter the density of states of the semiconductor and result in an improved semiconductor laser. He also realized that the laser wavelength could be changed merely by changing the thickness of the thin quantum well layers, whereas in a conventional laser, a change in wavelength requires a change in layer composition. On March 7, 1975, Henry and Dingle filed a patent entitled "Quantum Effects in Heterostructure Lasers," which was issued on Sept. 21, 1976. The story of the origin of the quantum well laser is told by Henry in the foreword to *Quantum Well Lasers*, edited by Peter S. Zory, Jr. (1993).

CARL FRIEDRICH GAUSS

Johann Carl Friedrich Gauss (30 April 1777 – 23 February 1855) was a German mathematician and scientist who contributed significantly to many fields, including number theory, statistics, analysis, differential geometry, geodesy, electrostatics, astronomy, and optics. Sometimes known as the *princeps mathematicorum* (Latin, usually translated as "the Prince of Mathematicians", although Latin *princeps* also can simply mean "the foremost") and "greatest mathematician since antiquity", Gauss had a remarkable influence in many fields of mathematics and science and is ranked as one of history's most influential mathematicians.

Gauss was a child prodigy. There are many anecdotes pertaining to his precocity while a toddler, and he made his first ground-breaking mathematical discoveries while still a teenager. He completed *Disquisitiones Arithmeticae*, his magnum opus, in 1798 at the age of 21, though it would not be published until 1801. This work was fundamental in consolidating number theory as a discipline and has shaped the field to the present day.

Early Years (1777–1798)

Gauss was born in Braunschweig, in the Electorate of Brunswick-Luneburg, now part of Lower Saxony, Germany, as the only son of poor working-class parents. There are several stories of his early genius, all of them open to doubt; according to one, his gifts became very apparent at the age of three when he corrected, in his head, an error his father had made on paper while calculating finances. Another famous story, and one that has evolved in the telling, has it that in primary school his teacher, J.G. Buttner, tried to occupy pupils by making them add a list of integers. The young Gauss reputedly produced the correct answer within seconds, to the astonishment of his teacher and his assistant Martin Bartels. Gauss's presumed method, which supposes the list of numbers was from 1 to 100, was to realise that pairwise addition of terms from opposite ends of the list yielded identical intermediate sums: 1 + 100 = 101, 2 + 99 = 101, 3 + 98 = 101, and so on, for a total sum of 50 × 101 = 5050 (*see arithmetic series and summation*). However whilst the method works, the incident itself is probably apocryphal; some, such as Joseph Rotman in his book *A first course in Abstract Algebra*, question whether it ever happened.

As his father wanted him to follow in his footsteps and become a mason, he was not supportive of Gauss's schooling in mathematics and science. Gauss was primarily supported by his mother in this effort and by the Duke of Braunschweig, who awarded Gauss a fellowship to the Collegium Carolinum (now Technische Universitat Braunschweig), which he attended from 1792 to 1795, and subsequently he moved to the University of Gottingen from 1795 to 1798. While in university, Gauss independently rediscovered several important theorems; his breakthrough occurred in 1796 when he was able to show that any regular polygon with a number of sides which is a Fermat prime (and, consequently, those polygons with any number of sides which is the product of distinct Fermat primes and a power of 2) can be constructed by compass and straightedge. This was a major discovery in an important field of mathematics; construction problems had occupied mathematicians since the days of the Ancient Greeks, and the discovery ultimately led Gauss to choose mathematics instead of philology as a career. Gauss was so pleased by this result that he requested that a regular heptadecagon be inscribed on his tombstone. The stonemason declined, stating that the difficult construction would essentially look like a circle.

The year 1796 was most productive for both Gauss and number theory. He discovered a construction of the heptadecagon on March 30. He invented modular arithmetic, greatly simplifying manipulations in number theory. He became the first to prove the quadratic reciprocity law on April 8. This remarkably general law allows mathematicians to determine the solvability of any quadratic equation in modular arithmetic. The prime number theorem, conjectured on May 31, gives a good understanding of how the prime numbers are distributed among the integers. Gauss also discovered that every positive integer is representable as a sum of at most three triangular numbers on July 10 and then jotted down in his diary the famous words, "Heureka! num = A + A + A." On October 1 he published a result on the number of solutions of polynomials with coefficients in finite fields, which ultimately led to the Weil conjectures 150 years later.

CHRISTIAN DOPPLER

Christian Andreas Doppler (November 29, 1803 – March 17, 1853) was an Austrian mathematician and physicist, most famous for the hypothesis of what is now known as the Doppler effect which is the apparent change in frequency and wavelength of a wave that is perceived by an observer moving relative to the source of the waves.

Christian Doppler was born in Salzburg, Austria as the son of a stone-mason. However he could not work in his father's business because of his generally weak physical condition. After completing high school he studied astronomy and mathematics in Vienna and Salzburg and started to work at the Prague Polytechnic (now Czech Technical University), where he was appointed professor for mathematics and physics in 1841. (Note: At that time, the present Czech Republic was ruled by the Empire of Austria.)

Only one year later at the age of 39 he published his most notable work on the Doppler effect (for instance to be noticed in the change of sound of a quickly passing vehicle). The German title was "Uber das farbige Licht der Doppelsterne und einige andere Gestirne des Himmels-Versuch einer das Bradleysche Theorem als integrirenden Theil in sich schliessenden allgemeineren Theorie" (English translation: On the coloured light of the binary refracted stars and other celestial bodies-Attempt of a more general theory including Bradley's theorem as an integral part). An English translation can be found in the book by Alec Eden together with the original German version (see reference). In this work, Doppler postulated his principle that the observed frequency depends on the speed of the source and the observer, and he tried to use it for explaining the colour of binary stars. The Doppler effect of sound was verified by Buys Ballot in 1845. In his time in Prague as professor he published more than 50 articles in mathematics, physics and astronomy.

His research career in Prague was interrupted by the revolutionary incidents of March 1848, when he fled to Vienna. There he was appointed head of the Institute for Experimental Physics at the University of Vienna in 1850. During his presence at the University of Vienna, Doppler, along with Franz Unger, played an influential role in the development of young Gregor Mendel, known as the founding father of genetics, who was a student at the University of Vienna from 1851 to 1853.

Doppler died on March 17, 1853 at age 49 from a pulmonary disease in Venice (also at that time part of the Austrian Empire). His tomb can be found just inside the entrance of the Venetian island cemetery of San Michele.

CLINTON DAVISSON

Clinton Joseph Davisson (22 October 1881 – 1 February 1958), was an American physicist who won the 1937 Nobel Prize in Physics for his discovery of electron diffraction. Davisson shared the Nobel Prize with George Paget Thomson, who independently discovered electron diffraction at about the same time as Davisson.

Life

Davisson was born in Bloomington, Illinois. He graduated from Bloomington High School in 1902, and entered the University of Chicago on scholarship. Upon the recommendation of Robert A. Millikan, in 1905 Davisson was hired by Princeton University as Instructor of Physics. He completed the requirements for his B.S.

degree from Chicago in 1908, mainly by working in the summers. While teaching at Princeton, he did doctoral thesis research with Owen Richardson. He received his Ph.D. in physics from Princeton in 1911; in the same year he married Richardson's sister, Charlotte.

Davisson was then appointed as an assistant professor at the Carnegie Institute of Technology. In 1917 he took a leave from the Carnegie Institute to do war-related research with the Engineering Department of the Western Electric Company (later Bell Telephone Laboratories). At the end of the war, Davisson accepted a permanent position at Western Electric after receiving assurances of his freedom there to do basic research. He had found that his teaching responsibilities at the Carnegie Institute largely precluded him from doing research. Davisson remained at Western Electric (and Bell Telephone) until his formal retirement in 1946. He then accepted a research professor appointment at the University of Virginia that continued until his second retirement in 1954. Clinton and Charlotte Davisson had four children, including the American physicist Richard Davisson.

CHARLES-AUGUSTIN DE COULOMB

Charles Augustin de Coulomb (born June 14, 1736, Angouleme, France-died August 23, 1806, Paris, France) was a French physicist. He is best known for developing Coulomb's law: the definition of the electrostatic force of attraction and repulsion. The SI unit of charge, the coulomb, was named after him.

Life

Coulomb was born in Angouleeme, France, to a well-to-do family. His father, Henri Coulomb, was inspector of the Royal Fields in Montpellier. His mother, Catherine Bajet, came from a wealthy family in the wool trade. When Coulomb was a boy the family moved to Paris, and there Coulomb studied at the prestigious College des Quatre-Nations. The courses in mathematics there, under Pierre Charles Monnier, determined him to pursue mathematics and similar subjects as a career. From 1757 to 1759 he joined his father's family in Montpellier and took part in the work of the academy of the city, directed by the mathematician Augustin Danyzy. With his father's approval, Coulomb returned to Paris in 1759 where he was successful in the entrance examination for the military school at Mezieres.

After he left the school in 1761, he initially took part in the survey for the British coastal charts, and was then sent on a mission to Martinique in 1764 to take part in the construction of the Fort Bourbon under the orders of the lieutenant-colonel of Rochemore, as the French colony was insulated in the middle of the English and Spanish possessions following the Seven Years' War. Coulomb spent eight years directing the work, contracting tropical fever. He carried out several experiments on the resistance of masonries and the behaviour of the walls of escarpe (supportings), which were inspired by the ideas of Pieter van Musschenbroek on friction.

Upon his return, with the rank of Captain, he was employed at La Rochelle, the Isle of Aix and Cherbourg. He discovered an inverse relationship of the force between electric charges and the square of its distance, later named after him as Coulomb's law.

In 1781, he was stationed permanently at Paris. On the outbreak of the Revolution in 1789, he resigned his appointment as *intendant des eaux et fontaines*, and retired to a small estate which he possessed at Blois. He was recalled to Paris for a time in order to take part in the new determination of weights and measures, which had been decreed by the Revolutionary government. He was one of the first members of the National Institute; he was appointed inspector of public instruction in 1802. His health was already very feeble, and four years later he died in Paris, France.

Coulomb leaves a legacy as a hero in the field of geotechnical engineering for his contribution to retaining wall design.

C. H. D. BUYS BALLOT

Christophorus Henricus Diedericus Buys Ballot (October 10, 1817, Kloetinge – February 3, 1890, Utrecht) was a Dutch chemist and meteorologist after whom Buys-Ballot's law and the

Buys Ballot table are named. The son of a Dutch Reformed minister, Buys Ballot attended the Gymnasium at Zaltbommel and the Hogeschool (now University) of Utrecht. After receiving his doctorate in 1844, he became lecturer in mineralogy and geology at Utrecht; he added theoretical chemistry in 1846. In 1847 he was appointed professor of mathematics and from 1867 until his retirement he was professor of physics. Buys Ballot tested the Doppler effect for sound waves in 1845 by using a group of musicians playing a calibrated note on a train in the Utrecht-Amsterdam line.

Buys Ballot is best known for his accomplishments in the field of meteorology, specifically the explanation of the direction of air flow in large weather systems. Furthermore, he founded the Royal Dutch Meteorological Institute in 1854 and he remained its chief director until his death. He was one of the first to see the need for international cooperation, and in 1873 became the first chairman of the International Meteorological Committee, a precursor of the World Meteorological Organization (WMO). Buys-Ballot's law states that if a person in the Northern Hemisphere stands with his back to the wind, the low atmospheric pressure is found to his left. His main research effort in meteorology went into examining long-time series for regularities; he was more concerned with establishing the regularities than in explaining them. He made no contributions to the theory of meteorology which is perhaps surprising given his training in physics. The contrast with his American contemporary, William Ferrel, who discovered Buy-Ballot's law slightly earlier, is striking. Buys Ballot devised a tabular method for investigating periodicity in time series. In 1847 he used the table now named after him to determine the period of the sun's rotation from daily observations of temperature in the Netherlands from 1729 to 1846.

CARL DAVID ANDERSON

Carl David Anderson (3 September 1905 – 11 January 1991) was an American physicist. He is best known for his discovery of the positron, an achievement for which he received the Nobel Prize in Physics in 1936.

Biography

Anderson was born in New York City, the son of Swedish immigrants. He studied physics and engineering at Caltech (B.S., 1927; Ph.D., 1930). Under the supervision of Robert A. Millikan, he began investigations into cosmic rays during the course of which he encountered unexpected particle tracks in his cloud chamber photographs that he correctly interpreted as having been created by a particle with the same mass as the electron, but with opposite electrical charge. This discovery, announced in 1932 and later confirmed by others, validated Paul Dirac's theoretical prediction of the existence of the positron. Anderson obtained the first direct proof that positrons existed by shooting gamma rays produced by the natural radioactive nuclide ThC" (^{208}Tl) into other materials, resulting in creation of positron-electron pairs. For this work, Anderson shared the Nobel Prize in Physics for 1936 with Victor Hess.

Also in 1936, Anderson and his first graduate student, Seth Neddermeyer, discovered the muon (or 'mu-meson', as it was known for many years), a subatomic particle 207 times more massive than the electron. Anderson and Neddermeyer at first believed that they had seen the pion, a particle which Hideki Yukawa had postulated in his theory of the strong interaction. When it became clear that what Anderson had seen was *not* the pion, theoretical physicist I. I. Rabi, puzzled as to how the unexpected discovery could fit into any logical scheme of particle physics, famously asked "Who ordered *that*?" (sometimes the story goes that he was dining with colleagues at a Chinese restaurant at the time).

The muon was the first of a long list of subatomic particles whose discovery initially baffled theoreticians who could not make the confusing 'zoo' fit into some tidy conceptual scheme. Willis Lamb, in his 1955 Nobel Lecture, joked that he had heard it said that "the finder of a new elementary particle used to be rewarded by a Nobel Prize, but such a discovery now ought to be punished by a $10,000 fine."

Carl Anderson spent all of his career at Caltech. During World War II he conducted research in rocketry. He died on 11 January 1991, and is interred in the Forest Lawn, Hollywood Hills Cemetery in Los Angeles, California.

CHARLES STEEN

Charles A. Steen (1919 – 2006-01-01), was a geologist who made and lost a fortune after discovering a rich uranium deposit in Utah during the Uranium boom of the early 1950s.

Early Years

Steen was born in Caddo, Texas and attended high school in Houston. He went on to study at John Tarleton Agricultural College in Stepenville and in 1940 transferred to the Texas College of Mines and Metallurgy (now named the University of Texas at El Paso), receiving a B.A. degree in geology in 1943.

Ineligible for the draft because of his poor eyesight, Steen spent World War II working as a geologist in Bolivia and Peru. Returning to Texas in 1945, he married Minnie Lee ("M.L.") Holland. He started graduate school at the University of Chicago but after a year returned to Houston to take a job doing field work for the Standard Oil Company of Indiana. However, within two years he had been fired for insubordination and had trouble getting any job as a geologist anywhere in the oil industry.

The Uranium Boom

Down on his luck, Steen read in the December 1949 issue of *The Engineering and Mining Journal* that the United States federal government had issued incentives for domestic uranium prospectors. Under the Atomic Energy Act of 1946, the U.S. Atomic Energy Commission had the authority to withdraw lands from the private sector in order to examine them as possible sites for uranium mining. During World War II, the Manhattan Project had received most of its uranium from foreign sources in Canada and the Belgian Congo. However, it had also received some from vanadium miners in the American Southwest, where uranium was often a by-product of mining (uranium was not, before the atomic bomb, a valuable metal). There was a concern that the United States would not have enough domestic supply of uranium for its nuclear weapons programme.

In the late 1940s and early 1950s the Atomic Energy Commission established itself as the only legal buyer of uranium in the U.S., and artificially manipulated prices to reflect their current uranium needs. By raising the price of uranium, they created an incentive for prospectors in the Four Corners region.

Despite the fact that his three sons, Johnny, Andy and Charles Jr., were all less than four years old, and his wife was expecting, Steen borrowed $1,000 from his mother and headed for the Colorado Plateau, determined to strike it rich.

Steen could not afford the standard radiation-detecting equipment used by uranium prospectors-the Geiger counter. Instead, he used a secondhand diamond drill rig and his geologic training for his prospecting. At the time, each prospector had his own idiosyncratic theory on where to find uranium. The uranium industry was composed primarily of individual prospectors and geologists who would attempt to find a large deposit and either mine it for themselves or mine it for a large company (such as Union Carbide) who would then transport the ore from the mine to the uranium mill where it could be converted into yellowcake. Steen's theory on uranium deposits was that they would collect in anticlinal structures in the same manner as oil, which others on the Plateau dismissed as "Steen's Folly." His family moved into a small trailer at Dove Creek, Colorado, and then later into a tarpaper shack near Cisco, Utah. Steen fed his family on poached venison and cereal, in a highly marginalized state of existence, for two years.

Mi Vida

But on July 6, 1952, Steen hit it big, finding a massive, relatively highly-enriched uranium deposit in the Big Indian Wash of Lisbon Valley, southeast of Moab, Utah. He named it the "Mi Vida" mine

(*My Life*), and it was the first big strike of the uranium boom. Steen made millions off his claims, and provoked a "Uranium Rush" of prospectors into the Four Corners region, similar to the Gold Rush of the 1850s in California. In Moab, Steen built a $250,000 hilltop mansion to replace his tarpaper shack, with a swimming pool, greenhouse, and servants' quarters. He formed a number of companies to continue his uranium work, including the Utex Exploration Company, the Moab Drilling Company, the Mi Vida Company, Big Indian Mines, Inc., and later the Uranium Reduction Company. He made his money well known, inviting the entire population of Moab to annual parties in a local airport hangar, having his original worn prospecting boots bronzed, and flying to Salt Lake City in his private plane for weekly rumba lessons. He donated $50,000 towards a new hospital in Moab and gave land for churches and schools.

Steen was elected to the Utah State Senate in 1958, but quickly became disillusioned with politics. He resigned from office in 1961 and moved to a ranch near Reno, Nevada, building a 16,000 square foot (1500 m^2) mansion near the residence of the Comstock millionaire miner, Sandy Bowers. He sold the Utex Exploration Company and the Uranium Reduction Company in 1962. By the late 1950s, the U.S. government had enough uranium for its needs and had stopped supporting high prices of the ore, killing the market by 1960. Steen attempted to diversify his interests by investing in Arabian horse breeding, a marble quarry, an airplane factory, a pickle plant, and real estate. He met with financial losses and misfortune. In 1968 he declared bankruptcy after the Internal Revenue Service seized his assets to pay for back taxes. In 1971 he suffered a severe head injury working on a copper prospect. Long suffering from Alzheimer's, Steen died on January 1, 2006, in Loveland, Colorado. Minnie Lee died in 1997.

CHARLES R. STELCK

Charles Richard Stelck (born 1917) is an award-winning Canadian petroleum geologist, paleontologist, stratigrapher and emeritus professor. His research has yielded many large oil and gas finds in western Canada. Stelck was born in Edmonton, Alberta. As a teenager he worked on summer geological field parties. With the help of a Tegler Scholarship, Stelck attended the University of Alberta. He switched into the geology programme when his friend, Robert Folinsbee, convinced him that it was an exciting field. He obtained a BSc (1937) and a MSc (1941). He moved to California and obtained his PhD at Stanford University.

Career

In the early 1940s, he took a position at the University of Alberta. While there he hypothesized that coral reefs had once lived in what is now the Arctic. He further hypothesized that this would mean there would be oil there now. He discovered reef material while conducting geological research in a mountainous region near Norman Wells, Northwest Territories with a dog team. Most geologists were shocked by his findings as the theory of continental drift had yet to be proposed. The next leap of discovery was to apply his knowledge to find if a reef had existed in Alberta. He worked with his students to develop an understanding of western Canada's sedimentary basin and the Leduc oilfields. Many of his former students discovered oil, including; Doug Layer (Leduc No. 1), and Arne Rudolph Nielsen and Tony Mason (Pembina oil field-the largest pool of oil in Canada).

CHARLES FRANCIS RICHTER

Charles Francis Richter (April 26, 1900 – September 30, 1985), was an American seismologist and physicist. Richter is most famous as the creator of the Richter magnitude scale which, until the development of the moment magnitude scale in 1979, quantified the size of earthquakes. Inspired by Kiyoo Wadati's 1928 paper on shallow and deep earthquakes, Richter first used the scale in 1935 after developing it in collaboration with Beno Gutenberg; both worked at California Institute of Technology, California, USA. The quote "logarithmic plots are a device of the devil" is attributed to Richter.

Career

Richter went to work at the Carnegie Institute in 1927 after receiving a job offer to be a research assistant there from Robert Millikan. Here he began a collaboration with Beno Gutenberg. The Seismology lab at the California Institute of Technology was hoping to begin publishing regular reports on earthquakes in southern California, and had a pressing need to have a system of measuring the strength of earthquakes for these reports. Together they had devised the scale that would become known at the Richter scale to fill this need, based on measuring quantitatively the displacement of the earth due to seismic waves, as had been suggested by Kiyoo Wadati.

The pair designed a seismograph that measured this displacement, and developed a logarithmic scale to measure intensity. The name "magnitude" for this measurement came from Richter's childhood interest in Astronomy, where the intensity of stars is measured in magnitudes. Gutenberg's contribution was substantial, but his aversion to interviews contributed to his name being left off the scale. After publishing the proposed scale in 1935, it was quickly adopted for use in measuring the intensity of earthquakes.

He remained at the Carnegie Institute until 1936 when he obtained a post at the California Institute of Technology, where Beno Gutenberg worked. Gutenberg and Richter published *Seismicity of the Earth* in 1941. Its revised edition, published in 1954, is considered a standard reference in the field.

Richter became a full professor at the California Institute of Technology in 1952. In 1958, he published *Elementary Seismology* based on his undergraduate teaching notes. As Richter never published in peer reviewed journals, this is often considered his most important contribution to seismology. Richter spent 1959 and 960 in Japan as a Fulbright scholar. Around this time in his career, he became involved in the development of building codes for earthquake prone areas. The city government of Los Angeles removed many ornaments and cornices from municipal buildings in the 1960s as a result of

Richter's awareness campaigns. After the 1971 Los Angeles Earthquake, the city cited Richter's warnings as important in preventing many deaths. Richter retired in 1970.

He was also a naturist, and travelled to many nudist communities with his wife.

Richter died of congestive heart failure on September 30, 1985 in Pasadena, California.

CHARLES LYELL

Sir Charles Lyell, 1st Baronet, (November 14, 1797 – February 22, 1875) was a Scottish lawyer, geologist, and protagonist of uniformitarianism. He was the foremost geologist of his day, and an influence on the young Charles Darwin.

Life

Charles Lyell was born in Kinnordy, Forfarshire (now Angus), the eldest of ten children. Lyell's father, also named Charles, was a lawyer and botanist of minor repute and first exposed the younger Charles to the study of nature. Charles spent much of his childhood at the family's other home, Bartley Lodge in the New Forest, England, where his interest in the natural world was sparked.

After being sent down from Exeter College, Oxford in 1820, Lyell learnt geology under the wing of the naturalist William Buckland. After graduation he took up law as a profession, and completed a circuit through rural England, where he could observe geology. As his eyesight began to fail him he turned to geology as a full time profession. His first paper, "On a recent formation of freshwater limestone in Forfarshire", was presented in 1822. By 1827, he had abandoned the law and embarked on a geological career that would result in fame and the acceptance of ideas, mainly uniformitarianism, proposed by James Hutton a few decades earlier.

In 1832, Lyle married Mary Horner of Bonn, daughter of Leonard Horner (1785-1864), also associated with the Geological Society of London. The new couple spent their honeymoon in

Switzerland and Italy on a geological tour of the area. During the 1840s, he travelled to the United States and Canada, and wrote two popular travel-and-geology books: *Travels in North America* (1845) and *A Second Visit to the United States* (1849). After the Great Chicago Fire, Lyell was one of the first to donate books to help found the Chicago Public Library.

Lyell's wife Mary died in 1873, and two years later Lyell himself died as he was revising the twelfth edition of *Principles*. He is buried in Westminster Abbey. Lyell was rewarded by the State with a knighthood (KT), and later by a baronetcy (Bt), which is an hereditary honour.

He was awarded the Copley Medal in 1858 and the Wollaston Medal in 1866. Lyell crater on the Moon and a crater on Mars were named in his honour. In addition, Mount Lyell in western Tasmania, Australia, located in a profitable mining area, bears Lyell's name.

CLARENCE KING

Clarence King (January 6, 1842 – December 24, 1901) was an American geologist and mountaineer. He was the first director of the United States Geological Survey, from 1879-1881. Clarence King was noted for his exploration of the Sierra Nevada. He was born in Newport, Rhode Island.

Career

In 1862, King graduated from the Sheffield Scientific School of Yale College with a Ph.B. in chemistry. While at Yale, he studied with James Dwight Dana. After graduation King travelled on horseback to California with his good friend and classmate, James Terry Gardiner. In California he joined the California Geological Survey without pay where he worked with William H. Brewer, Josiah D. Whitney and Richard D. Cotter. In October 1872, he uncovered a diamond and gemstone hoax perpetrated by Philip Arnold. In 1864, King and Richard Cotter reported the first ascent of Mount Tyndall, at the time labeling it mistakenly as the highest peak in the Sierra Nevada.

In 1867, King was named U.S. Geologist of the Geological Exploration of the Fortieth Parallel, commonly know as the Fortieth Parallel Survey, a position for which he strongly lobbied. King spent six years in the field exploring areas form Wyoming to the border of California. During that time he also published his famous "Mountaineering in the Sierra Nevada" (1872). After the completion of the field work, in 1878 King published "Systematic Geology."

While conducting field work for the Survey, King met and befriended Henry Brooks Adams. Their friendship lasted for the rest of King's life, and he is often mentioned by Adams in the autobiographical *The Education of Henry Adams* (1907). In 1879, the US Congress consolidated the number of geological surveys exploring the American West and created the United States Geological Survey. King was chosen its first director, however he served for only twenty months.

His common law marriage in 1888 to a black woman, Ada Copeland, was kept secret by his keeping a double identity. King didn't even reveal his true name to his wife until he was on his deathbed. He was survived by four children.

King died of tuberculosis in Phoenix, Arizona, and is buried in Newport, Rhode Island. Kings Peak in Utah and Mount Clarence King in Kings Canyon National Park are named in his honour.

CLAUDE HILLAIRE-MARCEL

Professor Claude Hillaire-Marcel FRSC (born April 1, 1944) is a Canadian geoscientist of great distinction and a world leader in Quaternary research. He is known for his groundbreaking research on the environment, climate change, and oceanography. He is a Fellow of the Royal Society of Canada and professor at l'Universite du Quebec a Montreal. Dr. Hillaire-Marcel was born and educated in France. He received advanced degrees at the Sorbonne in 1968, and the University of Paris in 1979.

He moved to Canada and became a professor at l'Universite du Quebec a Montreal. From between 1970 and 2003, Claude Hillaire-

Marcel authored or co-authored over 150 scientific papers. He supervised 20 doctoral dissertations and 37 M.Sc. & D.E.A. theses, and in addition he had 13 scientists working with him as postdoctoral fellows from Belgium, Canada, Denmark, France, Germany, Mexico, the UK & the U.S.

His early papers covered Pleistocene marine fauna and isostatic rebound near Montreal. Later he broadened his geographic scope to include Ungava Bay and Hudson Bay. In 1976, he began writing about oxygen and carbon isotopes. By 1980 he was involved in dating studies utilizing isotopes of uranium and thorium.

Between 1985 and 1991, Mr. Hillaire-Marcel participated in, or was chief scientist on various scientific marine expeditions, including six cruises on Canadian ships (CSS Dawson & CSS Hudson) and a cruise aboard the French research ship Marion-Dufresne in Greenland waters in 1999.

In 1994, a special issue of the Canadian Journal of Earth Sciences featured Labrador Sea studies. Nine of the 12 articles were co-authored by Claude Hillaire-Marcel. In 2001, he was lead author on a paper in Nature entitled "Absence of deep-water formation in the Labrador Sea during the last interglacial period", and he was one of several authors of an EOS article entitled "New Record Shows Pronounced Changes in Arctic Ocean Circulation and Climate".

Most of his work has been around the shores of Canada, but he has carried out field studies or been involved in research in Africa (Algeria, Burundi, Egypt, Ethiopia, Kenya, Libya, Mali, Niger, Tanzania and Tunisia, the Middle East (Israel and Syria, Latin America (Chile, Mexico, Peru, and Uruguay), and Europe (France, Greece and Spain (including the Balearic and Canary island.

Between 1977 and 2002 he co-authored 24 non-Quaternary scientific papers in the fields of agriculture, nutrition, and physical exercise. One involved testing the authenticity of maple syrup. All papers were peer-reviewed. Professor Claude Hillaire-Marcel served on the following committees; the Royal Society of Canada, Canadian

Quaternary Association, International Union for Quaternary Research, Ocean Drilling Programme, International Marine Global Change Study (IMAGES), the World Climate Research Programme (WCRP), and the Joint Global Oceans Flux Studies (JGOFS).

He is a member of the Consultative Committee for the Environment of Hydro-Quebec, the Canadian Scientific Committee for the Integrated ODP, the Scientific Committee of the Institut du Sahel, and the Executive Committee of Fonds quebecois de la recherche sur la nature et les technologies (FONDS FCAR) and Vice-President of the Sub-commission for the Americas of the INQUA Commission on Shorelines.

Dr. Hillaire-Marcel performs editorial duties for GpQ, CJES and QSR.

Claude Hillaire-Marcel was the Founding Director (1981-1989, 1997-1999) of The Centre de recherche en geochimie et geodynamique, or GEOTOP. He served twice as Chairman of the Department of Earth Sciences at UQAM (1983-1985 and 1987-1989)

Dr. Hillaire-Marcel has held two endowed chairs: from 1989 to 2000 the Industrial Chair Hydro-Quebec-NSERC-UQAM and from 2000 on the International Chair UNESCO.

CLARENCE DUTTON

Clarence Edward Dutton (May 15, 1841 – January 4, 1912) was an American geologist and US Army officer. Dutton was born in Wallingford, Connecticut on May 15, 1841. He graduated from Yale College in 1860 and took postgraduate courses there until 1862, when he enlisted in the 21st Connecticut Volunteers; he fought at Fredericksburg, Suffolk, Nashville and Petersburg.

In 1875 he began work as a geologist for the U.S. Geological Survey. Working chiefly in the Colorado Plateau region, he wrote several classic papers, including geological studies of the high plateaus of Utah (1879-80), the Tertiary history of the Grand Canyon district (1882), and the Charleston, SC earthquake of 1886. As head of the division of volcanic geology at the USGS, he studied volcanism in Hawaii, California, and Oregon. He helped coordinate the scientific response to a large earthquake in Sonora, Mexico, in 1887. He was elected a member of the National Academy of Sciences in 1884.

In 1886, Dutton led a USGS party to Crater Lake, Oregon. His team carried a half-ton survey boat, the *Cleetwood*, up the steep mountain slope and lowered it 2,000 feet into the lake. From the *Cleetwood*, Dutton used piano wire with lead weights to measure the depth of the lake at 168 different points.

The survey team determined the lake was 1,996 feet deep. The currently-accepted maximum depth figure, measured by sonar, is 1,943 feet (592 meters).

In 1889, Dutton proposed the term "isostasy" for the concept of a general balance within the earth's crust, with lighter weight blocks coming to stand higher than adjacent blocks with higher density, an idea first expressed by Pratt and Airy in the 1850s.

Dutton was a close associate of John Wesley Powell and G.K. Gilbert at the USGS. He was an energetic and effective field geologist: in 1875-1877 Dutton's field party mapped 12,000 square miles of the high plateaus of southern Utah, an area of rugged topography and poor access.

Dutton had a distinctive flair for literary description, and is best remembered today for his colourful (and sometimes flamboyant) descriptions of the geology and scenery of the Grand Canyon region of Arizona. "Dutton first taught the world to look at that country and see it as it was... Dutton is almost as much the *genius loci* of the Grand Canyon as Muir is of Yosemite"—Wallace Stegner, *Beyond the Hundredth Meridian.*

In 1891 he retired from the USGS to serve as commander of the arsenal of San Antonio, Texas; then as ordnance officer of the department of Texas. After retiring from the Army in 1901, he returned to the study of geology. Dutton spent his last years at the home of his son in Englewood, New Jersey.

COLIN CAMPBELL

Colin J. Campbell, (born in Berlin, Germany in 1931) is a retired British petroleum geologist who predicts that oil production will peak by 2007.

The consequences of this are uncertain but drastic, due to the world's dependence on fossil fuels for the vast majority of its energy. His theories have received wide attention, but are disputed by some in the oil industry and have not significantly changed U.S. governmental energy policies at this time. In order to deal with declining global oil production, he has proposed the Rimini protocol.

Influential papers by Campbell include *The Coming Oil Crisis*, which he wrote with Jean Laherrere in 1998, and is credited with convincing the International Energy Agency of the coming peak; and *The End of Cheap Oil*, which was published the same year in *Scientific American*. He was referred to as a "doomsayer" in the *The Wall Street Journal* in 2004.

Association for the Study of Peak Oil and Gas founded by Campbell is gaining recognition in the recent years. They have organized yearly international conferences since 2002. The last one was held in Cork, Ireland on 17th-18th September 2007. The next conference is scheduled for 20-22th October 2008 in Barcelona, Spain.

Background

The most famous peak oil petrogeologist is M. King Hubbert, who successfully predicted in 1956 that oil production would peak in the United States between 1965 and 1970. His theories became popular during the 1973 energy crisis, and during 1979 energy crisis when even the United States Secretary of Energy, James Schlesinger, announced that the peak had arrived.

In December 2000 Colin Campbell warned in a public lecture held in Clausthal University of a possible ill-conceived military intervention in the Middle East.

DENNIS GABOR

Dennis Gabor (original Hungarian name: **Gabor Denes**), FRS, (June 5, 1900, Budapest – February 9, 1979, London) was a Hungarian electrical engineer and inventor, most notable for inventing holography, for which he later received the Nobel Prize in Physics.

Biography

Born Gabor Denes, Dennis Gabor studied at the Technical University of Budapest and, in Germany, at the Charlottenburg Technical University in Berlin, now known as the Technical University of Berlin. At the start of his career, he analyzed the properties of high voltage electric transmission lines by using cathode-beam oscillographs, which led to his interest in electron optics. Studying the fundamental processes of the oscillograph, Gabor was led to other electron-beam devices such as electron microscopes and TV tubes. He eventually wrote his Ph.D. thesis concerning the cathode ray tube in 1927, and worked on plasma lamps.

Having fled from Nazi Germany in 1933, Gabor was invited to Britain to work at the development department of the British Thomson-Houston company in Rugby, Warwickshire. During his time in Rugby, he met Marjorie Butler, and they married in 1936. It was while working at British Thomson-Houston that he invented holography, in 1947.

Gabor's research focused on electron optics, which led him to the invention of holography. The basic idea was that for perfect optical imaging, the total of all the information has to be used; not only the amplitude, as in usual optical imaging, but also the phase. In this manner a complete holo-spatial picture can be obtained. Gabor published his theories of optical imaging and holography in a series of papers between 1946 and 1951.

Gabor also researched how human beings communicate and hear; the result of his investigations was the theory of granular synthesis, although Greek composer Iannis Xenakis claimed that he was actually the first inventor of this synthesis technique.

At the time Gabor developed holography, coherent light sources were not available, so the theory had to wait more than a decade until its first practical applications were realized, though he experimented with a heavily filtered mercury arc light source. The invention in 1960 of the laser, the first coherent light source, was followed by the first hologram, in 1963, after which holography became commercially available.

In 1948 Gabor moved from Rugby to Imperial College London, and in 1958 became professor of Applied Physics until his retirement in 1967. While spending much of his retirement in Italy, he remained connected with Imperial College as a Senior Research Fellow and also became Staff Scientist of CBS Laboratories, in Stamford, Connecticut; there, he collaborated with his life-long friend, CBS Labs' president Dr. Peter C. Goldmark in many new schemes of communication and display. He developed an interest in social analysis and published *The Mature Society: a view of the future* in 1972. Gabor wrote, "The best way to predict the future is to invent it."

Following the rapid development of lasers and a wide variety of holographic applications (*e.g.* art, information storage, recognition of patterns), Gabor achieved acknowledged success and worldwide attention during his lifetime. He received numerous awards besides the Nobel Prize. The International Society for Optical Engineering (SPIE) presents its *Dennis Gabor award* annually, "in recognition of outstanding accomplishments in diffractive wavefront technologies, especially those which further the development of holography and metrology applications." The NOVOFER Foundation of the Hungarian Academy of Sciences annually presents its *International Dennis Gabor Award*, for young scientists researching in the fields of physics and applied technology.

DANIEL GABRIEL FAHRENHEIT

Daniel Gabriel Fahrenheit (24 May 1686 – 16 September 1736) was a German physicist and engineer who worked most of his life in the Dutch Republic. The Fahrenheit (**°F**) temperature scale is named after him.

Biography

Fahrenheit was born in 1686 in Danzig (Gdansk), Poland. The Fahrenheits were a merchant family who had moved from one Hanseatic League city to another. Fahrenheit's great-grandfather had lived in Rostock, and research suggests that the Fahrenheit family originated in Hildesheim. Daniel's grandfather, Reinhold Friedrich Fahrenheit (1703-1781), moved from Kneiphof (in Konigsberg) to Danzig and settled there as a merchant in 1650. By widespread trading, he became the richest man in eastern Prussia. His son, Daniel Fahrenheit (the father of the subject of this article), married Concordia (widowed name, Runge), daughter of the well-known Danzig business family of Schumann. Daniel Gabriel was the eldest of the five Fahrenheit children (two sons, three daughters) who survived childhood.

Upon the accidental early death of his parents, by consumption of poisonous mushrooms in 1702, sixteen-year-old Gabriel Daniel Fahrenheit began training as a merchant in Amsterdam. However, his interest in natural science caused him to take up studies and experimentation in that field. From 1707 onwards, he travelled to Berlin, Halle, Leipzig, Dresden, Kopenhagen, and also to his hometown. During that time, Fahrenheit met or was in contact with Ole Romer, Christian Wolff, and Gottfried Leibniz. In 1717, Fahrenheit settled in The Hague with the trade of glassblowing, making barometers, altimeters, and thermometers. From 1718 onwards, he gave lectures in chemistry in Amsterdam. In 1724, he visited England and became a member of the Royal Society. (On this occasion, he signed himself as "Polonus", indicating that he was born a Polish subject.) Fahrenheit died in The Hague and was buried there at the Kloosterkerk (Cloister Church).

DEMOCRITUS

Democritus was a pre-Socratic Greek materialist philosopher (born at Abdera in Thrace ca. 460 BC-died ca 370 BC). Democritus was a student of Leucippus and co-originator of the belief that all matter is made up of various imperishable, indivisible elements which he called *atoma* (sg. *atomon*) or "indivisible units", from which we get the English word atom. It is virtually impossible to tell which of these ideas were unique to Democritus and which are attributable to Leucippus.

Life

Democritus was born in Abdera in Thrace, an Ionian colony of Teos, although some called him a Milesian. His year of birth was 460 BC according to Apollodorus, who is probably more reliable than Thrasyllus who placed it ten years earlier. John Burnet has argued that the date of 460 is "too early", since according to Diogenes Laertius 9.41 Democritus said that he was a "young man (*neos*)" during Anaxagoras' old age (circa 440-428). It was said that Democritus' father was so wealthy that he received Xerxes on his march through Abdera. Democritus spent the inheritance which his father left him on travels into distant countries, to satisfy his thirst for knowledge. He travelled to Asia, and was even said to have reached India and Ethiopia. We know that he wrote on Babylon and Meroe; he must also have visited Egypt, and Diodorus Siculus states that he lived there for five years. He himself declared, that among his contemporaries none had made greater journeys, seen more countries, and met more scholars than himself. He particularly mentions the Egyptian mathematicians, whose knowledge he praises. Theophrastus, too, spoke of him as a man who had seen many countries. During his travels, according to Diogenes Laertius, he became acquainted with the Chaldean magi. A certain "Ostanes", one of the magi accompanying Xerxes was also said to have taught him.

After returning to his native land he occupied himself with natural philosophy. He travelled throughout Greece to acquire a knowledge of its culture. He mentions many Greek philosophers in his writings, and his wealth enabled him to purchase their writings. Leucippus, the founder of the atomism, was the greatest influence upon him. He also praises Anaxagoras. The tradition that he was friends with Hippocrates seems to have been based on spurious letters. He may have been acquainted with Socrates, but Plato does not mention him and Democritus himself is quoted as saying, "I came to Athens and no one knew me.". Though Aristotle viewed him as a pre-Socratic., it should be noticed that since Socrates was born in ca. 469 BC (about 9 years before Democritus), it is very possible that Aristotle's remark was not meant to be a chronological one, but directed towards his philosophical similarity with other pre-Socratic thinkers.

The many anecdotes about Democritus, especially in Diogenes Laertius, attest to his disinterestedness, modesty, and simplicity, and show that he lived exclusively for his studies. One story has him deliberately blinding himself in order to be less disturbed in his pursuits; it may well be true that he lost his sight in old age. He was cheerful, and was always ready to see the comical side of life, which later writers took to mean that he always laughed at the foolishness of people.

He was highly esteemed by his fellow-citizens, "because," as Diogenes Laertius says, "he had foretold them some things which events proved to be true," which may refer to his knowledge of natural phaenomena. According to Diodorus Siculus, Democritus died at the age of 90, which would put his death around 370 BC, but other writers have him living to 104, or even 109.

DAVID M. DENNISON

David Mathias Dennison (1900 in Oberlin, Ohio – April 3, 1976) was an American physicist who made contributions to quantum mechanics, spectroscopy, and the physics of molecular structure.

Education

In 1917, Dennison entered Swarthmore College, where he graduated in 1921. He then went to the University of Michigan, in Ann Arbor, for graduate studies in physics with Walter F. Colby and Oskar Klein. Klein, already associated with the Kaluza-Klein theory (1921), joined the faculty at Michigan in 1922, after a six-year stay at the Institute for Theoretical Physics, under Niels Bohr, at the

University of Copenhagen. It was through Klein that Dennison heard and leaned much about the current theoretical physics being developed in Europe, which created a yearning in him to go to Copenhagen for further study. Dennison's thesis was on the molecular structure and infrared spectrum of the methane molecule, and he was awarded his doctorate in 1924.

From 1924 to 1926, Dennison had an International Education Board (IEB) Fellowship to do postgraduate study and research in Europe. By the end of that time, Harrison McAllister Randall, chairman of physics department at the University of Michigan, had arranged for Dennison to stay in Europe another year on a University of Michigan fellowship. Dennison arrived at the Institute of Theoretical Physics at the University of Copenhagen, in October 1924. During his three years in Europe, he mostly did postdoctoral research in Copenhagen, where he had associations with other visiting physicists working there, such as Paul Dirac, Samuel Abraham Goudsmit, Werner Heisenberg, Walter Heitler, Ralph H. Fowler, Friedrich Hund, Hendrik Anthony Kramers, Yoshio Nishina, Wolfgang Pauli, and George Eugene Uhlenbeck. In the last half of 1925, Heisenberg and Max Born published their matrix mechanics formulation of quantum mechanics. In the fall of 1926 he went to the University of Zurich to study and work with Erwin Schrodinger, who had early in the year published his papers on his wave mechanics formulation of quantum mechanics. In early spring of 1927, Dennison went back to Copenhagen, and in late spring he went to the University of Cambridge to work with Ralph Fowler for six weeks – there at the time were Ernest Rutherford, Nevill Francis Mott, Pyotr Kapitsa, Patrick Blackett, and John Cockcroft. The last few weeks of his fellowship were spent at the University of Leiden with Paul Ehrenfest.

In 1925, George Eugene Uhlenbeck and Samuel Abraham Goudsmit had proposed spin, and Wolfgang Pauli had proposed the Pauli exclusion principle. In 1926, Enrico Fermi and Paul Dirac introduced Fermi-Dirac statistics. While at Cambridge, Dennison used quantum mechanicals calculations on molecular hydrogen to show that protons, like electrons, were subject to Fermi-Dirac statistics, or had spin-½, and therefore obeyed the Pauli exclusion principle.

DEREK ABBOTT

Derek Abbott (3 May 1960, in South Kensington, London, UK) is a physicist and electronic engineer. He is a Professor of Electrical and Electronic Engineering at the University of Adelaide, Australia. He is notable for leading theoretical work in the development of Parrondo's paradox, contributions to the field of stochastic resonance, and experimental contributions to T-ray imaging.

Early Years

In the period 1963-1965 Abbott attended the famous Norland College pre-school, Chislehurst, Kent, UK, as a boarder. Then during 1965-1967 he attended Oakfield School, Dulwich, UK, at the same time as the singer Kim Wilde. In 1968, he attended the Ecole de Ferney-Voltaire, France, and the Ecole Seminaire de Collonges-sous-Saleve, France. In 1969 he did a stint at Bassett House School, London, UK.

In the 1969-1971 period, he was a boarder at Copthorne Preparatory School, Sussex, UK. He attended Copthorne Preparatory School at the same time as the deputy editor of *Private Eye,* Francis Wheen.

During 1971-1978 he attended the infamous Holland Park School, London, UK, known as the "socialist Eton." At Holland Park School, the singer Yazz was one of his classmates. Here, he was taught English Literature by the comedian Mike Walling and music by Andy Mackay who later became the saxophonist of Roxy Music. In the early 1970s he lived next door to Cat Stevens' drummer Gerry Conway in Holland Park, London.

Career

In 1978, he began work at GEC Hirst Research Centre, Wembley, UK, performing research in the area of CCD and microchip design for imaging systems. Whilst working, he graduated in 1982 with a

BSc in Physics from Loughborough University, where his key intellectual influence was Nicholas J. Phillips. In 1986, at the time when the mysterious GEC deaths started, he began work as a microchip designer at Austek Microsystems in Adelaide, Australia. In 1987, he joined the University of Adelaide completing his PhD thesis in Electrical & Electronic Engineering in 1995, entitled *GaAs MESFET Photodetectors for Imaging Arrays*, under Kamran Eshraghian and Bruce R. Davis.

Teaching

He is currently a full professor at the University of Adelaide, where he has won a number of teaching awards. In the late 1990s, Abbott wore two watches, one on each wrist. When asked why, he would reply, "It is a way of identifying the best students—to check their powers of observation." In the 1990s, during undergraduate lectures, if a student raised a hand and spotted a mistake in the lecture material, Abbott would open his wallet and give the student the lowest coin or note that he happened to be carrying. On occasion, if he forgot to bring coins, he had to part with a high denomination. Around 1998, he also adopted the same prize money approach for the "most perceptive question" asked in a lecture.

DAVID STRANGWAY

David William Strangway, is a Canadian geophysicist and university administrator. Strangway is the founder and Chancellor of Quest University Canada, a private non-profit liberal arts and sciences university in Squamish, British Columbia which opened in September 2007.

Strangway studied at the University of Toronto, earning a B.A. in physics and geology in 1956, an M.A. in physics and a Ph.D in physics in 1960. After work in the field of geology and three years on the faculty at M.I.T, in 1970, he joined NASA as the Chief of the Geophysics Branch and was responsible for the geophysical aspects of the Apollo missions. In 1972, he was awarded the NASA Exceptional Scientific Achievement Medal for his scientific contribution to NASA. He was a vice-president at the University of Toronto and the chairman of its geology department from 1973 to 1983. Upon the retirement of James Ham in 1983, Strangway was appointed the acting president of the University of Toronto. He was unexpectedly elevated to become the university's eleventh president after the designated successor, Donald Forster, suddenly died of a heart attack in August of that year.

From 1985 to 1997, he was the tenth President of the University of British Columbia. From 1998 to 2004, he was the President and Chief Executive Officer of the Canada Foundation for Innovation, an independent corporation created by the Government of Canada to fund research infrastructure.

DAVID M. RAUP

David M. Raup is a University of Chicago paleontologist. Raup studied the fossil record and the diversity of life on Earth. Raup contributed to the knowledge of extinction events along with his colleague Jack Sepkoski. They suggested that the extinction of dinosaurs 65 mya was part of a cycle of mass extinctions that may have occurred every 26 million years.

In addition to his time at the University of Chicago, Raup has taught at Caltech, Johns Hopkins, and the University of Rochester. He was also a curator and Dean of Science at the Field Museum of Natural History in Chicago as well as a visiting professor in Germany at Tubingen and on the faculty of the College of the Virgin Islands. Raup was heavily involved through his career in joint programmes with biology and in promoting training of paleontologists in modern marine environments. In 1994, he retired to Washington Island in northern Lake Michigan. Currently, he assists the Santa Fe Institute to develop methods and approaches to dealing with the evolutionary exploration of morphospace.

Early Life

Born in 1933 and raised in Boston, Raup's interest in the fossil record did not begin at a young age, having had very little contact with such things until later in life. He focused instead on leisure activities such as skiing and camping. His first mentor was John Clark, a vertebrate paleontologist and sedimentologist at the University of Chicago while starting his education. Raup began his academic career at Colby College in Maine before transferring two years later to the University of Chicago where he earned his Bachelor of Science degree. From there, he went to Harvard for graduate studies where he majored in geology while focussing on palaeontology and biology; he earned his MA and PhD degrees there.

DAN MCKENZIE

Daniel (Dan) Peter McKenzie, (b. 1942) is a Professor of Geophysics at Cambridge University, and one-time head of the Bullard Laboratories. He wrote the first paper defining the principles of plate tectonics, and his early work on mantle convection created the modern discussion of planetary interiors.

Early Life

Born in Cheltenham 1942, the son of an Ear Nose and Throat surgeon, he first attended Westminster Under School and later Westminster School, London.

Education and Career

Dan McKenzie attended King's College, Cambridge where he read Physics, obtaining a 2:1 in his final degree. As a graduate student, he worked with Edward "Teddy" Bullard who suggested he work on the subject of thermodynamic variables. He was awarded a Research Fellowship at King's College at the beginning of his second year which enabled him to study anything he wanted. As such, he gave up doing what Teddy had suggested and became interested in how the interior of the earth convects, something completely speculative at that time. McKenzie taught himself fluid mechanics and then went to the Scripps Oceanography Institute at the University of California, San Diego, on the invitation of Freeman Gilbert and Walter Munk. After eight months he returned to the

Cambridge, submitting his PhD in 1966. He has since said that nothing in his early life as a scientist had such a profound effect on him as those eight months in California.

Plate Tectonics

Spending time between Cambridge and a Fellowship held in Caltech, Dan was invited, along with with Teddy Bullard, to a conference in New York which initiated his revolutionary work on plate tectonics. After listening to separate talks from Fred Vines and Lynn Sykes he came back to Cambridge and started work on the first paper to be published on plate tectonics, looking at the thermal structure of oceanic plates as they formed and cooled.

Following this, he published a seminal paper with Bob Parker, which employed the Euler Theorem, in conjunction with magnetic anomalies and earthquakes to determine a precise mathematical theory on plate tectonics. This work was published some 3-4 months after the same work had been carried out by Jason Morgan at Princeton. Allegations were subsequently made suggesting that McKenzie was at Morgan's spring AGU talk where he presented his plate tectonics work. Later in 1968 he went to Princeton where he found that he and Morgan had solved two or three problems using identical mathematics in exactly the same way – plate tectonics was one, another was the thermal structure of the oceans and another was looking at earthquake mechanisms in a different way to seismologists.

Working with John Sclater, McKenzie determined the entire geological history of the Indian Ocean, the publication of which eventually resulted in them both receiving Fellowships at the Royal Society.

Mantle Convection and Sedimentary Basins

McKenzie was awarded a University position and took it up in 1971. At this point he decided to move away from plate tectonics, choosing instead to focus on the behavior of fluids below the plates. He studied cellular convection and motions in the mantle whilst at the same time pursuing yet another new avenue of research; the development of sedimentary basins. It was from this work that he produced a classic paper that has been widely accepted by oil companies as the "McKenzie Model of Sedimentary Basins."

McKenzie was elected a Fellow of the Royal Society in 1976 at just 34 years of age, and by 1978 was awarded a University Readership position.

Later Career

Dan McKenzie continues to work at the Bullard Laboratories in Cambridge where he holds a Royal Society Research Professorship, awarded in 1996. Most recently his research has provided new insights into the tectonic evolution of Mars and Venus.

In 2002 he was awarded the prestigious Crafoord Prize from the Royal Swedish Academy of Sciences for his contributions to research in the field of plate tectonics, sedimentary basin formation and mantle melting.

DIGBY MCLAREN

Dr. Digby Johns McLaren (December 11, 1919 – December 8, 2004) was a Canadian geologist and palaeontologist.

Born in Carrickfergus, Ireland and educated at Sedbergh School, he received a Bachelor of Arts in geology from the University of Cambridge. During World War II, he fought in the Middle East and Europe with the Royal Regiment of Artillery. After the war, he received a Master of Arts in geology from the University of Cambridge in 1948. In 1948, he moved to Canada and joined the Geological Survey of Canada (GSC). In 1951, he received a Ph.D. from the University of Michigan.

From 1959 to 1967, he was the head of the palaeontology section of the GSC. In 1967, he became the first director of the Institute of Sedimentary and Petroleum Geology of the GSC and in 1973 he was appointed Director of the Geological Survey of Canada. In 1981, he became Assistant Deputy Minister of Science and Technology for Energy, Mines and Resources Canada. He was the author of over 100 publications and maps in the fields of palaeontology, biostratigraphy and regional geology. He was one of the early theorist of the Cretaceous-Tertiary extinction event.

From 1987 to 1990, he was the president of the Royal Society of Canada. He was also President of the Geological Society of America. In 1942, he married to Phyllis Matkin with whom he had three children: Ian, Patrick, and Alison.

DOUGLAS MAWSON

Sir Douglas Mawson,(5 May 1882 – 14 October 1958) was an Australian Antarctic explorer and geologist. With Roald Amundsen, Robert Falcon Scott, and Ernest Shackleton, Mawson was a key expedition leader during the Heroic Age of Antarctic Exploration.

He was appointed geologist to an expedition to the New Hebrides (now Vanuatu) in 1903; his report *The geology of the New Hebrides*, was one of the first major geological works of Melanesia. Also that year he published a geological paper on Mittagong, New South Wales. His major influences in his geological career were Professor Edgeworth David and Professor Archibald Liversidge. He then became a lecturer in petrology and mineralogy at the University of Adelaide in 1905. He identified and first described the mineral Davidite, named for Edgeworth David.

In 1907, Mawson joined the *British Antarctic Expedition* led by Ernest Shackleton as an expedition geologist. With his mentor and fellow geologist, Edgeworth David, he was on the first ascent of Mount Erebus. Later, he was a member of the first team to reach the South Magnetic Pole, assuming the leadership of the party from David on their perilous return.

Mawson's Australian Antarctic Expedition

Dawson turned down an invitation to join Robert Falcon Scott's Terra Nova Expedition in 1910; Australian geologist Griffith Taylor went instead. Dawson chose to lead his own expedition, the *Australian Antarctic Expedition*, to King George V Land and Adelie Land, the sector of the Antarctic continent immediately south of Australia, which at the time was almost entirely unexplored. The objectives were to carry out geographical exploration and scientific studies, including visiting the South Magnetic Pole.

The expedition, using the ship *Aurora* commanded by Captain John King Davis, departed Hobart on 2 December 1911, and landed at Cape Denison on Commonwealth Bay on 8 January 1912 and established the Main Base. A second camp was located to the west on the ice shelf in Queen Mary Land. Cape Denison proved to be unrelentingly windy; the average wind speed for the entire year was about 50 mph (80 km/h). They built a hut on the rocky cape and wintered through nearly constant blizzards. On pg. 133 in "The Home of the Blizzard Mawson wrote "...on the evening of May 24, in the form of Herculean gusts....the momentary velocity of these doubtlessly approached two hundred miles per hour."

Mawson's exploration programme was carried out by five parties from the Main Base and two from the Western Base. Mawson's team, which was to trek east, consisted of Xavier Mertz, Lieutenant B. E. S. Ninnis and himself. Nearing the end of this team's trek, Ninnis, his dog team and sledge with most of the provisions fell through a crevasse and were lost.

Mawson and Mertz turned back immediately. Mertz died during the return journey and Mawson continued alone. On one occasion during his return trip to the Main Base, he fell through the lid of a crevasse and was saved only by his sledge wedging itself into the ice above him. When he finally made it back to Cape Denison, the ship Aurora had left only a few hours before. Using wireless communication the ship was recalled only to have bad weather thwart the rescue effort. Mawson, and six men who had remained behind to look for him, wintered a second year until December 1913. In Mawson's book, *Home of the Blizzard*, he describes his experiences. His party, and those at the Western Base, had explored large areas of the Antarctic coast, describing its geology, biology and meteorology, and more closely defining the location of the south magnetic pole.

Dog Livers and Hypervitaminosis

The dogs became a food resource after Ninnis, his dog team and the sledge they were pulling fell into a crevasse and were lost, along with most of the food supply. The liver of one dog contains enough vitamin A to produce the condition called hypervitaminosis A. Mawson did not know this and fed more of the dog livers to Mertz, as the latter was the weaker of the two men, thus causing vitamin A poisoning and facilitating Mertz's demise.

The words of his first rescuer upon finding Mawson were "My God, which one are you?"

DUNCAN R. DERRY

Duncan R. Derry (1906–1987) was an internationally known Canadian economic geologist. He was largely responsible for the creation of the *World Atlas of Geological and Mineral Deposits.*

Derry was born in England. He obtained an honour science degree from University of Cambridge before moving to Canada. He attended the University of Toronto and obtained his M.A. and Ph.D. degrees in geology.

In 1935, he started work at Ventures Ltd., which later became Falconbridge Ltd.. Derry worked closely with Thayer Lindsley. He supervised exploration and mining programmes in Canada and many other countries, including South Africa, Greece, Guyana, Chile, Peru, and Greenland. His work at Venture was interrupted by World War II. He enlisted and served as a squadron leader navigation training officer. In 1950, he compiled a tectonic map of Canada with John Sinclair Stevenson. It was the first time in Canada that structural data from government, university, and industry sources were combined and synthesized.

In 1954, Derry became president of Rio Tinto Exploration. He was apart of the acquisition and development of the Rio Algom's bit uranium mines in the Elliot Lake area of Ontario. In 1960, he left Rio to be a founding partner of the consulting firm Derry Michener Booth & Wahl.

Dr. Derry spent three years researching, compiling, funding and publishing the *World Atlas of Geological and Mineral Deposits*. In reference to his work on this textbook and his induction, the representative of the Canadian Mining Hall of Fame expressed that he, "added immeasurably not only to the advancement of the geological sciences and their practical application to mining development in Canada and elsewhere, but to the publication of world literature in the field."

Dr. Derry was a past-president of the Society of Economic Geologists. He was a part of founding Geological Association of Canada, the Canadian Geological Foundation, and the Canadian Geoscience Council.

DAVID SLOAN WILSON

David Sloan Wilson (1949-) is an American evolutionary biologist. Son of the author Sloan Wilson, David Sloan Wilson is a distinguished professor at Binghamton University. He is a prominent proponent of the concept of group selection (aka multi-level selection) in evolution. He has, along with Elliott Sober in their book *Unto Others* proposed a framework called multilevel selection theory, which incorporates the more orthodox approach of gene-level selection and individual selection. This framework argues that while genes serve as the means by which organisms' designs are transmitted across generations, individuals and groups are vehicles for those genes and both are arenas for genes to act on. Indeed, genes themselves can be affected by selection, not just because of their effects on the design of their vehicle (the organism) but also because of their effect on the functioning of the DNA on which they reside. Hence, the notion of multilevel selection. Wilson has also coined the concept of a trait-group, a group of organisms linked not permanently as a group but having a shared fate due to interactions that they have.

Wilson's book *Darwin's Cathedral* proposes that religion is a multi-level adaptation, a product of cultural evolution developed through a process of multi-level selection. His latest book *Evolution for Everyone: How Darwin's Theory Can Change the Way We Think About Our Lives* attempts to give an introduction to evolution for a broad audience, detailing the various ways in which evolution can be applied to everyday affairs.

Wilson started the Evolutionary Studies (EvoS) programme at Binghamton University to provide a programme that unifies diverse disciplines under the theory of evolution. Students in the programme take evolution-themed courses in a variety of disciplines including biology, anthropology, psychology, bioengineering, and philosophy. SUNY New Paltz has started a similar programme.

DAVID WEATHERALL

Sir David John Weatherall (born 9 March 1933) is a British physician and researcher in molecular genetics, haematology, pathology and clinical medicine. His research concentrated on the genetics of the haemoglobinopathies and, in particular, a group of inherited haematological disorders known as the thalassemias that are associated with abnormalities in the production of globin (the protein component of haemoglobin). Weatherall is one of the world's experts on the clinical and molecular basis of the thalassemias and the application of this information for the control and prevention of these diseases in the developing countries.

Weatherall was educated at Calday Grange Grammar School and then graduated from the Medical School at the University of Liverpool in 1956. After house staff training, he joined the Army for 2 years. Returning from military service, he took a fellowship at Johns Hopkins University before returning to Liverpool, where he rose to the rank of Professor of Haematology.

In 1974 Weatherall was appointed Nuffield Professor of Clinical Medicine at the University of Oxford, and, in 1992, he assumed the most prestigious chair, that of Regius Professor of Medicine, from 1992 to 2000. He was knighted in 1987.

In 1989 Weatherall founded the Institute of Molecular Medicine at Oxford, which was renamed the Weatherall Institute of Molecular

Medicine in his honour in the year 2000 upon his retirement. He then became Chancellor of Keele University.

In 2002 Weatherall wrote a major report on the application of genomics for global health for the World Health Organization. Sir David is a Distinguished Supporter of the British Humanist Association.

In 2006 a working group report under the Chairmanship of Professor David Weatherall concludes that there is a strong scientific case to maintain biomedical research activities using non-human primates in carefully selected areas.

DAVID SUZUKI

David Takayoshi Suzuki (born March 24, 1936), is a Canadian science broadcaster and environmental activist. Since the mid-1970s, Suzuki has been known for his TV and radio series and books about nature and the environment. He is best known as host of the popular and long-running CBC Television science magazine, *The Nature of Things*, seen in syndication in over 40 nations. He is also well known for criticizing governments for their lack of action to protect the environment.

A long time activist to reverse global climate change, Suzuki co-founded the David Suzuki Foundation in 1990, to work "to find ways for society to live in balance with the natural world that sustains us." The Foundation's priorities are: oceans and sustainable fishing, climate change and clean energy, sustainability, and David Suzuki's Nature Challenge. He also served as a director of the Canadian Civil Liberties Association from 1982-1987.

Early Life

Suzuki had a twin sister named Marcia, as well as two other siblings, Geraldine (now known as Aiko) and Dawn. They were born to Setsu Nakamura and Kaoru Carr Suzuki in Vancouver, Canada. Suzuki's maternal and paternal grandparents had immigrated to Canada at the beginning of the 20th century.

A third-generation Japanese-Canadian ("Canadian Sansei"), Suzuki and his family suffered internment in British Columbia during the Second World War from when he was six (1942) until after the war ended. In June 1942, the government sold the Suzuki family's dry-cleaning business, then interned Suzuki, his mother, and two sisters in a camp at Slocan in the British Columbia Interior. His father had been sent to a labour camp in Solsqua two months earlier. Suzuki's sister, Dawn, was born in the internment camp.

After the war, Suzuki's family, like other Japanese Canadian families, was forced to move east of the Rockies. The Suzukis moved to Islington, Leamington, and London, Ontario. David Suzuki, in interviews, has many times credited his father for having interested and sensitized him to nature.

Suzuki attended Mill Street Elementary School and Grade 9 at Leamington Secondary School before moving to London, where he attended London Central Secondary School, eventually winning the election to become Students' Council President in his last year there by more votes than all of the other candidates combined.

In 2006, David Suzuki was the recipient of the Bradford Washburn Award presented at the Museum of Science in Boston, Massachusetts.

DAVID STATES

David J. States is a Professor of Human Genetics at the University of Michigan. His research group is using computational methods to understand the human genome and how it relates to the human proteome. He is the Director of the Michigan NIH Bioinformatics Training Programme and a Senior Scientist in the National Centre for Integrative Biomedical Informatics.

Dr. States earned his BA ('75), MD ('83) and PhD ('83) degrees at Harvard University. He was a Staff Scientist at the National Magnet Laboratory at MIT and a resident in internal medicine at UCSD Medical Centre. He then moved to the NIH as a Clinical Associate and Senior Staff Fellow where he joined the National

Centre for Biotechnology Information (NCBI). While at NCBI, he and Warren Gish enhanced BLAST, one of the most widely used programmes in bioinformatics. In 1992, Dr. States was recruited to Washington University as Director of the Institute for Biomedical Computing, and in 2001, he moved to the University of Michigan to establish the University of Michigan Bioinformatics Programme. He was a member of the founding Board of Directors and Treasurer of the International Society for Computational Biology and Chair of the 1996 and 2005 Intelligent Systems for Molecular Biology Conferences. Dr. States is also known for his work in nuclear magnetic resonance where he developed pure absorption phase multi-dimensional spectroscopy, a technique now widely used in protein structure determination. Dr. States also contributed to computational biophysics as an author of the CHARMM molecular dynamics simulation programme. He combined NMR spectroscopy and modeling to demonstrate for the first time the presence of native-like structure in the folding intermediates of bovine pancreatic trypsin inhibitor and the first demonstration of a conformationally trapped folding intermediate.

DAVID T. LYKKEN

David Thoreson Lykken (June 18, 1928-September 15, 2006) was a behavioural geneticist and Professor Emeritus of Psychology and Psychiatry at the University of Minnesota. He is best known for his work on twin studies.

Life

Born in Minneapolis, Minnesota, at 17, Lykken joined the United States Navy, then attended University of Minnesota on the G.I. Bill, earning his bachelor of arts (psychology, philosophy and mathematics) 1949, his masters degree in psychology and statistics in 1952, and his doctorate in clinical psychology and neuropsychiatry in 1955. He remained on Minnesota's permanent faculty for his entire career and taught as a visiting professor at Deep Springs College. He was an emeritus professor from 1998 until his death.

Work

Lykken was also known for his work on twins, which he began in 1970. He was a principal investigator on the Minnesota Twin Family Study, which examines heritability of certain psychological traits based on evidence found in identical and fraternal twins. He was a signatory of a collective statement in response to *The Bell Curve* titled "Mainstream Science on Intelligence", written by *Intelligence* editor Linda Gottfredson and published in the *Wall Street Journal* in 1994 and in *Intelligence* in 1997.

Lykken was the proponent of a set-point theory of happiness, which argues that one's sense of well-being is half determined by genetics and half determined by circumstances, and has been the subject of international media attention. His research findings suggest that a person's baseline levels of cheerfulness, contentment, and psychological satisfaction are largely a matter of heredity.

He was elected a Fellow of the American Psychological Association (Division 1), a Charter Fellow of the American Psychological Society and a Fellow of the American Association for the Advancement of Science. He was also a member of the Behaviour Genetics Association and the International Society for Twin Research. Throughout his career, he consulted with government and industry. He frequently testified as an expert witness on polygraph testing and personality assessment in the wake of Daubert standard requirements.

DOROTHY CROWFOOT HODGKIN

Dorothy Mary Hodgkin, (12 May 1910 – 29 July 1994) was a British chemist, credited with the discovery of protein crystallography

She pioneered the technique of X-ray crystallography, a method used to determine the three dimensional structures of biomolecules. Among her most influential discoveries are the determination of the structure of penicillin and vitamin B12, for which she was awarded the Nobel Prize in Chemistry. In 1969, after 35 years of work and five years after winning the Nobel Prize in Chemistry, Hodgkin was able to decipher the structure of insulin. She is regarded as one of the foremost scientists in the field of X-Ray crystallography studies of natural molecules. Besides her extraordinary scientific abilities, she was unassuming, very communicative, and passionate about social inequalities and peace.

Early Years

She was born Dorothy Mary Crowfoot in May 12, 1910 in Cairo, Egypt, to John Crowfoot, excavator and scholar of classics, and Grace Mary Crowfoot *nee* Hood. For the first four years of her life she lived as an English expatriate in Asia Minor, returning to England only a few months each year. She spent the period of World War I in the UK under the care of relatives and friends, but separated from her parents. After the war, her mother decided to stay home in England and educate her children, a period that Hodgkin later described as the happiest in her life.

In 1921, she entered the Sir John Leman Grammar School in Beccles, Suffolk. She travelled abroad frequently to visit her parents in Cairo and Khartoum. Both her father and her mother had a strong influence with their Puritan ethic of selflessness and service to humanity which reverberated in her later achievements.

Education and Research

She developed a passion for chemistry from a young age, and her mother fostered her interest in science in general. Her excellent early education prepared her well for university. At age 18 she started studying chemistry at Somerville College, Oxford, then one of the University of Oxford colleges for women only.

She also studied at the University of Cambridge under the tutelage of John Desmond Bernal, where she became aware of the potential of X-ray crystallography to determine the structure of proteins.

In 1934, she moved back to Oxford and two years later, in 1936, she became a research fellow at Somerville College, a post which she held until 1977. In 1960 she was appointed Wolfson Research Professor at the Royal Society.

EMIL WOLF

Emil Wolf (born July 30, 1922) is a Czech born American physicist who made advancements in physical optics, including diffraction, coherence properties of optical fields, spectroscopy of partially coherent radiation, and the theory of direct scattering and inverse scattering.

He is the co-author, along with Max Born, of one of the standard textbooks of optics, *Principles of Optics*. He also co-authored, along with Leonard Mandel, *Optical Coherence and Quantum Optics*. He is the author of *Introduction to the Theory of Coherence and Polarization of Light* and *Selected Works of Emil Wolf with Commentary*.

He also predicted a new mechanism that produces redshift and blueshift, that is not due to moving sources (Doppler effect), that has subsequently been confirmed experimentally (called the Wolf Effect). Technically, he found that two non-Lambertian sources that emit beamed energy, can interact in a way that causes a shift in the spectral lines.

It is analogous to a pair of tuning forks with similar frequencies (pitches), connected together mechanically with a sounding board; there is a strong coupling that results in the resonant frequencies getting "dragged down" in pitch. The Wolf Effect can produce either redshifts or blueshifts, depending on the observer's point of view, but is redshifted when the observer is head-on. A subsequent 1999 article by Sisir Roy *et al* have suggested that the Wolf Effect may explain discordant redshift in certain quasars Ref.

Wolf was born in Prague, Czechoslovakia. He was forced to move out of his native country when the Germans invaded the country. After having left Czechoslovakia, he went to France for a few years. Eventually, he came to England. He received his B.Sc. in Mathematics and Physics (1945), and PhD in Physics from Bristol University, England, in 1948. In the early 1950s he worked at the University of Edinburgh. He is currently (2006) Professor of Optics at the University of Rochester, USA, having first come to Rochester in 1959. He is a naturalized US citizen.

EUGENE WIGNER

Eugene Paul "E.P." Wigner (Hungarian **Wigner Pal Jeno**) (November 17, 1902 – January 1, 1995) was a Hungarian physicist and mathematician.

He received the Nobel Prize in Physics in 1963 "for his contributions to the theory of the atomic nucleus and the elementary particles, particularly through the discovery and application of fundamental symmetry principles". Some contemporaries referred to Wigner as *the Silent Genius* and some even considered him the intellectual equal to Albert Einstein, though without his prominence. Wigner is important for having laid the foundation for the theory of symmetries in quantum mechanics as well as for his research into atomic nuclei, and for his several theorems.

Early Life

Wigner was born in Budapest, Austria-Hungary (now Hungary) to a middle class Jewish family. At age 11, Wigner contracted what his parents believed was tuberculosis. They sent him for six weeks to a sanitarium in the Austrian mountains. During this period, Wigner began to develop an interest in mathematical problems. From 1915 till 1919, concurrently with John von Neumann, Wigner studied at the Lutheran Fasori Evangelikus Gimnazium where they both greatly benefited from encouragement by the legendary mathematics teacher Laszlo Ratz. In 1919, to escape the Bela Kun Communist regime, the family briefly moved to Austria, returning after Kun's downfall. Partly as a reaction to the prominence of Jews in the Kun regime, the family converted to Lutheranism.

In 1921, Wigner studied chemical engineering at the Technische Hochschule in Berlin (today the Technische Universitat Berlin). He also attended the Wednesday afternoon colloquia of the German Physical Society. These colloquia featured such luminaries as Max Planck, Max von Laue, Rudolf Ladenburg, Werner Heisenberg, Walther Nernst, Wolfgang Pauli, and Albert Einstein. Wigner also met physicist Leo Szilard, who at once became Wigner's closest friend. A third experience in Berlin was formative. Wigner worked at the Kaiser Wilhelm Institute for Physical Chemistry and Electrochemistry (now Fritz Haber Institute), and there met Michael Polanyi, who became, after Laszlo Ratz, Wigner's greatest teacher.

EMIL WIECHERT

Emil Johann Wiechert (26 December 1861 – 19 March 1928) was a German geophysicist. Wiechert was born in Tilsit, Province of Prussia, the son of Johann and Emilie Wiechart. After his father died, Emilie moved to Konigsberg so that Emil could study at the University of Konigsberg. Due to economic difficulties he took longer than normal to complete his education, but he was awarded a Ph.D. in 1889.

The following year he became qualified to lecture in physics at a university-level in Germany. He became an assistant to Paul Volkmann at Konigsberg University, teaching there, and during the next seven years performed research in physics until 1897, when he received a call to Georg-August-Universitat in Gottingen. He started as an assistant of Woldemar Voigt, in physics, and In 1898 he was named professor of geophysics and Director of the Geophysical Laboratory at Gottingen. He became a full professor at the institution in 1905, and would remain there for the remainder of his career. He would be married to Helene Ziebarth, a lawyer's daughter, in 1908, but the couple did not have children.

During his career he made important contributions to the discovery of the electron, the physics of cathode rays, and Lienard-Wiechert Potentials. He was the first geophysicist to present a verifiable model of the Earth's interior as a series of shells. He wrote a number of scientific papers, including a pioneering work on how seismic waves propagate through the Earth. He also devised an improved seismograph and created the field of geological prospecting using small, artificially-created earthquakes.

Toward the end of his life he became increasingly deaf and would suffer from a number of ailments before finally passing away. He died in Gottingen.

ERNEST WALTON

Ernest Thomas Sinton Walton (October 6, 1903 – June 25, 1995) was an Irish physicist and Nobel laureate for his work with John Cockcroft with "atom-smashing" experiments done at Cambridge University in the early 1930s. Walton is the only Irishman to have won a Nobel Prize in science.

Early Years

Ernest Walton was born in Abbeyside, County Waterford, Ireland, to a Methodist minister father, Rev. John Walton (1874-1936) and Anna Sinton (1874-1906), growing up mostly in Ulster. In those days a general clergyman's family moved once every three years, and this practice carried Ernest and his family, while he was a small child, to counties Limerick and County Monaghan. He attended day schools in counties Down, Tyrone, and Wesley College Dublin before becoming a boarder at Methodist College Belfast in 1915, where he excelled in science and mathematics.

In 1922 Walton won scholarships to Trinity College, Dublin for the study of mathematics and science. He was awarded bachelor's and master's degrees from Trinity in 1926 and 1927, respectively. During these years at college, Walton received numerous prizes for excellence in physics and mathematics (seven prizes in all). Following graduation he was accepted as a research student at Trinity College, Cambridge, under the supervision of Sir Ernest Rutherford, Director of Cambridge University's Cavendish Laboratory. At the time there were four Nobel Prize laureates on the staff at the Cavendish lab and a further five were to emerge, including Walton and John Cockcroft. Walton was awarded his Ph.D. in 1931 and remained at Cambridge as a researcher until 1934.

During the early 1930s Walton and John Cockcroft collaborated to build an apparatus that split the nuclei of lithium atoms by bombarding them with a stream of protons accelerated inside a high-voltage tube (700 kilovolts). The splitting of the lithium nuclei produced helium nuclei. This was experimental verification of theories about atomic structure that had been proposed earlier by Rutherford,

George Gamow, and others. The successful apparatus—a type of particle accelerator now called the Cockcroft-Walton generator—helped to usher in an era of particle-accelerator-based experimental nuclear physics. It was this research at Cambridge in the early 1930s that won Walton and Cockcroft the Nobel Prize in physics in 1951.

Career at Trinity College Dublin

Ernest Walton returned to Ireland in 1934 to became a Fellow of Trinity College Dublin in the physics department, and in 1946 was appointed professor with the grand old title *Erasmus Smith's Professor of Natural and Experimental Philosophy*. Walton's lecturing was considered outstanding as he had the ability to present complicated matters in simple and easy-to-understand terms. His research interests were pursued with very limited resources, but yet he was able to study, in the late 1950s, the phosphorescent effect in glasses, secondary-electron emissions from surfaces under positive-ion bombardment, radiocarbon dating and low-level counting, and the deposition of thin films on glass.

Family Life

Ernest Walton married Freda Wilson, daughter of an Irish Methodist Minister, on August 23, 1934. They had five children, Dr. Alan Walton (college lecturer in physics, Magdalene College, Cambridge), Mrs Marian Woods, Professor Philip Walton, Professor of Applied Physics, National University of Ireland, Galway, Jean Clarke and Winifred Walton. Walton was a longtime member of the board of governors of Wesley College, Dublin. As a boy he attended Methodist College Belfast.

Later Years

On his retirement from Trinity College Dublin in 1974, Walton returned to Northern Ireland, where he had grown up as a child, and for the remaining twenty years of his life lived in Belfast. He died in there on June 25, 1995, aged 91. He was widely respected, much admired, and regarded as a modest, unassuming man.

EVANGELISTA TORRICELLI

Evangelista Torricelli (Listen to the pronunciation (help info)) (October 15, 1608 – October 25, 1647) was an Italian physicist and mathematician, best known for his invention of the barometer.

Biography

Torricelli was born in Faenza, then part of the Papal States. He was left fatherless at an early age and educated under the care of his uncle, a Camaldolese monk, who first entered young Torricelli in a Jesuit College in 1624 to study mathematics and philosophy until 1626, when he sent Torricelli to Rome in 1627 to study science under the Benedictine Benedetto Castelli, professor of mathematics at the Collegio della Sapienza in Pisa.

In 1632, shortly after the publication of Galileo's *Dialogues of the New Science*, Torricelli wrote to Galileo of reading it "with the delight [...] of one who, having already practised all of geometry most diligently [...] and having studied Ptolemy and seen almost everything of Tycho [Brahe], Kepler and Longomontanus, finally, forced by the many congruences, came to adhere to Copernicus, and was a Galileian in profession and sect". (The Vatican condemned Galileo in June 1633, and this was the only known occasion on which Torricelli openly declared himself to hold the Copernican view.)

Aside from several letters, little is known of Torricelli's activities in the years between 1632 and 1641, when Castelli sent Torricelli's monograph of the path of projectiles to Galileo, then a prisoner in his villa at Arcetri. Although Galileo promptly invited Torricelli to visit, he did not accept until just three months before Galileo's death.

During his stay, however, he wrote out Galileo's Discourse of the Fifth day. After Galileo's death on January 8, 1642, Grand Duke Ferdinando II de' Medici asked him to succeed Galileo as the grand-ducal mathematician and professor of mathematics in the University of Pisa. In this role he solved some of the great mathematical problems of the day, such as finding a cycloid's area and centre of gravity. He also designed and built a number of telescopes and simple microscopes; several large lenses, engraved with his name, are still preserved at Florence. In 1644, he famously wrote in a letter: "We live submerged at the bottom of an ocean of air."

Torricelli died in Florence a few days after having contracted typhoid fever, and was buried in San Lorenzo. The asteroid 7437 Torricelli was named in his honour.

ERNEST WILLIAM TITTERTON

Sir Ernest (Ernie) William Titterton Ph. D. (born March 4, 1916 in Tamworth, UK, died 8 February 1990) was a nuclear physicist and professor.

Early Years

Ernest William Titterton, was born of William Alfred and Elizabeth Titterton in Kettlebrook, Tamworth on March 4, 1916.

Titterton's primary education that began next door to the family home in Kettlebrook at a single-room school for infants, starting at the age of four. After two years, his studies moved to a boys-only school in Glastcote, Tamworth. This council school in a mining town had basic science facilities (uncommon at that time), and it was there that his interest in science was first kindled. At ten, Titterton won a scholarship to attend Queen Elizabeth's Grammar school (Tamworth), where he performed consistently well. After topping the class frequently, he entered to sixth form, which was at that time reserved for gifted students expected to continue to study at a tertiary level. Ernest studied mathematics, physics and chemistry, and under the tutelage of physics teacher William Summerhayes, he thrived.

In 1934, Titterton was accepted into University of Birmingham on a scholarship basis. Due to his achievements at secondary school, Ernest was allowed to begin his tertiary studies with second-year subjects, and even then he was said to have found them easy. He obtained his Bachelor of Science in 1936 with distinctions in both pure and applied mathematics and, of course, physics. An honours year quickly followed, and Titterton topped the year in Physics. One year later, Ernest was presented with a University scholarship, and worked in a research position under Professor Mark Oliphant. The project he shared with another student was to determine if the weak alpha activity of samarium was due to the electron or gamma ray components of cosmic rays. Upon completion of these experiments, Titterton was awarded a Master of Science in 1938. As a requirement of his scholarship, Ernest was required to become a teacher for a year. This met a lukewarm reception, but he graduated from the Diploma in Education, and was even awarded the Elizabeth Cadbury Prize for achieving top in the class.

After a call from Oliphant, who wanted to develop a small wavelength radiation generator, Titterton worked as a research officer with the British Admiralty for the early part of the second world war, working on radar systems. Though the work was classed top-secret, he was allowed to submit it to Birmingham and was awarded a PhD in physics in 1941.

EDWARD TELLER

Edward Teller (original Hungarian name *Teller Ede*) (January 15, 1908 – September 9, 2003) was a Hungarian-born American theoretical physicist, known colloquially as "the father of the hydrogen bomb," even though he claimed that he did not care for the title.

Teller is best known for his work on the American nuclear programme, specifically as a member of the Manhattan Project during World War II, his role in the development of the hydrogen bomb, and his long association with Lawrence Livermore National Laboratory (which he co-founded and served as a director). He invited contention in the 1950s by his controversial testimony in the security clearance hearing of his former Los Alamos colleague Robert Oppenheimer, and thus became ostracized by much of the scientific community. He continued to find support from the U.S. government and military research establishment, particularly for his advocacy for nuclear energy development, a strong nuclear arsenal, and a vigorous nuclear testing programme.

In his later years he became especially known for his advocacy of controversial technological solutions to both military and civilian problems, including a plan to excavate an artificial harbour in Alaska using thermonuclear explosives. He was a vigorous advocate of Ronald Reagan's Strategic Defense Initiative, though he was accused of overselling the feasibility of the project. Over the course of his life, Teller was known both for his scientific ability and his difficult interpersonal relations and volatile personality, and is considered one of the inspirations for the character Dr. Strangelove in the 1964 movie of the same name.

Early Life and Education

Teller was born in Budapest, Austria-Hungary to a Jewish family. He left Hungary in 1926. The political climate and revolutions in Hungary during his youth instilled a lingering animosity for both Communism and Fascism in Teller. When he was a young student, his leg was severed in a streetcar accident in Munich, requiring him to wear a prosthetic foot and leaving him with a life-long limp. Teller graduated in chemical engineering at the University of Karlsruhe and received his Ph.D. in physics under Werner Heisenberg at the University of Leipzig. Teller's Ph.D. dissertation dealt with one of the first accurate quantum mechanical treatments of the hydrogen molecular ion. In 1930 he befriended Russian physicists George Gamow and Lev Landau. Very important for Teller's scientific and philosophical development was his life-long close friendship with a Czech physicist George Placzek. It was Placzek who arranged for young Teller a summer stay in Rome with Enrico Fermi and oriented his scientific career to nuclear physics.

He spent two years at the University of Gottingen and left Germany in 1933 through the aid of the Jewish Rescue Committee. He went briefly to England and moved for a year to Copenhagen, where he worked under Niels Bohr. In February 1934, he married "Mici" (Augusta Maria) Harkanyi, the sister of a longtime friend.

In 1935, thanks to George Gamow's incentive, Teller was invited to the United States to become a Professor of Physics at the George

Washington University (GWU), where he worked with Gamow until 1941. Prior to the discovery of fission in 1939, Teller was engaged as a theoretical physicist working in the fields of quantum, molecular, and nuclear physics. In 1941, after becoming a naturalized citizen of the United States, his interest turned to the use of nuclear energy, both fusion and fission.

At GWU, Teller predicted the Jahn-Teller Effect (1937), which distorts molecules in certain situations; this affects the chemical reactions of metals, and in particular the coloration of certain metallic dyes. Teller and Hermann Arthur Jahn analyzed it as a piece of purely mathematical physics. In collaboration with Brunauer and Emmet, Teller also made an important contribution to surface physics and chemistry; the so-called Brunauer-Emmett-Teller (BET) isotherm.

When World War II began, Teller wanted to contribute to the war effort. On the advice of the well-known Caltech aerodynamicist and fellow Hungarian emigre Theodore von Karman, Teller collaborated with his friend Hans Bethe in developing a theory of shock-wave propagation. In later years, their explanation of the behaviour of the gas behind such a wave proved valuable to scientists who were studying missile re-entry.

ERNST STUECKELBERG

Ernst Carl Gerlach Stueckelberg (February 1, 1905, Basel-September 4, 1984, Basel) was a Swiss mathematician and physicist. In 1926 Stueckelberg got his Ph. D. at Munich under Arnold Sommerfeld. He qualified as a university lecturer together with Konrad Bleuler under supervision from Gregor Wentzel at the University of Zurich. In 1934 he devised a fully covariant perturbation theory for quantum fields. To quote this paper, "The approach proposed by Stueckelberg was far more powerful, but was not adopted by others at the time". Now, despite its benefits, this approach has been all but forgotten. However, besides being explicitly covariant, Stueckelberg's methods avoid vacuum bubbles. See also here.

Independently from Hideki Yukawa, he gave vector boson exchange as the theoretical explanation of the strong nuclear force in 1935.

In 1938 he recognized that massive electrodynamics contains a hidden scalar, and formulated an affine version of what would become known as the Abelian Higgs mechanism.

The evolution parameter theory he presented in 1941 and 1942 is the basis for recent work in Relativistic dynamics.

In 1942 he proposed the interpretation of the positron as a negative energy electron travelling backward in time.

In 1943 he came up with a renormalization programme to attack the problems of infinities in quantum electrodynamics (QED), but his paper was rejected by the Physical Review.

In 1953 he and Andre Peterman discovered the renormalization group.

In 1976 he was awarded the Max Planck medal.

Although his work was mostly well respected, later work that was only superficially different and only marginally more advanced would win the Nobel prize for others.

EMILIO G. SEGRE

Emilio Gino Segre (February 1, 1905 – April 22, 1989) was a Italian physicist and Nobel laureate in physics, who with Owen Chamberlain, discovered antiprotons, a sub-atomic antiparticle.

Biography

Segre was born in Tivoli, near Rome, and enrolled in the University of Rome La Sapienza as an engineering student. He switched to physics in 1927 and earned his doctorate in 1928, having studied under Enrico Fermi.

After a stint in the Italian Army from 1928 to 1929, he worked with Otto Stern in Hamburg and Pieter Zeeman in Amsterdam as a Rockefeller Foundation fellow in 1930. Segre was appointed assistant professor of physics at the University of Rome in 1932 and served until 1936. From 1936 to 1938 he was Director of the Physics Laboratory at the University of Palermo. After a visit to Ernest O. Lawrence's Berkeley Radiation Laboratory, he was sent a molybdenum strip from the laboratory's cyclotron deflector in 1937 which was emitting anomalous forms of radioactivity. After careful chemical and theoretical analysis, Segre was able to prove that some of the radiation was being produced by a previously unknown element, dubbed technetium, and was the first artificially synthesized chemical element which does not occur in nature.

He was a colleague and close friend of Ettore Majorana, who disappeared mysteriously in 1938.

While Segre was on a summer visit to California in 1938, Mussolini's fascist government passed anti-Semitic laws barring Jews from university positions. As a Jew, Segre was now rendered an indefinite emigre. At the Berkeley Radiation Lab, Lawrencc offered him a job as a Research Assistant—a relatively lowly position for someone who had discovered an element—for US$300 a month. However, in Segre's recollection, when Lawrence learned that Segre was lcgally trapped in California, he reduced his salary to US$116 a month which many, including Segre, saw as exploiting the situation. Segre also found work as a lecturer of the physics department at the University of California, Berkeley.

While at Berkeley, he helped discover the element astatine and the isotope plutonium-239 (which was later used to make Fat Man, the atom bomb dropped on Nagasaki). He found in April 1944 that Thin Man, the proposed plutonium "gun-type" bomb, would not work (because of the presence of Pu-240 impurities), and priority was given to Fat Man, the plutonium "implosion" bomb.

Segre's ID badge photo from Los Alamos.

From 1943 to 1946 he worked at the Los Alamos National Laboratory as a group leader for the Manhattan Project. In 1944, he became a naturalized citizen of the United States. He taught at Columbia University, University of Illinois and University of Rio de Janeiro. On his return to Berkeley in 1946, he became a professor of physics and of the history of science, serving until 1972. In 1974 he returned to the University of Rome as a professor of nuclear physics.

In 1970, Segre published a biography of Fermi (Enrico Fermi: Physicist, University of Chicago Press)

Segre was also active as a photographer, and took many photos documenting events and people in the history of modern science. The American Institute of Physics named its photographic archive of physics history in his honour. Segre died at the age of 84 of a heart attack.

ERWIN SCHRODINGER

Erwin Rudolf Josef Alexander Schrodinger (August 12, 1887 – January 4, 1961) was an Austrian physicist who achieved fame for his contributions to quantum mechanics, especially the Schrodinger equation, for which he received the Nobel Prize in 1933. In 1935, after extensive correspondence with personal friend Albert Einstein, he proposed the Schrodinger's cat thought experiment.

Biography

In 1887 Schrodinger was born in Vienna, Austria to Rudolf Schrodinger (cerecloth producer, botanist) and Georgine Emilia Brenda (daughter of Alexander Bauer, Professor of Chemistry, k.u.k. Technische Hochschule Vienna). His mother was half Austrian and half English; the English side of her family came from Leamington Spa.

Schrodinger learned English and German almost at the same time due to the fact that both were spoken in the family household. His father was a Catholic and his mother was a Lutheran. In 1898 he attended the Akademisches Gymnasium. Between 1906 and 1910 Schrodinger studied in Vienna under Franz Serafin Exner (1849-1926) and Friedrich Hasenohrl (1874-1915). He also conducted experimental work with Friedrich Kohlrausch. In 1911, Schrodinger became an assistant to Exner.

Death and Legacy

On January 4, 1961, Schrodinger died in Vienna of tuberculosis at the age of 73. He left a widow, Anny (born Annemarie Bertel on December 3, 1896, died October 3, 1965), and was buried in Alpbach (Austria).

The philosophical issues raised by Schrodinger's cat are still debated today and remains his most enduring legacy in *popular* science (Schrodinger's equation being his most enduring legacy at a more technical level). The huge Schrodinger crater on the far side of the Moon was posthumously named after him by the IAU. The Erwin Schrodinger International Institute for Mathematical Physics was established in Vienna in 1993.

EDWARD RAMBERG

Edward G. Ramberg (June 14, 1907 in Florence, Italy – January 9, 1995) was an American physicist who contributed to the early development of electron microscopy and colour television. He was the uncle of Mario Capecchi, a 2007 Nobel laureate. His mother was an American painter, Lucy Dodd Ramberg (nee Dodd), and his father a German archaeologist, Walter Ramberg. His father was killed while serving in World War I.

Education

Ramberg and his mother moved from Italy to Munich for the remainder of World War I, and in 1920 they moved to his mother's family home in Portland, Oregon. He graduated from Lincoln High School in 1922.

That year he enrolled in Reed College, but two years later he transferred to Cornell University. During the years 1925 to 1927, he took a hiatus and worked for Bausch & Lomb on optical computing. Upon receipt of his bachelor's degree from Cornell in 1928, he stayed at the University to work with K. F. Richtmyer. In 1930, Ramberg went to study with Arnold Sommerfeld at the Ludwig Maximilians University of Munich. He was granted his Ph.D. in 1932.

Career

Upon return to the United States from Munich, Ramberg returned to Cornell and continued the work on which he based his thesis: X-ray satellites and line widths. In 1935, he left Cornell to take a position at RCA to work on both theoretical and experimental work on secondary emission, pickup tubes, and field emission. He later took part in the development of the theory of thermoelectric refrigeration and image tube aberrations and in demonstrating the mathematical operability of a multistage electrostatic electron multiplier. He also took part in construction of one of the first electron microscopes in the mid-1940s. He remained at RCA until 1972.

In addition to working at RCA, he was a visiting professor at the University of Munich in 1949 and, he was a Fulbright lecturer a the Technische Hochschule Darmstadt 1960-1961. In addition to co-authoring a number of books, he also translated *Electrodynamik*, Arnold Sommerfeld's third volume in his six-volume *Lectures on Theoretical Physics*.

EDWARD MILLS PURCELL

Edward Mills Purcell (August 30, 1912 – March 7, 1997) was an American physicist who shared the 1952 Nobel Prize for Physics for his independent discovery (published 1946) of nuclear magnetic resonance in liquids and in solids. Nuclear magnetic resonance (NMR) has become widely used to study the molecular structure of pure materials and the composition of mixtures.

Biography

Born and raised in Taylorville, Illinois, Purcell received his BE in electrical engineering from Purdue University, followed by his M.A. and Ph.D. in physics from Harvard University. After spending the years of World War II working at the MIT Radiation Laboratory on the development of microwave radar, Purcell returned to Harvard to do research. In December 1945, he discovered nuclear magnetic resonance (NMR) with his colleagues Pound and Torrey. NMR provides scientists with an elegant and precise way of determining chemical structure and properties of materials, and is widely used in physics and chemistry.

It also is the basis of magnetic resonance imaging (MRI), one of the most important medical advances of the 20th century. For his discovery of NMR, Purcell shared the 1952 Nobel Prize in physics with Felix Bloch of Stanford University.

Purcell also made contributions to astronomy as the first to detect radio emissions from neutral galactic hydrogen (the famous 21 cm line due to hyperfine splitting), affording the first views of the spiral arms of the Milky Way.

This observation helped launch the field of radio astronomy, and measurements of the 21 cm line are still an important technique in modern astronomy. He has also made other seminal contributions to solid state physics, with studies of spin-echo relaxation, nuclear magnetic relaxation, and negative spin temperature (important in the development of the laser). With Norman F. Ramsey, he was the first to question the CP symmetry of particle physics.

Purcell was the recipient of many awards for his scientific, educational, and civic work. He served as science advisor to Presidents Dwight D. Eisenhower, John F. Kennedy, and Lyndon B. Johnson. He was president of the American Physical Society, and a member of the American Philosophical Society, the National Academy of Sciences, and the American Academy of Arts and Sciences. He was awarded the National Medal of Science in 1979. Purcell was also inducted into his Fraternity's (Phi Kappa Sigma) Hall of Fame as the first Phi Kap ever to receive a Nobel Prize.

Purcell is the author of *Electricity and Magnetism* (1965) — originally *Volume 2* of the *Berkeley Physics Course.* (A 1984 second edition is meant to stand on its own.) This elegant text, which showcases Purcell's skill as a teacher, is still one of the standard introductory electricity and magnetism textbooks in college physics. Purcell is also remembered by biologists for his famous lecture "Life at Low Reynolds Number".

EGON OROWAN

Egon Orowan (Hungarian: **Orovan Egon**) (August 2, 1902 — August 3, 1989) was a Hungarian/British/U.S. physicist and metallurgist.

Life

Orowan was born in the Obuda district of Budapest. His father, Berthold, was a mechanical engineer and factory manager, and his mother, Josze Spitzer Sagvari was the daughter of an impoverished land owner. In 1928, Orowan commenced his education at the Technical University of Berlin in mechanical and electrical engineering but soon transferred to physics, completing his doctorate on the fracture of mica in 1932. He seems to have experienced some difficulty in finding immediate employment and spent the next few years living with his mother and ruminating on his doctoral research.

In 1934, Orowan, roughly contemporarily with G. I. Taylor and Michael Polanyi, realised that the plastic deformation of ductile materials could be explained in terms of the theory of dislocations developed by Vito Volterra in 1905. Though the discovery was neglected until after World War II, it was critical in developing the modern science of solid mechanics.

After working for a short while on the extraction of krypton from the air for the manufacture of light bulbs, in 1937 Orowan moved to the University of Birmingham, UK where he worked on the theory of fatigue collaborating with Rudolf Peierls.

In 1939, he moved to the University of Cambridge where William Lawrence Bragg inspired his interest in x-ray diffraction. During World War II, he worked on problems of munitions production, particularly that of plastic flow during rolling. In 1944, he was central to the reappraisal of the causes of the tragic loss of many Liberty ships during the war, identifying the critical issues of the notch sensitivity of poor quality welds and the aggravating effects of the extreme low temperatures of the North Atlantic. In 1950, he moved to the Massachusetts Institute of Technology where, in addition to continuing his metallurgical work, he developed his interests in geological and glacialogical fracture and in what he termed *socionomy*. In the latter study, Orowan developed the writings of the 14th century Tunisian historian Ibn Khaldun to forecast an eventual failure of market demand similar to that predicted by Karl Marx. His ideas found little acceptance among the majority of economists.

Throughout his life, he patented many inventions.

ERNST MACH

Ernst Mach (February 18, 1838 – February 19, 1916) was an Austrian physicist and philosopher and is the namesake for the "Mach number" (also known as Mach speed) and the optical illusion known as Mach bands.

Biography

Ernst Mach was born in Chrlice (then part of the Austrian empire, now part of Brno, Czech Republic). His father was tutor to the Brethon noble family in Zlin having graduated from Prague University]. Some sources state that Mach' birthplace was Tuoany, but this was where the Chrlice registry office was situated.

Up to the age of 14 he was educated at home by his parents. He then joined a Gymnasium in Kromioiz where he studied for three year. In 1855 he entered the University of Vienna. There he studied physics and for one semester medical physiology, receiving his doctorate in physics in 1860 and his Habilitation the following year. His early work focused on the Doppler effect in optics and acoustics. In 1864 he took a job as Professor of Mathematics in Graz, and in 1866 he was appointed as Professor of Physics.

During that period Mach continued his work in psycho-physics and in sensory perception. In 1867 he took the chair of Professor of Experimental Physics at Charles-Ferdinand University, Prague, where he stayed for 28 years. Mach's main contribution to physics was his description and photographs of spark shock waves and then ballistic shock waves. He described how passing the sound barrier compressed air in front of bullets and shells. Using a so-called "schlierenmthod" he and his son Ludwig were able to photograph the shadows of the invisible shock waves.

During the early 1890's Ludwig was able to invent an interferometer which allowed for much clearer photographs. But Mach also made many contributions to psychology and physiology including his anticipation of gestalt phenomena, his discovery of Mach bands an inhibition influenced type of visual illusion, and especially his discovery of a non-acoustic function of the inner ear which helped control human balance.

Mach is also well-known for his philosophy, which was a type of phenomenalism as if only sensations were real. Unfortunately, this position was not compatible with the reality of atoms and molecules, and from about 1908 to 1911 his views were criticized by Max Planck as being incompatible with physics. Some of Mach's criticisms of Newton's position on space and time influenced Einstein, but later Einstein realized that Mach was basically opposed to Newton's philosophy and that his physical criticism was not sound. As an experimental physicist Mach tended to think that scientific theories were only provisional and had no lasting place in physics. This attitude made it hard for him to accept Einstein's special theory of relativity, especially since the second axiom seemed like an absolute of the kind Mach opposed, which was criticized in the preface to a posthumously published book on light which appeared in 1921.

In 1898 he suffered a stroke and in 1901 retired from the University of Vienna and was appointed to the upper chamber of the Austrian parliament. On leaving Vienna in 1913 he moved to his son's home in Vaterstetten, near Munich where he continued writing and corresponding until his death in 1916.

EVGENY LIFSHITZ

Evgeny Mikhailovich Lifshitz (February 21, 1915 – October 29, 1985) was a leading Soviet physicist from a Jewish origin and the brother of Ilya Mikhailovich Lifshitz. (Some commonly encountered alternative transliterations of his names include Yevgeny or Evgenii and Lifshits or Lifschitz.)

Lifshitz is well known in general relativity for coauthoring the BKL conjecture concerning the nature of a *generic curvature singularity*. As of 2006, this is widely regarded as one of the most important open problems in the subject of classical gravitation.

With Lev Landau, Lifshitz co-authored an ambitious series of physics textbooks, in which the two aimed to provide a graduate-level introduction to the entire field of physics. These books are still considered invaluable and continue to be widely used. Lifshitz was the second of only 43 people ever to pass Landau's "Theoretical Minimum" examination.

The wife of Lev Landau strongly criticized his scientific abilities, hinting at how much of the two of them was done by Lifshitz, and how much by Landau. (Of their textbooks, the joke is made, "Not one word of Landau, not one thought of Lifshitz.") Despite the sniping, he is well known for many invaluable contributions, in particular to quantum electrodynamics, where he calculated the Casimir force in an arbitrary macroscopic configurations of metals and dielectrics.

ERNEST LAWRENCE

Ernest Orlando Lawrence (August 8, 1901 – August 27, 1958) was an American physicist and Nobel Laureate best known for his invention, utilization, and improvement of the cyclotron beginning in 1929, and his later work in uranium-isotope separation in the Manhattan Project.

He had a long career at the University of California, Berkeley where he was a professor of physics. In 1939, Lawrence was awarded the Nobel Prize in Physics for his work on the cyclotron and its applications. Chemical element number 103 is named "lawrencium" in his honour. He was also the first recipient of the Sylvanus Thayer Award. His brother John H. Lawrence is known for pioneering the field of nuclear medicine.

Early Life

Born in Canton, South Dakota, Lawrence attended St. Olaf College in Minnesota, but transferred to the University of South Dakota after his first year. He earned his bachelor's degree in 1922. He received his Master's Degree in Physics from the University of Minnesota in 1923. He spent a year at the University of Chicago, and received his Ph.D. in physics at Yale University in 1925, making him somewhat unusual in his field—a very promising young scientist who had received his entire education in the United States, in a day when study at one of the great science institutions of Europe was considered essential for someone who truly wished to make a significant contribution. He remained at Yale as a researcher on the photoelectric effect, becoming an assistant professor in 1927. In 1928 he was appointed Associate Professor of Physics at the University of California, Berkeley, and two years later he became a full Professor, being the youngest at Berkeley. There, he was called the "Atom Smasher,"; the man who "held the key" to atomic energy. "He wanted to do 'big physics,' the kind of work that could only be done on a large scale with a lot of people involved," said Herbert York, the first director of the Lawrence Livermore laboratory, as quoted on the lab's official Web site.

ERWIN FUES

Erwin Richard Fues (January 17, 1893 in Stuttgart, Germany – 1970 in Germany) was a German theoretical physicist who made contributions to atomic physics and molecular physics, quantum wave mechanics, and solid-state physics.

Education and Career

During the period 1912 to 1914, Fues studied at the University of Berlin and then the University of Munich. He served in the military 1914 to circa 1915, and then attended the University of Tubingen from 1916 to 1918. During 1918, he became a student of Arnold Sommerfeld, and he received the *doctor rerum naturalium* from the University of Munich in 1920. From 1922 he did postgraduate work at the Stuttgart Technische Hochschule, under Paul Peter Ewald, also a former student of Arnold Sommerfeld, and he completed his Habilitation in 1924. At Stuttgart he served as a Privatdozent and assistant to Ewald until 1929, during which time he worked on atomic and molecular structure and spectroscopy based on the Sommerfeld-Bohr theory.

During his tenure under Ewald, he was absent during the period 1925 to 1927, when, as an International Education Board fellow, he was first an assistant to Erwin Schrodinger at the University of Zurich, and then a research assistant at the University of Copenhagen at Neils Bohr's Institute of Theoretical Physics. At that time three major centres for the development of quantum mechanics were the Theoretical Physics Institute at the University of Munich, under Arnold Sommerfeld, the Institute of Theoretical Physics at the University of Gottingen, under Max Born, and the Institute of Theoretical Physics, under Niels Bohr.

From 1929 to 1934, he served as ordinarius professor at the Hanover Technische Hochschule. From 1934 to 1943, he served as ordinarius professor jointly at the University of Breslau and the Breslau Technische Hochschule, after which, he went to the Vienna Technische Universitat, where he remained until 1947. In that year, he went back to the Stuttgart Technische Hochschule, where the Institute for Theoretical and Applied Physics (Institut fur Theoretische und Angewandte Physik) had been formed with two chairs. Fues became ordinarius professor for theoretical physics as well as director of the institute; the other joint director was Ulrich Dehlinger. The institute followed the tradition of both Sommerfeld and Ewald in carrying on with both theoretical and experimental research and teaching.

After the death of Sommerfeld in 1951, Fues edited and supplemented multiple editions of two volumes of Sommerfeld's six-volume *Vorlesungen uber theoretische Physik*.

In his career, Fues made contributions to theoretical physics, especially in atomic structure, quantum wave mechanics, and solid-state physics. In 1960, Hermann Haken took over from Fues at the Institute for Theoretical and Applied Physics.

ENRICO FERMI

Enrico Fermi (September 29, 1901 – November 28, 1954) was an Italian physicist most noted for his work on the development of the first nuclear reactor, and for his contributions to the development of quantum theory, nuclear and particle physics, and statistical mechanics. Fermi was awarded the Nobel Prize in Physics in 1938 for his work on induced radioactivity and is today regarded as one of the top scientists of the 20th century. He is acknowledged as a unique physicist who was highly accomplished in both theory and experiment. Fermium, a synthetic element created in 1952 is named after him.

Biography

Enrico Fermi was born in Rome, Italy. His father was Alberto Fermi, a Chief Inspector of the Ministry of Communications, and his mother was Ida de Gattis, an elementary school teacher. As a young boy he enjoyed learning physics and mathematics and shared his interests with his older brother, Giulio. When Giulio died unexpectedly of a throat abscess in 1915, Enrico was distraught, and immersed himself into scientific study to distract himself. According to his own account, each day he would walk in front of the hospital where Giulio died until he became inured to the pain. Later, Enrico befriended another scientifically inclined student named Enrico Persico, and the two together engaged in scientific projects such as building gyroscopes, and measuring the magnetic field of the earth. Fermi's interest in physics was further encouraged when a friend of his father's gave him several books on physics and mathematics, which he read and assimilated.

Fermi received his undergraduate and doctoral degree from the Scuola Normale Superiore in Pisa. There was an entrance exam which candidates had to take in order to enter the prestigious institute, which included an essay. For his essay on the given theme

Characteristics of Sound, 17-year-old Fermi chose to derive and solve the Fourier analysis based partial differential equation for waves on a string. The examiner interviewed Fermi and concluded that his essay would have been commendable even for a doctoral degree. At the Scuola Normale Superiore, Fermi teamed up with a fellow student named Franco Rasetti with whom he used to indulge in light hearted pranks. Later, Rasetti became Fermi's close friend and collaborator.

Fermi's Ph.D advisor was Luigi Puccianti. In 1924 Fermi spent a semester in Gottingen, and then stayed for a few months in Leiden with Paul Ehrenfest. From January 1925 to the autumn of 1926 he stayed at the University of Florence. In this period he wrote his work on the Fermi-Dirac statistics. When he was only 24 years old, Fermi took a professorship in Rome (the first for atomic physics in Italy, which he won in a competition created by Professor Orso Mario Corbino, director of the Institute of Physics). Corbino helped Fermi in selecting his team, which soon was joined by notable minds like Edoardo Amaldi, Bruno Pontecorvo, Franco Rasetti and Emilio Segre.

For the theoretical studies only, Ettore Majorana also took part in what was soon nicknamed "the Via Panisperna boys" (after the name of the road in which the Institute had its labs). The group went on with its now famous experiments, but in 1933 Rasetti left Italy for Canada and the United States, Pontecorvo went to France and Segre left to teach in Palermo.

During their time in Rome, Fermi and his group made important contributions to many practical and theoretical aspects of physics. Some of these include the theory of beta decay, and the discovery of slow neutrons, which was to prove pivotal for the working of nuclear reactors. His group also systematically bombarded elements with slow neutrons, and during their experiments with uranium, narrowly missed observing nuclear fission.

At that time, fission was thought to be improbable, if not impossible, mostly on theoretical grounds. While people expected elements with higher atomic number to form from neutron bombardment of lighter elements, nobody expected neutrons to have enough energy to actually split a heavier atom into two light element fragments. However, the chemist Ida Noddack had criticised Fermi's work and had suggested that some of his experiments could have produced lighter elements. At the time, Fermi dismissed this possibility on the basis of calculations.

Fermi was well-known for his simplicity in solving problems. He began his inquiries with the simplest lines of mathematical reasoning, then later produced complete solutions to the problems he deemed worth pursuing. His abilities as the greatest combined theoretical and applied nuclear physicist of all time were acknowledged by and influenced many physicists who worked with him, such as Hans Bethe, who spent two semesters working with Fermi in the early 1930s. From the time he was a boy, Fermi meticulously recorded his calculations in notebooks, and later used to solve many new problems that he encountered based on these earlier known problems.

When Fermi submitted his famous paper on beta decay to the prestigious journal *Nature*, the journal's editor turned it down because "it contained speculations which were too remote from reality". Thus, Fermi saw the theory published in Italian and in German before it was published in English. *Nature* eventually did publish Fermi's report on beta decay on January 16, 1939.

ERNEST COURANT

Ernest Courant (born 1920) has been called the "father of modern particle accelerators". A fundamental contributor to the field, he has also been mentor to several generations of students. In this kind of generative academic influence, he can be compared to his father, the mathematician Richard Courant.

Currently, Ernest Courant is a member the National Academy of Sciences, and remains active as a distinguished scientist emeritus at Brookhaven National Laboratory. He has played a part in the work of Brookhaven for sixty years.

Early Life

The first of their four children, he was born in Gottingen, Germany in 1920, to Richard Courant and Nerina Runge Courant, a year after their marriage.

He has written that he "came by science naturally". His mother's father, Carl Runge, is credited with the Runge-Kutta method for numerical solutions of differential equations. A maternal great-grandfather (Runge's father-in-law) was Emil DuBois-Reymond, a pioneer in electrophysiology. Affinity for science and mathematics extended further than his biological family. Ernest Courant's childhood neighbours included the mathematician David Hilbert (his father's thesis director, in whose honour Ernest received the middle name of David) and the physicists Max Born and James Franck. Further, his father's students and colleagues became friends of the family, and frequented their home.

Ernest's early interests centred on chemistry. "I had a lab at home full of test tubes, Bunsen burners, and chemicals. Once there was a small fire (easily put out), but I got a sense of how things were put together."

Adolf Hitler came to power in 1933, and the neighborhood and its intellectual society were disrupted-along with the mathematics department at the University. Ernest's father had been born to a Jewish family of small businessmen, and he was now now identified as a Jew, and an undesirable, by the new regime. Expelled from his position at the University of Gottingen, Richard Courant took a temporary teaching position in England, and the family abandoned Gottingen in favour of Cambridge for a few months. Forewarned by a Nazi acquaintance that the anti-Semetic storm would not settle-but intensify, the family made plans to emigrate permanently. They returned only briefly to Germany before embarking to New York City, where his father had secured a post at New York University-and immigration visas to the USA.

Fluent in English from both early lessons and the recent period enrolled at the Perse School in Cambridge, Ernest was accepted at the Fieldston School of the School for Ethical Culture, with scholarship, thanks to intervention by family friend (and Fieldston alumnus), J. Robert Oppenheimer.

Career

Courant graduated from the Fieldston School in 1936, received a physics degree from Swarthmore College, and earned a Ph.D. in physics from the University of Rochester in 1943. Courant has worked at Brookhaven National Laboratory from 1948 to the present, first as an associate scientist in the Proton Synchrotron Division. He received tenure in 1955, and was promoted to senior scientist in 1960. In addition, he taught as an Adjunct Professor at SUNY Stony Brook from 1966 to 1986.

His most notable discovery is his 1952 work with M Stanley Livingston and Hartland Snyder on the Strong Focusing Principle, a critical step in the development of modern particle accelerators.

EDWARD CONDON

Edward Uhler Condon (March 2, 1902 – March 26, 1974) was a distinguished American nuclear physicist, a pioneer in quantum mechanics, a participant in the development of radar and nuclear weapons in World War II, research director of Corning Glass, director of the National Bureau of Standards, and president of the American Physical Society (as well as, late in his life, professor of physics at the University of Colorado, where he directed a controversial Air Force-funded scientific study of UFOs). He was born in Alamogordo, New Mexico, United States, and earned a Ph.D. from University of California, Berkeley in 1926.

In 1943, Condon joined the Manhattan Project; however, within six weeks, he resigned as a result of conflicts with General Leslie R. Groves, the project's military leader.

Condon was one of the physicists whose loyalty to the United States was challenged by members of Congress — including Congressman Richard M. Nixon, who called for the revocation of his security clearance — in the late 1940s and early 1950s. The superpatriotic chairman of the House Committee on Un-American Activities (HUAC), Rep. J. Parnell Thomas, would call the physicist "Dr. Condon," the "weakest link" in American security, and even the "missing link."

In 1948, U.S. President Harry Truman — at the Annual Meeting of the American Association for the Advancement of Science, and with Condon sitting beside him — denounced Rep. Thomas and HUAC on the grounds that vital scientific research "may be made impossible by the creation of an atmosphere in which no man feels safe against the public airing of unfounded rumours, gossip and vilification." He called HUAC's activities "the most un-American thing we have to contend with today. It is the climate of a totalitarian country."

Carl Sagan, once a student of Condon, documented Condon's own account of being brought up before a loyalty review board: *'Dr. Condon, it says here that you have been at the forefront of a revolutionary movement in physics called" — and here the inquisitor read the words slowly and carefully — "quantum mechanics. It strikes this hearing that if you could be at the forefront of one revolutionary movement...you could be at the forefront of another."*

Condon replied that the accusation was unfounded, since he most emphatically was *not* a "revolutionary". He raised his right hand and solemnly declared, "I believe in Archimedes' Principle, formulated in the third century B.C. I believe in Kepler's laws of planetary motion, discovered in the seventeenth century. I believe in Newton's laws...." He continued in this vein, listing a long sequence of scientists whose work, done centuries before, was still valid and respected: The Bernoulli family, Fourier, Ampere, Boltzmann, and Maxwell. HUAC did not appreciate his sense of humour; however, fortunately for Condon, the most severe charge they could confirm was that in high school he had a paper route delivering a socialist newspaper.

From 1966 to 1968, Condon directed the University of Colorado UFO Project. Though plagued with infighting and controversy, the project's conclusion—that all unidentified flying objects had prosaic explanations—have been cited as a key factor in the generally low levels of interest in UFOs among most mainstream scientists and academics. See Condon Report. In his negative critique of the Condon Report, astronomer J. Allen Hynek hoped that Condon's reputation would not be soured by the Condon Report, writing, "It is unfortunate that, almost certainly, popular history will henceforth link Dr. Condon's name with UFOs, and only the arcane history of physics will accord him his true place and record his brilliant career in contributing to the understanding... of the nature of the physical world. These contributions UFOs cannot take away from him, even though his work with this problem is analogous to that of a Mozart producing an uninspired pot-boiler, unworthy of his talents." (Clark, 605)

Following his death, Condon crater on the Moon was named after him.

FREDERICK SEITZ

Frederick Seitz (2008-07-04–2008-03-02) was an American physicist and a pioneer of solid state physics. Seitz studied under Eugene Wigner at Princeton University, graduating in 1934. He, along with Wigner, came up with the concept of the Wigner-Seitz unit cell. He also founded the Frederick Seitz Materials Research Laboratory at the University of Illinois at Urbana-Champaign as well as several other material research laboratories across the United States.

Biography

Born in San Francisco on 2008-07-04, Seitz graduated from Lick-Wilmerding High School in the middle of his senior year. He went on to study physics at Standford University obtaining his bachelor's degree in three years, and then moved to Princeton University to study metals under Eugene Wigner. He and Wigner pioneered one of the first quantum theory of crystals, and developed concepts such as the Wigner-Seitz unit cell. After his graduate studied, Seitz continued to work on solid state physics, publishing

The Modern Theory of solids in 1940, motivated by a desire to "write a cohesive account of the various aspects of solid-state physics in order to give the field the kind of unity it deserved". *The Modern Theory of Solids* helped unify and understand the relations between the fields of metallurgy, ceramics, and electronics. He was also a consultant on many World War II related projects in metallurgy, radiation damage to solids and electronics amongst others.

He, along with Hillard Huntington, made the first calculation of the energies of formation and migration of vacancies and interstitials in copper, inspiring many works on point defects in metals.

He was the president of Rockefeller University from 1968 to 1978 during which he helped to launch new research programmes in molecular biology, cell biology, and neuroscience as well as creating a joint MD-PhD programme with Cornell University. Shortly before his retirement from Rockefeller University in 1979, Seitz began working as a paid permanent consultant for the R.J. Reynolds Tobacco Company, advising their research programme.

In 1994, Seitz authored *Global warming and ozone hole controversies. A challenge to scientific judgment.*, a report published by the George C. Marshall Institute, of which he was a founder and chairman of the board, titled "" In a broader discussion of environmental toxins, he concluded "there is no good scientific evidence that passive inhalation is truly dangerous under normal circumstances."

Seitz questioned whether global warming is anthropogenic. He supported the position of the Oregon Institute of Science and Medicine (OISM) on global warming and in an open letter invited scientists to sign the OISM's global warming petition. He also signed the 1995 Leipzig Declaration and questioned the view that CFCs "are the greatest threat to the ozone layer".

Seitz died March 2, 2008 in New York. He was said to have a "wry sense of humour" and to be "a kind and generous person, giving untold and unacclaimed time and energy to help young scientists and young science along their way".

FULVIO MELIA

Fulvio Melia (born 2 August 1956) is an Italian-American physicist/astrophysicist and author. He is Professor of Physics and Astronomy at the University of Arizona and Associate Editor of the Astrophysical Journal Letters. A former Presidential Young Investigator and Sloan Research Fellow, he is the author of six books and more than 230 articles on theoretical astrophysics.

Career

Melia was educated at Melbourne University and The Massachusetts Institute of Technology, and held a post-doctoral research position at the University of Chicago before taking an assistant professorship at Northwestern University in 1987. Moving to the University of Arizona as an associate professor in 1991, he became a full professor in 1993. From 1988 to 1995, he was a Presidential Young Investigator (under President Ronald Reagan), and then an Alfred P. Sloan Research Fellow from 1989 to 1992. He became a Fellow of the American Physical Society in 2002. He is also a Professorial Fellow in the School of Physics, Melbourne University.

From 1996 to 2002, he was a Scientific Editor with the Astrophysical Journal, and since then has been an Associate Editor with the Astrophysical Journal Letters. He is also the Chief Editor of the Theoretical Astrophysics series of books at the University of Chicago Press.

In a career that has seen him publish over 230 research papers and several books, Melia has made important contributions in High Energy Astronomy and the physics of supermassive black holes. He is especially known for his work on the Galactic centre, particularly developing a theoretical understanding of the central supermassive black hole, known as Sagittarius A*. With his students and collaborators, he was the first to propose imaging this object with millimeter-interferometry, which should be feasible within a few years, proving beyond any doubt that it possesses an event horizon, as predicted by Einstein's theory of general relativity. He is also a well-respected and popular publicist of astronomy and science in general, delivering many lectures at public venues, including museums and planetariums. His books have won several awards of distinction, including the designation of Outstanding Academic Books by the American Library Association, and selection as world-wide astronomy books of the year by Astronomy (magazine).

FRITZ HOUTERMANS

Friedrich Georg "Fritz" Houtermans (January 22, 1903 – March 1, 1966) was an atomic and nuclear physicist born in Zoppot (today Sopot, Poland) near Danzig (today Gdansk, Poland). Houtermans made important contributions to geochemistry and cosmochemistry.

Education

Houtermans began his studies at the Georg-August University of Gottingen in 1921, and he received his doctorate under James Franck in 1927, the same year Robert Oppenheimer received his doctorate under Max Born. He completed his Habilitation under Gustav Hertz at the Technische Hochschule Berlin, in 1932. Hertz and Franck were Nobel Prize laureates; they shared the 1925 Nobel Prize in Physics.

While at Gottingen, Houtermans met Enrico Fermi, George Gamow, Werner Heisenberg, Wolfgang Pauli, and Victor Frederick Weisskopf. Houtermans and Gamow did pioneering work on quantum tunneling in 1928. Houtermans, in 1929, with Robert d'Escourt Atkinson, made the first calculation of stellar thermonuclear reactions. Their pioneering calculations were the impetus for Carl Friedrich von Weizsacker and Hans Bethe, in 1939, to put forth the correct theory of stellar thermonuclear energy generation.

Charlotte Riefenstahl, who received her doctorate in physics at the University of Gottingen in 1927, the same year as Houtermans and Robert Oppenheimer, was courted by both men. She was no relation to Leni Riefenstahl, the notable German filmmaker. In 1930, she left her teaching position at Vassar College and went back to Germany. During a physics conference at the Black Sea resort of Batumi, Riefenstahl and Houtermans were married in August 1930, in Tbilisi, with Wolfgang Pauli and Rudolf Peierls as witnesses to the ceremony. (Three other references cite the year as being 1931.)

Career

From 1932 to 1933, Houtermans taught at the Technische Hochschule Berlin and was an assistant to Hertz. While there, he met Patrick Blackett, Max von Laue, and Leo Szilard.

Houtermans was a Communist; he had been a member of the German Communist Party since the 1920s. After Adolf Hitler came to power in 1933, Charlotte Houtermans insisted that they leave Germany. They went to Great Britain, near Cambridge, where he worked for the EMI (Electrical and Musical Instruments, Ltd.) Television Laboratory. In 1935 Houtermans emigrated to the Soviet Union, as the result of a proposal by Alexander Weissberg, who had emigrated to there in 1931. Houtermans took an appointment at the Khar'kov Physico-Technical Institute and worked there for two years with the Russian physicist Valentin P. Fomin. In the Great Purge, Houtermans was arrested by the NKVD in December 1937. He was tortured and confessed to being a Trotskyist plotter and German spy, out of fear from threats against Charlotte.

However, Charlotte had already escaped from the Soviet Union to Denmark, after which she went to England and finally the USA. After the Hitler-Stalin Pact of 1939, Houtermans was turned over to the Gestapo in May 1940 and imprisoned in Berlin. The Gestapo subjected him to brutal interrogation, accused of being a Soviet spy. Through efforts of Max von Laue, Houtermans was released in August 1940, whereupon he took a position at *Forschungslaboratoriums fur Elektronenphysik*, a private laboratory of Manfred Baron von Ardenne, in Lichterfelde, a suburb of Berlin. In 1944, Houtermans took a position as a nuclear physicist at the Physikalisch-Technische Reichsanstalt.

While imprisoned in the Soviet Union, a cellmate of Houtermans was the Kiev University historian Konstantine F. Shteppa. They would later write a book together, "Russian Purge and the Extraction of Confession", under the pseudonyms of Beck and Godin to protect their many friends and colleagues back in the USSR.

At the Forschunsinstitut Manfred von Ardenne, Houtermans showed that transuranic isotopes, such as neptunium and plutonium, could be used as fissionable fuels in substitution for uranium. Houtermans sent a telegram from Switzerland to Eugene Wigner at the Met Lab warning the USA's Manhattan Project of German work on fission: "Hurry up. We are on the track." During Houtermans' employment at the Physikalisch-Technische Reichsanstalt (PTR), he got himself into serious trouble as a result of his habit of being a chain-smoker and suffering great distress if he did not have a supply of tobacco. On official PTR stationery, he wrote to a Dresden cigarette manufacturer to obtain a kilogram of Macedonian tobacco, claiming the tobacco was "kriegswichtig", *i.e.*, important for the war effort.

When he had smoked the tobacco, he again wrote for more, however, the letter fell into the hands of an official at the PTR, who fired him. Werner Heisenberg and Carl Weizsacker came to the rescue of Houtermans and arranged an interview for him with Walter Gerlach, the plenipotentiary (Bevollmachtiger) for German nuclear research under the Reich Research Council. As a result, Houtermans moved to Gottingen in 1945, where Hans Kopferman and Richard Becker got him positions at the Institut fur Theoretische Physik and II. Physikalischen Institut der Universitat Gottingen. From 1952, Houtermans took a position as ordinarius professor of physics at the University of Bern. During his tenure there, he founded the internationally renowned *Berner Schule*, whose thrust was the application of radioactivity to astrophysics, cosmochemistry, and geosciences.

FRED HOYLE

Sir **Fred Hoyle** (24 June 1915 – 20 August 2001) was an English astronomer primarily remembered today for his contribution to the theory of stellar nucleosynthesis and his often controversial stance on other cosmological and scientific matters, in particular his rejection of the Big Bang hypothesis.

Hoyle was born in Gilstead, West Yorkshire, England, near Bradford, where his father, George Hoyle, worked in the wool trade. His mother, Mabel Pickard, had studied music at the Royal College of Music in London. Hoyle was educated at Bingley Grammar School and read mathematics at Emmanuel College, Cambridge. In addition to his work as an astronomer, Hoyle was a writer of science fiction, including a number of books co-authored with his son Geoffrey Hoyle. Hoyle spent most of his working life at the Institute of Astronomy at Cambridge and served as its director for a number of years. He died in Bournemouth, England, after a series of strokes.

Contribution to Cosmology

An early paper of Hoyle's made an interesting use of the anthropic principle. In trying to work out the routes of stellar nucleosynthesis, he observed that one particular nuclear reaction, the triple-alpha process, which generated carbon, would require the carbon nucleus to have a very specific energy for it to work. The large amount of carbon in the universe, which makes it possible for carbon-based lifeforms (*e.g.* humans) to exist, demonstrated that this nuclear reaction must work. Based on this notion, he made a prediction of the energy levels in the carbon nucleus that was later borne out by experiment. However, those energy levels, while needed in order to produce carbon in large quantities, were statistically very unlikely. Hoyle later wrote:

> *Would you not say to yourself, "Some super-calculating intellect must have designed the properties of the carbon atom, otherwise the chance of my finding such an atom through the blind forces of nature would be utterly minuscule." Of course you would... A common sense interpretation of the facts suggests that a superintellect ha monkeyed with physics, as well as with chemistry and biology, and that there are no blind forces worth speaking about in nature. The numbers one calculates from the facts seem to me so overwhelming as to put this conclusion almost beyond question.*

Hoyle, an atheist until that time, said that this suggestion of a guiding hand left him "greatly shaken." Consequently, he began to believe in a god and panspermia. Those who advocate the intelligent design hypothesis sometimes cite Hoyle's work in this area to support the claim that the universe was fine tuned in order to allow intelligent life to be possible.

His co-worker William Alfred Fowler eventually won the Nobel Prize for Physics in 1983 (with Subramanyan Chandrasekhar), but for some reason Hoyle's original contribution was overlooked, and many were surprised that such a notable astronomer missed out. Fowler himself in an autobiographical sketch affirmed Hoyle's pioneering efforts:

The concept of nucleosynthesis in stars was first established by Hoyle in 1946. This provided a way to explain the existence of elements heavier than helium in the universe, basically by showing that critical elements such as carbon could be generated in stars and then incorporated in other stars and planets when that star "dies". The new stars formed now start off with these heavier elements and even heavier elements are formed from them. Hoyle theorized that other rarer elements could be explained by supernovas, the giant explosions which occasionally occur throughout the universe, whose temperatures and pressures would be required to create such elements.

FRIEDRICH HASENOHRL

Friedrich Hasenohrl (November 30, 1874-October 7, 1915), was an Austro-Hungarian physicist.

Friedrich Hasenohrl was born in Vienna, Austria-Hungary in 1874. His father was a lawyer and his mother belonged to a prominent aristocratic family. After his elementary education, he studied natural science and mathematics at the University of Vienna under Stephan and Boltzmann. He worked under H. A. Lorentz in Leiden at the low temperature laboratory.

In 1907 he became Boltzmann's successor at the University of Vienna as the head of the Department of Theoretical Physics. He had a number of illustrious pupils there and had an especially significant impact on Erwin Schrodinger, who later won the Nobel Prize for Physics for his contributions to Quantum Mechanics.

When the war broke out in 1914, he volunteered at once into the Austria-Hungarian army. He fought as Oberleutnant against the Italians in Tyrol. He was wounded, recovered and returned to the front. He was then killed by a grenade in an attack on Mount Plaut on October 7, 1915 at the age of 40.

$E = mc^2$

In 1904 and 1905 he published two papers on the inertia of a cavity containing radiation. This was an entirely classical derivation (no use of special relativity) and used Maxwell's equation for the pressure of light.

In the first paper, Hasenohrl specifically associated mass via inertia with the energy concept through an equation. Hasenohrl first concluded that $m = (8 / 3)E / c^2$. The same formula appeared on the page 363 in his paper. The title of this paper, which in English is *On the radiation of the bodies in motion*, is very similar to the title of the Einstein's paper published a year later *On the electrodynamics of the bodies in motion.*

In the later paper Hasenohrl re-calculated this result and arrived at $m = (4 / 3)E / c^2$. Hasenohrl indicated that if the internal energy of a system consists of radiation, then, in general, the inertial mass of the system would depend upon that energy.

Thus, this new Hasenohrl calculation establishes that due to the radiant energy E contained in his system, to that inertial mass must be added an apparent mass m.

Indeed, in 1914 Cunningham showed that Hasenohrl had made an error in that he did not include the shell. If he had included the shell in his calculations in a way consistent with relativity, the pre-factor would have been 1, so yielding $m = E / c^2$. He could not have done this, since he did not have relativistic mechanics, with which he could model the shell.

FEZA GURSEY

Feza Gursey (April 7, 1921-April 13, 1992) was a Turkish mathematician and physicist. His best known contribution to theoretical physics is his work on the Nonlinear Chiral Lagrangian.

Biography

Feza Gursey was born on April 21, 1921 in Istanbul, to Reoit Sureyya Gursey, a military physician, and Remziye Hisar (tr:Remziye Hisar), a chemist and a pioneering female Turkish scientist. He graduated from Galatasaray Lisesi in 1940, and received his degree in Mathematics – Physics from Istanbul Fen Fakultesi in 1944.

Through a scholarship of the Turkish Ministry of Education he received while he was an assistant in Istanbul University, he pursued a doctorate degree at the Imperial College London in the United Kingdom. He completed his work on Application of Quaternions to Quantum Field Theory in 1950. After spending the period from 1950 – 1951 in postdoctoral research at Cambridge University, he worked as an assistant at Istanbul University, where he married Suha Pamir, also a physics assistant, in 1952, and in 1953 he acquired the title of Associate Professor.

During 1957 – 1961 he worked at Brookhaven National Laboratory, Institute for Advanced Study at Princeton, New Jersey, and Columbia University. In 1960s, he worked on the Nonlinear Chiral Lagrangian, and produced results of relevance to Quantum Chromodynamics.

Returning to Turkey in 1961, he accepted the title of Professor from Middle East Technical University (METU) and took part in the establishment of METU Department of Theoretical Physics. Continuing his work as a lecturer at METU until 1974, he formed a research group.

Being offered a position at Yale University in 1965, he started to work in both Yale University and METU, until 1974, when he decided to give up his position in METU and settle in the United States to continue with Yale. During these years, he took part in the formulation of E(6) grand unified theories. Gursey died in 1992, in New Haven, Connecticut. He is survived by his son, Yusuf Gursey. The Feza Gursey Institute, founded by the joint effort of Booazici University and TUBYTAK in Turkey, is named in his honour.

FELIX EHRENHAFT

Felix Ehrenhaft (April 24, 1879 – March 4, 1952) was an Austrian physicist who contributed to atomic physics, to the measurement of electrical charges and to the optical properties of metal colloids. He was known for his maverick and controversial style. His fearless iconoclasm was greatly admired by philosopher Paul Feyerabend.

Biography

Ehrenhaft was born in Vienna to physician Leopold Ehrenhaft and Louise Eggar, the daughter of an Hungarian industrialist. Ehrenhaft earned his doctorate from the University of Vienna in 1903, working on the optical properties of metallic colloids. He subsequently became assistant to Viktor von Lang.

Later Years

From the mid-1930s, Ehrenhaft's thinking started to diverge strikingly from the mainstream of physics. He observed many genuinely surprising and reproducible physical phenomena, usually of ultra-microscopic particles near the limits of perception. However, he was all too willing to adopt bizarre theories to explain experiments that were beset with interactions and multifactorial cause systems.

From the 1940s, Ehrenhaft's views became increasingly extreme and strident, eventually terminating his good friendship with Albert Einstein. He found it impossible to obtain either research funding or even a sympathetic hearing in the U.S.. In 1946, he returned to the University of Vienna where he held again his old position until his death. He became increasingly certain that he had observed magnetic monopoles; *magnetic currents*; and *magnetolysis*, the disassociation of liquids by magnets rather than electric current as in electrolysis.

A review of his life work can be found in the Austrian scientific journal "Acta physica Austriaca", and in the article by Rohatschek on photophoresis (see sources below).

FRIEDRICH ERNST DORN

Friedrich Ernst Dorn (27 July 1848 – 16 December 1916) was a German physicist who was the first to discover that a radioactive substance, later named radon, is emitted from radium.

Life and Work

Dorn was born in Guttstadt (Dobre Miasto), Province of Prussia, and died in Halle, Province of Saxony. He was educated at Konigsberg and went on to teach at the university level. In 1885, at Halle University, Dorn took over the position of personal *ordinarius* professor.for theoretical physics from Anton Oberbeck.

Since Dorn was already an *ordinarius* professor, he was allowed to assume the title so as to not appear as having been demoted. In 1895, Dorn succeeded Hermann Knoblauch at Halle as the *ordinarius* professor for experimental physics and director of the physics institute. Dorn's previous duties were assumed by Karl Schmidt, who had been a Privatdozent and was called as an *extraordinarius* professor for theoretical physics.

In 1900, Dorn published a paper in which he described experiments that repeated and extended some earlier work on thorium by Ernest Rutherford. Dorn verified Rutherford's observation that a radioactive material was emitted by thorium, and discovered that a similar emission arose from the element radium. Additional work by Rutherford and Soddy showed that the same emission came from both thorium and radium, that it was a gas, and that it was actually a new element.

Dorn called the radioactive gaseous product from radium simply "emanation", but in 1904 Rutherford introduced the name "radium emanation" for the same material. Ramsay later suggested "niton", from the Latin word "nitens" meaning "shining". In 1923 the name was again changed, this time to radon by an international body of scientists.

Marshall and Marshall have examined the original papers leading to radon's discovery and their work should be consulted for a full treatment and extensive references. They conclude that it is actually Rutherford who should be awarded credit for radon's discovery since he was the first to detect the element being emitted from any radioisotope (thorium) and the first to demonstrate radon's gaseous nature. Rutherford also was the first to integrate his own work on radon with that of others on radon's atomic mass, its spectrum, and its position on the periodic table.

FRANCOIS ARAGO

Francois Jean Dominique Arago (February 26, 1786 – October 2, 1853) was a French mathematician, physicist, astronomer and politician.

Early Life and Work

Arago was born at Estagel, a small village near Perpignan, in the *departement* of Pyrenees-Orientales, Catalan France. He was the eldest of four brothers. Jean (1788-1836) emigrated to North America and became a general in the Mexican army. Jacques Etienne Victor (1799-1855) took part in Louis de Freycinet's exploring voyage in the *Uranie* from as 1817 to 1821, and on his return to France devoted himself to his journalism and the drama. The fourth brother, Etienne Vincent de (1802-1892), is said to have collaborated with Honore de Balzac in *The Heiress of Birague*, and from 1822 to 1847 wrote a great number of light dramatic pieces, mostly in collaboration.

Showing decided military tastes, Francois Arago was sent to the municipal college of Perpignan, where he began to study mathematics in preparation for the entrance examination of the polytechnic school. Within two years and a half he had mastered all the subjects prescribed for examination, and a great deal more, and, on going up for examination at Toulouse, he astounded his examiner by his knowledge of J. L. Lagrange.

Towards the close of 1803 Arago entered the Ecole Polytechnique, Paris, but apparently found the professors there incapable of imparting knowledge or maintaining discipline. The artillery service was his ambition, and in 1804, through the advice and recommendation of Simeon Poisson, he received the appointment of secretary to the Paris Observatory. He now became acquainted with Pierre-Simon Laplace, and through his influence was commissioned, with Jean-Baptiste Biot, to complete the meridianal measurements which had been begun by J. B. J. Delambre, and interrupted since the death of P. F. A. Mechain in 1804). Arago and Biot left Paris in 1806 and began operations along the mountains of Spain. Biot returned to Paris after they had determined the latitude of Formentera, the southernmost point to which they were to carry the survey. Arago continued the work until 1809, his purpose being to measure a meridian arc in order to determine the exact length of a metre.

After Biot's departure, the political ferment caused by the entrance of the French into Spain extended to the Balearic Islands, and the population suspected Arago's movements and his lighting of fires on the top of mola de l'Esclop as the activities of a spy for the invading army. Their reaction was such that he was obliged to give himself up for imprisonment in the fortress of Bellver in June 1808. On July 28 he escaped from the island in a fishing-boat, and after an adventurous voyage he reached Algiers on August 3. From there he obtained a passage in a vessel bound for Marseille, but on August 16, just as the vessel was nearing Marseille, it fell into the hands of a Spanish corsair. With the rest the crew, Arago was taken to Roses, and imprisoned first in a windmill, and afterwards in a fortress, until the town fell into the hands of the French, when the prisoners were transferred to Palamos.

After three months' imprisonment, Arago and the others were released on the demand of the dey of Algiers, and again set sail for Marseille on the November 28, but then within sight of their port they were driven back by a northerly wind to Bougie on the coast of Africa. Transport to Algiers by sea from this place would have occasioned a weary delay of three months; Arago, therefore, set out over land, guided by a Moslem priest, and reached it on Christmas Day. After six months in Algiers he once again, on the June 21, 1809, set sail for Marseille, where he had to undergo a monotonous and inhospitable quarantine in the lazaretto, before his difficulties were over. The first letter he received, while in the lazaretto, was from Alexander von Humboldt; and this was the origin of a connection which, in Arago's words, lasted over forty years without a single cloud ever having troubled it.

FREDERICK VINE

Frederick John Vine (born June 17, 1939) is a marine geologist and geophysicist and was a key contributor to the theory of plate tectonics.

Early Life

Vine was born in London, W4 and educated at Latymer Upper School and St. John's College, Cambridge where he studied Natural Sciences (BA, 1962) and marine geophysics (PhD, 1965).

Plate Tectonics

As a graduate student Fred Vine's Ph.D was 'magnetism in the seafloor', on which he worked along with his supervisor Drummond Matthews. Having met Harry Hess he was fully aware of his theories on sea floor spreading where the ocean bed effectively acts as a 'conveyor belt' moving away from the central ridge.. Vine's work, along with that of Drummond Matthews and Lawrence Morley of the Geological Survey of Canada, helped put the variations in the magnetic properties of the ocean crust into proper context. Specifically Vine and Matthews supported Dietz's (*Nature* 1961) idea that sea floor spreading was occurring at mid ocean ridges. Vine and Matthews showed that basalt created at a mid-ocean ridge records earth's current magnetic field polarity (and strength), thus turning Hess's theoretical 'conveyor belt' into a 'tape recorder'. Furthermore, they showed that magnetic reversals, suggested by Allan Cox (*Nature* 1963), can be seen as parallel strips as you travel perpendicularly away from the ridge crest.

Academic Career

Professor Vine had a distinguished career. He did important research with E.M. Moores on the Ophiolite within the Troodos mountains of southern Cyprus. He worked with R.A. Livermore and A.G.Smith on the history of Earth's magnetic field. He then did groundbreaking work on the electrical conductivity of rocks from the lower continental crust with R. G. Ross. In 1967 he became assistant professor of geology and geophysics at Princeton University. In 1970 he worked at the School of Environmental Sciences at the University of East Anglia, U.K., firstly as a Reader, then as Professor in 1974, and was Dean from 1977–1980, and again from 1993–1998. Since 1998, Vine has been a Professorial Fellow of the University of East Anglia. As of 2008 he remains at the university as Emeritus Professor.

FELIX ANDRIES VENING MEINESZ

Felix Andries Vening Meinesz (the Hague July 30, 1887-Amersfoort August 10, 1966) was a Dutch geophysicist and geodesist. He is known for his invention of a precise method for measuring gravity. Thanks to his invention, it became possible to measure gravity at sea, which led him to the discovery of gravity anomalies above the ocean floor. He later attributed these anomalies to continental drift.

Named after him are:

- a gravimeter, an apparatus to measure gravity
- a mathematical function used in geodesy
- a medal of the European Geophysical Society/European Geosciences Union
- a research school at Utrecht University
- Vening Meinesz crater on the Moon.

Biography

Vening Meinesz' father, Sjoerd Anne Meinesz, was mayor, first of Rotterdam, then of Amsterdam. He grew up in a protected environment. In 1910 he graduated in civil engineering in Delft. The same year he started working for the Dutch gravitational survey. In 1915 he wrote his dissertation on the defects of the gravimeters used at that time.

Vening Meinesz then designed a new gravimeter, which the KNMI (Royal Dutch Meteorological Institute) built. The apparatus has two pendula of the same size hanging in a frame but moving in opposite phases. With mirrors and lightbeams the difference in amplitude of the two pendula is captured on a film. Vening Meinesz had discovered that horizontal accelerations (as by waves on a boat) had no influence on the difference in amplitude between the two pendula. The recorded difference then is the amplitude of a theoretical, undisturbed pendulum. Now it became possible to measure gravity more accurately. Vening Meinesz started with measuring gravity all over the Netherlands, for which a network of 51 monitoring stations was created. This became a success, which encouraged him to do measurements at sea. A perfected gravimeter, hanging in a 'swing', was designed. The experiment was successful.

Now measuring gravity at sea had become possible. Between 1923 and 1929 the tall (over 2 metres) Vening Meinesz embarked in small submarines for some uncomfortable expeditions. His goal was to establish the exact shape of the geoid and the Earth. When one of his expeditions was made into a movie in 1935, Vening Meinesz became a hero of the Dutch cinema public. Besides, his research was in the international scientific spotlight. In 1927 he become a parttime professor in geodesy, cartography and geophysics at Utrecht University, and in 1937 he became professor at the Delft University of Technology as well. In World War II, Vening Meinesz was involved in the Dutch resistance. After the war he could take up his tasks as a professor again. From 1945 to 1951 he was the director of the KNMI. He retired in 1957.

Research and Discoveries

The vast amounts of data that his expeditions yielded were analyzed and discussed together with other leading Dutch Earth scientists of the time J.H.F. Umbgrove, B.G. Escher and Ph.H. Kuenen, the results were published in 1948. An important result was the discovery of elongated belts of negative gravity anomalies along the oceanic trenches. The mean gravity force appeared to be the same on land and at sea, which was in agreement with the principle of isostasy. Vening Meinesz was especially intrigued by the oceanic trenches. The coexisitence of active volcanism, large negative gravity anomalies and the sudden difference in terrain elevation could only be explained by assuming the Earth's crust was somehow pushed together at these places. As a geophysicist, he was prejudiced that the crust was too rigid to deform at that scale in such a way. His discoveries could be explained only with the development of the theory of plate tectonics in the '50s.

FLAXMAN CHARLES JOHN SPURRELL

Flaxman Charles John Spurrell (6 September 1842-25 February 1915), the archaeologist, geologist and photographer, was born in Mile End, Stepney, London, the eldest son of Dr. Flaxman Spurrell, M.D., F.R.C.S., and Ann Spurrell (who were also cousins). Shortly after his birth, his father moved to Bexley, Kent; later, Flaxman (Junior) lived at The Priory, Picardy Road, Belvedere, now home to the Priory Conservative Club. In the 1860s he began to examine flint implements in and around Crayford in Kent, and over the following decades published a large number of articles for the Kent Archaeological Society (of which his father was a founding member), the Essex Archaeological Society and Royal Archaeological Society, as well as other societies and groups. In 1895 he presented a number of pre-historic remains to the Natural History Museum, and later donated material to the Norwich Castle Museum.

He was a close friend of the egyptologist William Matthew Flinders Petrie, whom he helped to record discoveries made in, for example, Naqada and Tell el-Amarna in Egypt.

Flaxman Spurrell was also interested in photography, and some of his photographs are currently held by English Heritage.

Some years before his death, he retired to Bessingham Manor House in Norfolk, one of the seats of the Spurrell family, and was no longer active in the archaeological world. He died at The Den, Bessingham, in 1915, having married his cousin, Katherine Anne Spurrell, on 27 March 1912.

Flaxman Spurrell was educated at Epsom College and was a Fellow of Geological Society.

He was a nephew of Rev. Frederick Spurrell and an uncle of the biologist and author Herbert George Flaxman Spurrell.

FERDINAND VON RICHTHOFEN

Ferdinand Freiherr von Richthofen (May 5, 1833 – October 6, 1905) was a German traveller, geographer and scientist.

Biography

He was born in Carlsruhe, Prussian Silesia, and was educated in Breslau and Berlin. He travelled or studied in the Alps of Tyrol (the portion of what is now Bolzano-Bozen, Italy) and the Carpathians in Transylvania. In 1860 he joined the Eulenburg Expedition, a Prussian expedition which visited Ceylon, Japan, Taiwan, the Celebes, Java, the Philippines, Siam, Burma between 1860 and 1862. From 1862-868 he worked as a geologist in the United States discovering Goldfields in California. This was followed by several more trips of China, Japan, Burma and Java. He published his geographical, geological, economic, and ethnological findings in three volumes with an atlas. In China he located the dried-up lake bed of Lopnur.

He was also Professor of Geology at the University of Bonn beginning in 1875, Professor of Geography at the University of Leipzig in 1883, and Professor of Geography at the Friedrich Wilhelm University of Berlin in 1886. Among his most famous students was Sven Hedin, the Swedish explorer. He served as President of the German Geographical Society for many years, and founded the

Berlin Hydrographical Institute. He is noted for coining the terms "Seidenstraße" and "Seidenstraßen" = "Silk Road(s)" or "Silk Route(s)" in 1877.

He died in 1905 in Berlin.

When William Gill consulted him about a planned trip to China, he remarked:

"Hour after hour he gave up his valuable time to me, and opened volumes from his rich store of information. ... Baron von Richtofen possesses in a remarkable manner the faculty of gathering up the details presented to his view; putting them together and generalising on them with rare judgement; forming out of what would be to a lesser genius, but scattered and unintelligible fragments, a uniform and comprehensive whole ... not one hint was given me that did not subsequently prove its value; his kind thoughts for my comfort and amusement were never ceasing, and his refined and cultivated intellect and genial manner rendered the recollections of my stay in the German capital some of the most pleasant of my life." Ferdinand von Richthofen was an uncle of the World War I flying ace Manfred von Richthofen, best known as the "Red Baron".

The mountain range on the southern edge of the Gansu corridor in western China was named Richthofen Range after him, although the modern name is now Qilian Mountains.

FRIEDRICH MOHS

Friedrich Mohs (January 29, 1773-September 29, 1839) was a German geologist/mineralogist.

Career

Mohs, born in Gernrode, Germany, studied chemistry, mathematics and physics at the University of Halle and also studied at the Mining Academy in Freiberg, Saxony. After assuming the position of a foreman at a mine in 1801, Mohs moved in 1802 to Austria, where he was employed in trying to identify the minerals in a private collection of a Banker.

Mineral Properties

As part of this task, he started classifying minerals by their physical characteristics, in spite of their chemical composition, as had been done traditionally.

This emphasis on physical characteristics was at odds with the prevailing chemical systematics. Minerals are now classified by chemical characteristics, but the physical properties are still useful in field examination.

Harness Scale

In 1812, Mohs became professor in Graz; in 1818, professor in Freiberg, Saxony; in 1826, professor in Vienna. In 1812, using relatively common minerals, he created a hardness scale that is still used today, called the Mohs' scale of mineral hardness. Mohs died during a trip to Italy, in Agordo near Belluno.

FREDERICK MCCOY

Sir Frederick McCoy, FRS (1817 – 16 May 1899) was a British palaeontologist and museum administrator, active in Australia.

Early Life

McCoy was the son of Dr. Simon McCoy, M.D. and was born in Dublin; some sources have his year of birth as 1823, but 1817 is the most likely. He was educated in that city and at Cambridge for the medical profession.

Palaeontology Career

McCoy's interests, however, became early centred in natural history, and especially in geology, and at the age of eighteen he published a *Catalogue of Organic Remains compiled from specimens exhibited in the Rotunda at Dublin* (1841). He assisted Sir RJ Griffith by studying the fossils of the carboniferous and silurian rocks of Ireland, and they prepared a joint *in 1844 appeared A Synopsis of the Character of Carboniferous Limestone Fossils of Ireland* (1844) and *Synopsis of the Silurian Fossils of Ireland* (1846).

In 1846 Sedgwick secured his services, and for at least four years he devoted himself to the determination and arrangement of the fossils in the Woodwardian Museum at Cambridge. Sedgwick wrote of him as "an excellent naturalist, an incomparable and most philosophical palaeontologist, and one of the steadiest and quickest workmen that ever undertook the arrangement of a museum" (*Life and Letters of Sedgwick*, ii. 194). Together they prepared the important and now classic work entitled *A Synopsis of the Classification of the British Palaeozoic Rocks, with a Systematic Description of the British Palaeozoic Fossils in the Geological Museum of the University of Cambridge* (1855). Meanwhile McCoy in 1850 had been appointed professor of geology in Queen's College, Belfast.

Late Life

To local societies he contributed many papers, and he continued his active scientific work for fifty-eight years—his last contribution, "Note on a new Australian Pterygotus," being printed in the *Geological Magazine* for May 1899. He was awarded the Murchison Medal of the Geological Society of London in 1879 and was elected F.R.S. in 1880, and was one of the first to receive the Hon. D.Sc. from the university of Cambridge. In 1886 he was made CMG, and in 1891 KCMG. He died in Melbourne on the 16 May 1899. Obituary (with bibliography) in Geol. Mag. 1899, p. 283.

FRED LONGSTAFFE

Dr. Fred J. Longstaffe is the Provost and VP Academic at the University of Western Ontario. He is a highly regarded leader in Earth Science research. His current focus is on applying knowledge of stable isotopes to various fields of study.

Longstaffe earned a BSc (Hon) from the University of Windsor and a PhD in Geology from McMaster University. In 1978, he attended the University of Alberta as a Killam Post-Doctoral Scholar. After that he joined that university's faculty in the Department of Geology. In 1987, Longstaffe moved to the University of Western as a full professor in Geology and opened the Laboratory for Stable

Isotope Science. The labs principal research areas are environmental geochemistry and clastic diagenesis, with special emphasis on the application of stable isotopes and other biogeochemical methods to studies of the environment and climate change. The Departments of Geology and Geophysics were merged in 1993. He became the Chair of the newly formed Department of Earth Sciences. Dr. Longstaffe gave up that position in 1999 to take on the larger role of Dean of the Faculty of Science. In July 2005, Longstaffe became the university's Provost and VP Academic.

Dr. Longstaffe's research has attracted substantial funding from Natural Sciences and Engineering Research Council, Social Science and Humanities Research Council and Canada Foundation for Innovation. His current research focuses on the use of stable isotopes to study earth and environmental science, ecosystems, oil sands, and anthropology.

Longstaffe has served as President of the Geological Association of Canada. He has frequently served on Natural Sciences and Engineering Research Council and Royal Society of Canada committees.

FRANC JOUBIN

Franc Renault Joubin (1911-1997) was a prospector and geologist most well known for a huge uranium discovery in northeastern Ontario, Canada in 1953.

Born in San Francisco, California to parents of French descent, his family emigrated to Canada when he was three years old.

A graduate of the University of British Columbia, (Masters,Geology (1942)), Joubin worked independently as a consultant and prospector/geologist for various mining promoters and exploration companies.

In 1953, as an employee and eventual partner of promoter Joseph Hirshhorn, he persuaded his partner to finance diamond drilling of a previously dismissed area of surface radioactivity near Blind River, Ontario. Joubin's insight, with help from Dr. Charles

Davidson, a leading British geologist, was that the presence of iron sulphide had leached the uranium mineral to a location deeper in the ground. Drilling results confirmed this and implied uranium deposits along a huge ninety mile Z-shaped geological formation extending north of the area. Known as the "Big Z" deposit, it became the hub of a frenzy of uranium exploration and mining activity. The town of Elliot Lake, Ontario, (incorporated 1955) was built from scratch to house employees of the various mines that sprung up in the area. By 1955, Joubin and Hirshhorn sold their interests to Rio Tinto of Great Britain and divided paper profits of $35 million. By the 1980s it was estimated Joubin's discovery and the subsequent mineral production had added up to $30 billion to the Canadian economy.

Joubin resumed his career as a consulting geologist. He travelled much of the world for Rio Tinto, other companies, and eventually the United Nations.

He received the Order of Canada in 1983.

FRANK HAWTHORNE

Frank Christopher Hawthorne (born 1946) is a Canadian mineralogist and crystallographer.

Born in Bristol, England, he received a Bachelor of Science degree from Imperial College London in 1968 and an Associateship of the Royal School of Mines (ARSM). In 1973, he received a Ph.D. from McMaster University.

From 1973 to 1975, he was a Post-Doctoral Fellow in the Department of Geological Science at the University of Manitoba. He was a research associate from 1975 to 1980 and University Research Fellow from 1980 to 1985. In 1985, he was appointed an Associate Professor and in 1986 he was appointed a Professor of Crystallography and Mineralogy. He currently holds the Canada Research Chair in Crystallography and Mineralogy.

Hawthorne's early work focused on structural and crystal-chemical problems of amphiboles. He had utilized several experimental techniques, including X-ray and neutron diffraction, infrared spectroscopy, and Mossbauer spectroscopy. He summarized his results in a 300-page paper on amphiboles, for which he was awarded the Hawley Medal of the Mineralogical Association of Canada in 1983.

Hawthorne then turned his attention to a series of complex crystal-chemistry problems involving rock-forming minerals, such as staurolite, vesuvianite, pyroxenes, beryl, and tourmaline. He utilized a multi-technique approach and applied novel analytical and spectroscopic methods to solve these mineralogical problems. These results have been used to provide indication of the conditions prevailing during the progressive crystallization of magmas.

Hawthorne's work on the energetic content of the chemical bonds in mineral structures has advanced solid-state chemistry and crystallography.

FERDINAND VANDEVEER HAYDEN

Dr. Ferdinand Vandeveer Hayden (September 7, 1829–December 22, 1887) was an American geologist noted for his pioneering surveying expeditions of the Rocky Mountains in the late 19th century. He was born at Westfield, Massachusetts. He graduated from Oberlin College in 1850 and from the Albany Medical College in 1853, where he attracted the notice of Professor James Hall, state geologist of New York, through whose influence he was induced to join in an exploration of Nebraska. In 1856 he was engaged under the United States government, and commenced a series of investigations of the 109 Western Territories, one result of which was his *Geological Report of the Exploration of the Yellowstone and Missouri Rivers in 1859–1860* (1869).

Biography

About this time, he also became identified with the Megatherium Club at the Smithsonian Institution in Washington, D.C. During the Civil War he was actively employed as an army surgeon. He rose to be chief medical officer of the Army of the Shenandoah. In 1867 he was appointed geologist-in-charge of the United States Geological and Geographical Survey of the Territories. From his twelve years of labour and annual survey journeys there resulted a most valuable series of volumes in all branches of natural history and economic science; and he issued in 1877 his *Geological and Geographical Atlas of Colorado.*

In 1872 Hayden was instrumental in convincing Congress to establish Yellowstone as the first U.S. National Park, aided by the stunning large-format photographs of William Henry Jackson. The last of the annual survey journeys was in 1878. Upon the reorganization and establishment of the United States Geological Survey in 1879 he acted for seven years as one of the geologists. He died at Philadelphia on the 22nd of December 1887. The town of Hayden, Colorado, located in the Yampa River valley, is named for him."he was also a helper of the fedarel department of law".

His other publications were:

- *Sun Pictures of Rocky Mountain Scenery* (1870)
- *The Yellowstone National Park*, illustrated by chromolithographic reproductions of water-colour sketches by Thomas Moran (1876)
- *The Great West: its Attractions and Resources* (1880)

With FB Meek, he wrote (*Smithsonian Institution Contributions*, v. 14. Art. 4) "Palaeontology of the Upper Missouri, Pt. 1, Invertebrate." His valuable notes on Native American dialects are in *The Transactions of the American Philosophical Society* (1862) in *The American Journal of Science* (1862) and in The Proceedings of the American Philosophical Society (1869). With ARC Selwyn he wrote North America (1883) for Stanford's *Compendium.*"he's also a person of the fedarel department of law".

FLORENCE BASCOM

Florence Bascom (1862 – 1945) was the first woman hired by the United States Geological Survey. She was of Huguenot and Basque ancestry.

She was born in Williamstown, Massachusetts. She came from an academic background as her father, John Bascom, was President of Williams College. In the 1880s she received her Bachelor's and Master's degrees from the University of Wisconsin-Madison. She received her doctorate from Johns Hopkins University in 1893 and two years taught at Bryn Mawr College. She received her position at the USGS in 1896 and continued there until 1936. She also had three students who would also become members of the USGS. Two of those students, Eleanora Bliss and Anna Jonas Stose, were also important in other respects to her story. A great deal of her work involved the crystalline rocks and geomorphology of the Piedmont. This led to an unusual, for the time, example of a scientific dispute solely among women. The two students of Florence Bascom's mentioned above came to a different conclusion than her regarding the age of Wissahickon schist/gneiss. She contradicted them in a dispassionate way and the dispute is recorded as civil on the part of the three. That said by the 1930s it had broadened to most of those studying Appalachian geology and at times these individuals became more vehement than the original disputants.

FETAL ALCOHOL SYNDROME

Fetal alcohol syndrome is a disorder of permanent birth defects that occurs in the offspring of women who drink alcohol during pregnancy. It is unknown whether amount, frequency or timing of alcohol consumption during pregnancy causes a difference in degree of damage done to the fetus. Thus, the current recommendation is not to drink at all during pregnancy. Alcohol crosses the placental barrier and can stunt fetal growth or weight, create distinctive facial stigmata, damage neurons and brain structures, and cause other physical, mental, or behavioural problems. The main effect of FAS is permanent central nervous system damage, especially to the brain. Developing brain cells and structures are underdeveloped or malformed by prenatal alcohol exposure, often creating an array of primary cognitive and functional disabilities (including poor memory, attention deficits, impulsive behaviour, and poor cause-effect reasoning) as well as secondary disabilities (for example, mental health problems, and drug addiction). The risk of brain damage exists during each trimester, since the fetal brain develops throughout the entire pregnancy.

Fetal alcohol exposure is the leading known cause of mental retardation in the Western world. In the United States the FAS prevalence rate is estimated to be between 0.2 and 2.0 cases per 1,000 live births, comparable to or higher than other developmental disabilities such as Down syndrome or Spina Bifida. The lifetime medical and social costs of each child with FAS are estimated to be as high as US$800,000. While prenatal alcohol exposure does not automatically result in FAS, the U.S. Surgeon General advises pregnant women to abstain from alcohol use due to the risk of the syndrome.

FREDERICK SANGER

Frederick Sanger, (born 13 August 1918) is an English biochemist and twice a Nobel laureate in chemistry. He is the fourth (and only living) person to have been awarded two Nobel Prizes.

Early Years

Sanger was born in Rendcomb, a small village in Gloucestershire, the second son of Frederick Sanger, a medical practitioner, and his wife, Cicely. He was born on August 13, 1918, and educated at Bryanston School and then completed his Bachelor of Arts in natural sciences from St John's College, Cambridge in 1939. Raised as a Quaker, he learned to abhor violence, and during the Second World War he was a conscientious objector, being allowed to continue his research for a PhD.

He originally intended to study medicine, but became interested in biochemistry because some of the leading biochemists in the world were at Cambridge at the time. He completed his PhD in 1943 under A. Neuberger, on lysine metabolism and a more practical problem concerning the nitrogen of potatoes. He went on to discover the structure of proteins, most famously that of insulin protein. He also contributed to the determination of base sequences in DNA.

FRIEDRICH MIESCHER

Johan Friedrich Miescher (13 August 1844, Basel-26 August 1895, Davos) was a Swiss biologist. He isolated various phosphate-rich chemicals, which he called *nuclein* (now nucleic acids), from the nuclei of white blood cells in 1869 at Felix Hoppe-Seyler's laboratory at the University of Tubingen, Germany, paving the way for the identification of DNA as the carrier of inheritance. The significance of the discovery, first published in 1871, was not at first apparent, and it was Albrecht Kossel who made the initial inquiries into its chemical structure.

Miescher came from a scientific family: his father and his uncle held the chair of anatomy at the University of Basel. As a boy he was shy but intelligent. He had a partial hearing impairment due to a severe attack of typhus. But this did not stop him from having an interest in music and his father performed publicly. Miescher himself studied medicine at Basel. In the summer of 1865 Friedrich worked for the organic chemist Adolf Stecker in Gottingen. His studies were interrupted for the year when he became ill with typhoid fever; however, he still received his M.D. in 1868.

Miescher felt that his partial deafness would be a disadvantage as a doctor so he turned to physiological chemistry. Miescher originally wanted to study lymphocytes but was encouraged by Felix Hoppe-Seyler to study leucocytes. Miescher was interested in studying the chemistry of the nucleus. Lymphocytes were difficult to obtain in sufficient enough numbers to study while leucocytes were known to be the one of the main components in pus and could be obtained from bandages at the nearby hospital. The problem was, however, washing the cells off the bandages without damaging them.

Miescher devised different salt solutions eventually producing one with sodium sulfate. The cells were filtered. Since centrifuges were not present at this time the cells were allowed to settle at the bottom of a beaker. He then tried to isolate the nuclei free of cytoplasm. He subjected the purified nuclei to an alkaline extraction followed by acidification resulting in a precipitate being formed which Miescher called *nuclein* (now known as DNA). He found that this contained phosphorus, nitrogen, and sulfur. The discovery was so unlike anything else at the time that Hoppe-Seyler repeated all Miescher's research himself before publishing it in his journal. Friedrich then went on to study physiology at Leipzig in the laboratory of Carl Ludwig for a year before returning to Basel where he was appointed professor of physiology.

Miescher and his students researched much of the nucleic acid chemistry but their function remained unknown. However, his discovery played an important part in the identification of nucleic acids as the carriers of inheritance. The importance of Miescher's discovery was not apparent until Albrecht Kossel (a German physiologist specializing in the physiological chemistry of the cell and its nucleus and of proteins) carried out research on the chemical structure of nuclein. Friedrich Miescher is also known for demonstrating that carbon dioxide concentrations in blood regulate breathing.

He died of tuberculosis in 1895 aged 51. He has had a laboratory of the Max Planck Society in Tubingen and a research institute in Basel named after him.

FRITZ ALBERT LIPMANN

Fritz Albert Lipmann (June 12, 1899 – July 24, 1986) was a German-American biochemist and a co-discoverer in 1945 of coenzyme A. For this, together with other research on coenzyme A, he was awarded half the Nobel Prize in Physiology or Medicine in 1953.

Lipmann was born in Konigsberg, Germany to a Jewish family.

Lipmann studied medicine at the University of Konigsberg, Berlin, and Munich, graduating in Berlin in 1924. He returned to Konigsberg to study chemistry under Professor Hans Meerwein. In 1926 he joined Otto Meyerhof at the Kaiser Wilhelm Institute, Berlin, for his Ph.D. thesis. After that he followed Meyerhof to Heidelberg to the Kaiser Wilhelm Institute for Medical Research.

From 1939 lived and worked in the USA. From 1949 to 1957 he was professor of biological chemistry at Harvard Medical School. From 1957 onwards, he taught and conducted research at Rockefeller University, New York City. He was awarded the National Medal of Science in 1966.

FRITZ LENZ

Fritz Lenz (March 9, 1887 in Pflugrade, Pommern – July 6, 1976 in Gottingen) was a German geneticist and influential specialist in "racial hygiene" (also called eugenics) during the Third Reich, one of the leading German theorists of "scientific racism" which legitimized the Nazi racial policies, starting with the 1935 Nuremberg Laws.

Biography

The pupil of Alfred Ploetz, Lenz took over the publication of the magazine "Archives for Racial and Social Biology" from 1913 to 1933 and received in 1923 the first chair in eugenics in Munich. In 1933 he came to Berlin where he established the first specific department devoted to eugenics, at the Kaiser Wilhelm Institute of Anthropology, Human Heredity, and Eugenics.

Lenz specialised in the field of the transmission of hereditary human diseases and "racial health". The results of his research were published in 1921 and 1932 in collaboration with Erwin Baur and Eugen Fischer in two volumes that were later combined under the title *Human Heredity Theory and Racial Hygiene* (1936).

This work and his theory of "race as a value principle" placed Lenz and his two colleagues in the position of Germany's leading racial theorists. Their ideas provided scientific justification for Nazi ideology, in particular its emphasis on the superiority of the "Nordic race" and the desirability of eliminating allegedly inferior strains of humanity-or "life unworthy of life" (*Lebensunwertes Leben*). Lenz was a member of the "Committee of Experts for Population and Racial Policy". After the war Lenz continued to work as a geneticist as Professor at the University of Goettingen. When questioned Lenz said that the Holocaust would undermine the study of human genetics and racial theory. He continued to consider that eugenic theories of racial differences had been scientifically proven.

Theories

For Lenz, human genetics established that the connection between racial identity and human nature was actually physical in character. This extended to political affiliations. Lenz even claimed that the revolutionary agitation in Germany after 1918 was caused by inferior racial elements, warning that the nation's racial superiority was threatened. He stated that "The German nation is the last refuge of the Nordic race...before us lies the greatest task of world history". For Lenz, this validated the racialised politics of the Nazis.

He justified the Nuremberg laws of 1935 in this way:

As important as the external features for their evaluation is the lineage of individuals. A blond Jew is also a Jew. Yes, there are Jews who have most of the external features of the Nordic race, but who nevertheless display Jewish mental tendencies. The legislation of the National Socialist state therefore properly defines a Jew not by external race characteristics, but by descent.

Likewise, Lenz took the view that Slavs were inferior to Nordic peoples, and that they threatened to "overrun the superior Volk." (People) In 1940, Lenz advised the SS that "The resettlement of the Eastern zone is...the most consequential task of racial policy. It will determine the racial character of the population living there for centuries to come."

FRANCIS GALTON

Sir Francis Galton (16 February 1822 – 17 January 1911), half-cousin of Charles Darwin, was an English Victorian polymath, anthropologist, eugenicist, tropical explorer, geographer, inventor, meteorologist, proto-geneticist, psychometrician, and statistician. He was knighted in 1909. Galton had a prolific intellect, and produced over 340 papers and books throughout his lifetime. He also created the statistical concept of correlation and widely promoted regression toward the mean. He was the first to apply statistical methods to the study of human differences and inheritance of intelligence, and introduced the use of questionnaires and surveys for collecting data on human communities, which he needed for genealogical and biographical works and for his anthropometric studies. He was a pioneer in eugenics, coining the very term itself and the phrase "nature versus nurture".

As an investigator of the human mind, he founded psychometrics (the science of measuring mental faculties) and differential psychology. He devised a method for classifying fingerprints that proved useful in forensic science. As the initiator of scientific meteorology, he devised the first weather map, proposed a theory of anticyclones, and was the first to establish a complete record of short-term climatic phenomena on a European scale. He also invented the Galton Whistle for testing differential hearing ability.

Biography

He was born at "The Larches", a large house in Sparkbrook, Birmingham, England, built on the site of "Fair Hill", the former home of Joseph Priestley, which the botanist William Withering had renamed. He was Charles Darwin's half-cousin, sharing the common grandparent Erasmus Darwin. His father was Samuel Tertius Galton, son of Samuel "John" Galton. The Galtons were famous and highly successful Quaker gun-manufacturers and bankers, while the Darwins were distinguished in medicine and science.

Both families boasted Fellows of the Royal Society and members who loved to invent in their spare time. Both Erasmus Darwin and Samuel Galton were founder members of the famous Lunar Society of Birmingham, whose members included Boulton, Watt, Wedgwood, Priestley, Edgeworth, and other distinguished scientists and industrialists. Likewise, both families boasted literary talent, with Erasmus Darwin notorious for composing lengthy technical treatises in verse, and Aunt Mary Anne Galton known for her writing on aesthetics and religion, and her notable autobiography detailing the unique environment of her childhood populated by Lunar Society members.

Galton was by many accounts a child prodigy — he was reading by the age of 2, at age 5 he knew some Greek, Latin and long division, and by the age of six he had moved on to adult books, including Shakespeare for pleasure, and poetry, which he quoted at length (Bulmer 2003, p. 4). He attended numerous schools, but chafed at the narrow classical curriculum. His parents pressed him to enter the medical profession, and he studied for two years at Birmingham General hospital and King's College London Medical School. He followed this up with mathematical studies at Trinity College, University of Cambridge, from 1840 to early 1844. A severe nervous breakdown altered his original intention to try for honours.

He elected instead to take a "poll" (pass) B.A. degree, like his cousin Charles Darwin (Bulmer 2003, p. 5). (Following the Cambridge custom, he was awarded an M.A. without further study, in 1847). He then briefly resumed his medical studies. The death of his father in 1844 left him financially independent but emotionally destitute, and he terminated his medical studies entirely, turning to foreign travel, sport and technical invention.

In his early years Galton was an enthusiastic traveler, and made a notable solo trip through Eastern Europe to Constantinople, before going up to Cambridge. In 1845 and 1846 he went to Egypt and travelled down the Nile to Khartoum in the Sudan, and from there to Beirut, Damascus and down the Jordan. In 1850 he joined the Royal Geographical Society, and over the next two years mounted a long and difficult expedition into then little-known South-Western Africa (now Namibia).

He wrote a successful book on his experience, "Narrative of an Explorer in Tropical South Africa". He was awarded the Royal Geographical Society's gold medal in 1853 and the Silver Medal of the French Geographical Society for his pioneering cartographic survey of the region (Bulmer 2003, p. 16). This established his reputation as a geographer and explorer. He proceeded to write the best-selling *The Art of Travel*, a handbook of practical advice for the Victorian on the move, which went through many editions and still reappears in print today.

FRED GAGE

Fred "Rusty" Gage is a professor in the Laboratory of Genetics at the Salk Institute, and has concentrated on the adult central nervous system and the unexpected plasticity and adaptability that remains throughout the life of all mammals. His work may lead to methods of replacing brain tissue lost to stroke or Alzheimer's disease and repairing spinal cords damaged by trauma. Interestingly, he is the descendant of Phineas Gage, a man who was famous for surviving a large tamping iron driven through his skull, drastically changing his personality and becoming one of the most famous patients in neurosurgery. In 1998, Fred H. Gage (Salk Institute for Biological Studies, La Jolla, California) and Peter Eriksson (Sahlgrenska University Hospital, Gothenburg, Sweden) discovered and announced that the human brain produces new nerve cells in adulthood. Until then, it had been assumed that humans are born with all the brain cells they will ever have.

Gage's lab showed that, contrary to years of dogma, human beings are capable of growing new nerve cells throughout life. Small populations of immature nerve cells are found in the adult mammalian brain, and Gage is working to understand how these cells can be induced to become mature nerve cells. His team is investigating how such cells can be transplanted back to the brain and spinal cord.

They have showed that physical exercise can enhance the growth of new brain cells in the hippocampus, a brain structure that is important for the formation of new memories. Furthermore, his team is examining the underlying molecular mechanisms that are critical to the birth of new brain cells, work that may lead to new therapeutics for neurodegenerative conditions.

Fred Gage received his Bachelor of Science degree from the University of Florida and a Ph.D. from Johns Hopkins University.

He serves as a member of the Science Advisory Board of the Genetics Policy Institute.

FELIX D'HERELLE

Felix d'Herelle (April 25, 1873 – February 22, 1949) was a French-Canadian microbiologist, the co-discoverer of bacteriophages (viruses that infect bacteria) and experimented with the possibility of phage therapy.

Biography

D'Herelle was born in Montreal, Quebec, the son of French emigrants. His father, 30 years older than his wife, died when Felix was 6 years old. Felix, his mother and his younger brother Daniel, moved back to Paris. When sixteen years old, he started to travel through western Europe on bike. When 17, after finishing school (he attended the Lycee Condorcet and Lycee Louis-le-Grand high schools), he travelled through South America. Afterwards, he continued his travels through Europe, including Turkey, where he met his wife, Marie Caire.

At age 24, now father of a daughter, he and his family moved back to Canada. He built a home laboratory and studied microbiology from books and his own experiments. He earned money by working for the Canadian government, studying the fermentation and distillation of maple syrup to schnapps. He also worked as a medic for a geological expedition, even though he had no medical degree or real experience. Together with his brother, he invested almost all his money in a chocolate factory, which soon went bankrupt.

FRANCIS COLLINS

Francis S. Collins (born April 14, 1950), M.D., Ph.D., is an American physician-geneticist, noted for his landmark discoveries of disease genes, and his leadership of the Human Genome Project (HGP). He was director of the National Human Genome Research Institute (NHGRI), one of the 27 institutes and centres that make up the National Institutes of Health in Bethesda, Maryland until

August 1, 2008 (he announced his resignation on May 28, 2008). With Collins at the helm, the HGP has attained several milestones, while running ahead of schedule and under budget. A working draft of the human genome was announced in June 2000, and Collins was joined by US President Bill Clinton and rival biologist Craig Venter in making the announcement. Venter and Collins thus shared the "Biography of the Year" title from A&E Network. An initial analysis was published in February 2001. HGP scientists continued to work toward finishing the sequence of all three billion base pairs by 2003, coinciding with the 50th anniversary of Watson and Crick's seminal publication of the structure of DNA.

In 2005 Collins and Venter were also honoured as two of "America's Best Leaders" by U.S. News & World Report and the Harvard Centre for Public Leadership Collins's commitment to free, rapid access to genomic information helped to make all data immediately available to the worldwide scientific community. With these data sets of DNA sequence and variation in hand, researchers around the globe work on the process of understanding the connection between genes and disease. Collins envisions as a new era of individualized, prevention-oriented medicine.

Early Years

Raised on a small farm in Virginia's Shenandoah Valley, Francis Sellers Collins was home-schooled by his mother until the sixth grade. He is the youngest of four sons, which includes his brother, Dr. Fletcher Collins, who currently holds the title of "Assistant Head of Middle School" and "Director of Curriculum" at Collegiate School in Richmond, Virginia. Throughout most of Francis's high school and college years, the aspiring chemist had little interest in what he then considered the "messy" field of biology. What he refers to as his "formative education" was received at the University of Virginia, where he earned a B.S. in Chemistry in 1970. He went on to attain a Ph.D. in physical chemistry at Yale University in 1974. While at Yale, however, a course in biochemistry sparked his interest in the molecules that hold the blueprint for life: DNA and RNA.

Collins recognized that a revolution was on the horizon in molecular biology and genetics. After consulting with his old mentor from the University of Virginia, Carl Trindle, he changed fields and enrolled in medical school at the University of North Carolina at Chapel Hill, earning there an M.D. in 1977.

From 1978 to 1981, Collins served a residency and chief residency in internal medicine at North Carolina Memorial Hospital in Chapel Hill. He then returned to Yale, where he was named a Fellow in Human Genetics at the medical school from 1981 to 1984. During that time, he developed innovative methods of crossing large stretches of DNA to identify disease genes.

After joining the University of Michigan in 1984 in a position that would eventually lead to a Professorship of Internal Medicine and Human Genetics, Collins heightened his reputation as a relentless gene hunter. That gene-hunting approach, which he named "positional cloning," has developed into a powerful component of modern molecular genetics.

In contrast to previous methods for finding genes, positional cloning enabled scientists to identify disease genes without knowing in advance what the functional abnormality underlying the disease might be. Collins' team, together with collaborators, applied the new approach in 1989 in their successful quest for the long-sought gene responsible for cystic fibrosis. Other major discoveries soon followed, including isolation of the genes for Huntington's disease, neurofibromatosis, multiple endocrine neoplasia type 1, and the M4 type of adult acute leukemia.

FRANK MACFARLANE BURNET

Sir Frank Macfarlane Burnet, (3 September 1899 – 31 August 1985), usually known as Macfarlane or Mac Burnet, was an Australian virologist best known for his contributions to immunology. Burnet received his M.D. degree from the University of Melbourne in 1924, and his PhD degree from the University of London in 1928. He went on to conduct pioneering research on bacteriophages and viruses at the Walter and Eliza Hall Institute, Melbourne, and served as director of the Institute from 1944 to 1965. His virology research resulted in significant discoveries concerning their nature and replication and their interaction with the immune system.

From the mid-1950s, he worked extensively in immunology and was a major contributor to the theory of clonal selection, which explains how lymphocytes target antigens for destruction. Burnet and Peter Medawar were co-recipients of the 1960 Nobel Prize in Physiology or Medicine for demonstrating acquired immune tolerance. This research provided the experimental basis for inducing immune tolerance, the platform for developing methods of transplanting solid organs.

Burnet left the Walter and Eliza Hall Institute in 1965, he continued to work at the University of Melbourne until his official retirement in 1978. During his working life he wrote 31 books and monographs and more than 500 scientific papers. Burnet played an active role in the development of public policy for the medical sciences in Australia and was a founding member, and later the president, of the Australian Academy of Science. He was the most highly decorated and honoured scientist to have worked in Australia.

For his contributions to Australian science, he was made the first Australian of the Year in 1960, and in 1978 a Knight of the Order of Australia. He was recognised internationally for his achievements: in addition to the Nobel, he received the Lasker Award and the Royal and Copley Medals from the Royal Society, honourary doctorates, and distinguished service honours from the Commonwealth and Japan.

Early Life

Burnet was born in Traralgon, Victoria; his father, Frank Burnet, a Scottish emigrant to Australia, was the manager of the Traralgon branch of the Colonial Bank. He was the second of seven children and from childhood was known as "Mac". The Burnets moved to Terang in 1909. Burnet was interested in the wildlife around the nearby lake; he joined the Scouts in 1910 and enjoyed all outdoor activates. While living in Terang, he began to collect beetles and study biology. He read biology articles in the *Chambers's Encyclopaedia*, which introduced him to the work of Charles Darwin. He was educated at Victorian state schools and later won a full scholarship to board and study at Geelong College, one of Victoria's most exclusive private schools.

From 1917, Burnet attended the University of Melbourne, where he lived in Ormond College on a residential scholarship and studied medicine. There, he read more of Darwin's work and was influenced by the ideas of science and society in the writings of H.G. Wells. While at university, he became an agnostic; he was sceptical of religious faith, which he regarded as "an effort to believe what common sense tells you isn't true." The length of time required to study medicine had been reduced to train doctors faster following the outbreak of World War I, and Burnet graduated with a Bachelor of Medicine and a Bachelor of Surgery in 1922, and as a Doctor of Medicine late in 1924. In 1924 he was appointed resident pathologist at the Melbourne Hospital; the laboratories were a part of the Walter and Eliza Hall Institute. He conducted research into the agglutinin reactions in typhoid fever, leading to his first scientific publications.

The director of the Institute, Charles Kellaway, thought that Burnet would need experience working in a laboratory in England before he could lead his own research group in Australia. Burnet left Australia for England in 1925 and served as ship's surgeon during his journey. On arrival, he took a paid position assisting the curator of the National Collection of Type Cultures at the Lister Institute in London. He was awarded the Beit memorial fellowship by the Lister Institute in 1926 and began full-time research on bacteriophage. For this work he received a PhD from the University of London in 1928 and was invited to write a chapter on phage for the Medical Research Council's *System of Bacteriology*. While in London, Burnet became engaged to fellow Australian Edith Linda Druce. They married in 1928 after returning to Australia, and had a son and two daughters.

Walter and Eliza Hall Institute

Virology and Medicine: When Burnet returned to Australia, he went back to the Walter and Eliza Hall Institute, where he was appointed assistant director. His first assignment was to investigate the "Bundaberg disaster", in which 12 children had died after receiving a contaminated diphtheria vaccine. He identified *Staphylococcus aureus* in the toxin-antitoxin mixture that had been administered to the children, although turned out to be another toxin that had caused the children's deaths; this work on staphylococcal toxin piqued his interest in immunology.

During this time, he continued to study bacteriophage, writing 32 papers on phages between 1924 and 1937. In 1929, Burnet and his graduate assistant Margot McKie wrote a paper suggesting that bacteriophage could exist as a stable non-infectious form that multiplies with the bacterial host. Their pioneering description of lysogeny was not accepted until much later, and was crucial to the work of Max Delbruck, Alfred Hershey and Salvador Luria on the replication mechanism and genetics of viruses, for which they were awarded the 1969 Nobel Prize in Physiology or Medicine.

Between 1932 and 1933, Burnet took leave of absence to undertake a fellowship at the National Institute for Medical Research in London. Significant breakthroughs in virology were made while he was there, including the isolation and first demonstration of the transmission of the influenza virus. His own research was on the canarypox virus, which he used in developing a chick embryo assay for the isolation and quantification of animal viruses. When Burnet returned to Australia, he continued his work on virology, including the epidemiology of herpes simplex. He was also involved in two projects that were not viral, the characterisation of the causative agents of psittacosis and Q fever.

During the time he worked on Q fever with Australian scientist E.H. Derrick, the causative organism of which was named *Coxiella burnetii* in Burnet's honour, he became the first person to acquire the disease in the lab. His epidemiological studies of herpes and Q fever displayed an appreciation of the ecology of infectious disease that became a characteristic of his scientific method.

During World War II, Burnet's research moved to influenza and scrub typhus. His first book, *Biological Aspects of Infectious Disease*, was published in 1940. In 1942 he was made a Fellow of the Royal Society, and in 1944 he travelled to Harvard University to deliver the Dunham Lectures. There he was offered a chair, but he refused and returned to Australia.

In 1944, he was appointed director of the Institute when Kellaway was appointed director of the Wellcome Foundation. Under his direction, scientists at the Institute made significant contributions to infectious disease research during a period that has been called the "golden age of virology". Virologists including Alick Isaacs, Gordon Ada, John Cairns, Stephen Fazekas de St. Groth, and Frank Fenner made significant contributions on Murray Valley encephalitis, myxomatosis, poliomyelitis, poxviruses, herpes and influenza.

Burnet made significant contributions to influenza research; he developed techniques to grow and study the virus, including hemagglutination assays. He worked on a live vaccine against influenza, but the vaccine was unsuccessful when tested during World War II.

His interest in the influenza receptor led him to discover the neuraminidase that is secreted by *Vibrio cholerae*, which later provided the foundation for Alfred Gottschalk's significant work on glycoproteins and the neuraminidase substrate, sialic acid. Between 1951 and 1956, Burnet worked on the genetics of influenza. He examined the genetic control of virulence and demonstrated that the virus recombined at high frequency; this observation was not fully appreciated until several years later, when the segmented genome of influenza was demonstrated.

GEORGE GABRIEL STOKES

Sir George Gabriel Stokes, (13 August 1819–1 February 1903), was a mathematician and physicist, who at Cambridge made important contributions to fluid dynamics (including the Navier-Stokes equations), optics, and mathematical physics (including Stokes' theorem). He was secretary, then president, of the Royal Society.

Biography

George Stokes was the youngest son of the Reverend Gabriel Stokes, rector of Skreen, County Sligo, Ireland, where he was born and brought up in an evangelical Protestant family. After attending schools in Skreen, Dublin and Bristol, he matriculated in 1837 at Pembroke College, Cambridge, where four years later, on graduating as senior wrangler and first Smith's prizeman, he was elected to a fellowship. In accordance with the college statutes, he had to resign the fellowship when he married in 1857, but twelve years later, under new statutes, he was re-elected. He retained his place on the foundation until 1902, when on the day before his 83rd birthday, he was elected to the mastership. He did not enjoy this position for long, for he died at Cambridge on 1 February the following year, and was buried in the Mill Road cemetery.

Career

In 1849, Stokes was appointed to the Lucasian professorship of mathematics at Cambridge. On June 1, 1899, the jubilee of this appointment was celebrated there in a brilliant ceremony, which was attended by numerous delegates from European and American universities.

A commemorative gold medal was presented to Stokes by the chancellor of the university, and marble busts of Stokes by Hamo Thornycroft were formally offered to Pembroke College and to the university by Lord Kelvin. Sir George Stokes, who was made a baronet in 1889, further served his university by representing it in parliament from 1887 to 1892 as one of the two members for the Cambridge University constituency.

During a portion of this period (1885–1890) he also was president of the Royal Society, of which he had been one of the secretaries since 1854. Since he was also Lucasian Professor at this time, Stokes was the first person to hold all three positions simultaneously; Newton held the same three, although not at the same time. Stokes was the oldest of the trio of natural philosophers, James Clerk Maxwell and Lord Kelvin being the other two, who especially contributed to the fame of the Cambridge school of mathematical physics in the middle of the 19th century. Stokes's original work began about 1840, and from that date onwards the great extent of his output was only less remarkable than the brilliance of its quality. The Royal Society's catalogue of scientific papers gives the titles of over a hundred memoirs by him published down to 1883. Some of these are only brief notes, others are short controversial or corrective statements, but many are long and elaborate treatises.

Contributions to Science

In content his work is distinguished by a certain definiteness and finality, and even of problems which, when he attacked them, were scarcely thought amenable to mathematical analysis, he has in many cases given solutions which once and for all settle the main principles. This fact must be ascribed to his extraordinary combination of mathematical power with experimental skill. From the time when in about 1840 he fitted up some simple physical apparatus in his rooms in Pembroke College, mathematics and experiment ever went hand in hand, aiding and checking each other. In scope his work covered a wide range of physical inquiry, but, as Marie Alfred Cornu remarked in his Rede lecture of 1899, the greater part of it was concerned with waves and the transformations imposed on them during their passage through various media.

G. B. PEGRAM

George Braxton Pegram (October 24, 1876-August 12, 1958) was an American physicist who played a key role in the technical administration of the Manhattan Project.

Life

Pegram was born in Trinity, North Carolina, one of the five children of William Howell Pegram, professor of chemistry at

Trinity College (now Duke University), and Emma, daughter of Rev. Braxton Craven, the college's president. His upbringing in the academic atmosphere of the campus left him with an appetite for careful methodical work and an inherent diplomacy.

Pegram graduated from Trinity in 1895 and taught high school before becoming a teaching assistant in physics at Columbia University in 1900. He was to spend the rest of his working life at Columbia, taking his doctorate in 1903 and becoming a full professor in 1918. His administrative career began as early as 1913 when he became the department's executive officer. By 1918, he was Dean of the Faculty of Applied Sciences but he resigned in 1930 to relaunch his research activities, performing many meticulous measurements on the properties of neutrons with John R. Dunning.

Returning to administration in 1936, as Dean and Chair of Columbia's physics department, Pegram was instrumental in bringing Enrico Fermi to the US to escape the Fascist regime of his native Italy. In 1940 he brokered a meeting between Fermi and the US Navy at which the prospect of an atomic bomb was raised with the military for the first time.

The Columbia physics department was home to many of the key technologies required for the bomb project and Pegram and his colleague Harold C. Urey soon found themselves on Vannevar Bush's S-1 Uranium Committee coordinating all technical research. In autumn 1941, Pegram and Urey led a diplomatic mission to England to establish co-operation on development of the atomic bomb.

Pegram died in Swarthmore, Pennsylvania.

GEORG OHM

Georg Simon Ohm (March 16, 1789 – July 6, 1854) was a German physicist. As a high school teacher, Ohm started his research with the recently invented electrochemical cell, invented by Italian Count Alessandro Volta. Using equipment of his own creation, Ohm determined that there is a direct proportionality between the potential difference (voltage) applied across a conductor and the resultant electric current which flows through it—which we now know as Ohm's law. Using the results of his experiments, Ohm was able to define the fundamental relationship among voltage, current, and resistance, which represents the true beginning of electrical circuit analysis.

Biography

Georg Simon Ohm was born at Erlangen, Kingdom of Bavaria, to Johann Wolfgang Ohm, a locksmith and Maria Elizabeth Beck, the daughter of a tailor in Erlangen. Although his parents had not been formally educated, Ohm's father was a respected man who had educated himself to a high level and was able to give his sons an excellent education through his own teachings. Some of Ohm's brothers and sisters died in their childhood and only three survived. The survivors, including Georg Simon, were his younger brother Martin, who later became a well-known mathematician, and his sister Elizabeth Barbara. His mother died when he was ten.

From early childhood, Georg and Martin were taught by their father who brought them to a high standard in mathematics, physics, chemistry and philosophy. Georg Simon attended Erlangen Gymnasium from age eleven to fifteen where he received little in the area of scientific training, which sharply contrasted with the inspired instruction that both Georg and Martin received from their father. This characteristic made the Ohms bear a resemblance to the Bernoulli family, as noted by Karl Christian von Langsdorf, a professor at the University of Erlangen.

GOTTFRIED LEIBNIZ

Gottfried Wilhelm Leibniz (July 1, 1646 [OS: June 21] – November 14, 1716) was a German polymath who wrote primarily in Latin and French.

He occupies an equally grand place in both the history of philosophy and the history of mathematics. He invented calculus independently of Newton, and his notation is the one in general use since then. He also discovered the binary system, foundation of virtually all modern computer architectures. In philosophy, he is mostly remembered for optimism, *i.e.* his conclusion that our universe is, in a restricted sense, the best possible one God could have made. He was, along with Rene Descartes and Baruch Spinoza, one of the three greatest 17th-century rationalists, but his philosophy also looks back to the scholastic tradition and anticipates modern logic and analysis. Leibniz also made major contributions to physics and technology, and anticipated notions that surfaced much later in biology, medicine, geology, probability theory, psychology, linguistics, and information science. He also wrote on politics, law, ethics, theology, history, and philology, even occasional verse. His contributions to this vast array of subjects are scattered in journals and in tens of thousands of letters and unpublished manuscripts. To date, there is no complete edition of Leibniz's writings.

Biography

Gottfried Leibniz was born on 1 July 1646 in Leipzig to Friedrich Leibniz and Catherina Schmuck. His father had passed away when he was six, so he learned his religious and moral values from his mother. These would exert a profound influence on his philosophical thought in later life. As an adult, he often styled himself "von Leibniz", and many posthumous editions of his works gave his name on the title page as "Freiherr [Baron] G. W. von Leibniz." However, no document has been found confirming that he was ever granted a patent of nobility.

When Leibniz was six years old, his father, a Professor of Moral Philosophy at the University of Leipzig, died, leaving a personal library to which Leibniz was granted free access from age seven onwards. By 12, he had taught himself Latin, which he used freely all his life, and had begun studying Greek.

He entered his father's university at age 14, and completed university studies by 20, specializing in law and mastering the standard university courses in classics, logic, and scholastic philosophy. However, his education in mathematics was not up to the French and British standards. In 1666 (age 20), he published his first book, also his habilitation thesis in philosophy, *On the Art of Combinations.* When Leipzig declined to assure him a position teaching law upon graduation, Leibniz submitted the thesis he had intended to submit at Leipzig to the University of Altdorf instead, and obtained his doctorate in law in five months. He then declined an offer of academic appointment at Altdorf, and spent the rest of his life in the service of two major German noble families.

GEORGES LEMAITRE

Georges Henri Joseph Eduard Lemaitre (July 17, 1894 – June 20, 1966) was a Belgian Roman Catholic priest, honourary prelate, professor of physics and astronomer at the Universite catholique de Louvain.

Lemaitre proposed what became known as the Big Bang theory of the origin of the Universe, which he called his 'hypothesis of the primeval atom'.

Work

He was a pioneer in applying Einstein's theory of general relativity to cosmology: suggesting a pre-cursor of Hubble's law in 1927, and then publishing his primeval atom theory in the pages of *Nature* in 1931. At the time Einstein believed in a static universe and had previously expressed his skepticism about Lemaitre's original 1927 paper. A similar solution to Einstein's equations, suggesting a changing radius to the size of the universe, had been proposed in 1922 by Alexander Alexandrovich Friedman, as Einstein informed Lemaitre when he approached him with the theory at the 1927 Solvay Conference (Friedman had also been criticized by Einstein), but it is Lemaitre, with his proposed mechanism, that made the theory famous for several reasons according to historians.

First, Friedman was a mathematician who was not working with astronomical data or concerned with the math as a description of physical reality. Secondly, Friedman died young and could not further work on his ideas. Thirdly, Lemaitre worked with astronomers and made his theory in accord with observations and had consequences which could be tested. Fourth, Arthur Eddington made sure that Lemaitre got a hearing in the scientific community.

Lemaitre also proposed the theory at an opportune time since Edwin Hubble would soon release his velocity-distance relation that strongly supported an expanding universe and, consequently, the Big Bang theory. In fact, Lemaitre derived what became known as Hubble's Law in his 1927 paper, two years before Hubble. However, since Lemaitre spent his entire productive life in Europe rather than emigrating to America, the contributions of scientists such as Hubble or Einstein, who can be claimed to have a US connection, are often more well known in the US.

Both Friedman and Lemaitre had found that the universe must be expanding. Lemaitre went further than Friedman, since he concluded that an initial "creation-like" event must have occurred. This is the Big Bang theory as we know it today, and this is why he is credited with its discovery.

Einstein at first dismissed Friedman and then (privately) Lemaitre out of hand, saying that not all mathematics leads to correct theories. After Hubble's discovery was published, Einstein quickly and publicly endorsed Lemaitre's theory, helping both the theory and priest get fast recognition.

In 1933 he found an important inhomogeneous solution of Einstein's field equations describing a spherical dust cloud, the Lemaitre-Tolman metric.

GUSTAV KIRCHHOFF

Gustav Robert Kirchhoff (March 12, 1824 – October 17, 1887) was a German physicist who contributed to the fundamental understanding of electrical circuits, spectroscopy, and the emission of black-body radiation by heated objects. He coined the term "black body" radiation in 1862, and two sets of independent concepts in both circuit theory and thermal emission are named "Kirchhoff's laws" after him.

Life and Work

Gustav Kirchhoff was born in Konigsberg, East Prussia, the son of Friedrich Kirchhoff, a lawyer, and Johanna Henriette Wittke. He graduated from the Albertus University of Konigsberg in 1847 where he attended the mathematico-physical seminar directed by Franz Ernst Neumann and Friedrich Julius Richelot. He married Clara Richelot, the daughter of his mathematics professor Richelot. In the same year, they moved to Berlin, where he stayed until he received a professorship at Breslau.

Kirchhoff formulated his circuit laws, which are now ubiquitous in electrical engineering, in 1845, while still a student. He completed this study as a seminar exercise; it later became his doctoral dissertation.

He proposed his law of thermal radiation in 1859, and gave a proof in 1861. He was called to the University of Heidelberg in 1854, where he collaborated in spectroscopic work with Robert Bunsen. Together Kirchhoff and Bunsen discovered caesium and rubidium in 1861.

At Heidelberg he ran a mathematico-physical seminar, modelled on Neumann's, with the mathematician Leo Koenigsberger. Among those who attended this seminar were Arthur Schuster and Sofia Kovalevskaya. In 1875 Kirchhoff accepted the first chair specifically dedicated to theoretical physics at Berlin.

In 1862 he was awarded the Rumford Medal for his researches on the fixed lines of the solar spectrum, and on the inversion of the bright lines in the spectra of artificial light.

He contributed greatly to the field of spectroscopy by formalizing three laws that describe the spectral composition of light emitted by incandescent objects, building substantially on the discoveries of David Alter and Anders Jonas Angstrom (see also: spectrum analysis)

Kirchhoff died in 1887, and was buried in the St. Matthaus Kirchhof Cemetery in Schoneberg, Berlin, only a few meters from the graves of the Brothers Grimm.

GEORGE FITZGERALD

George Francis FitzGerald (3 August 1851 – 21 February 1901) was an Irish professor of "natural and experimental philosophy" (*i.e.*, physics) at Trinity College, Dublin, in the late 19th century.

FitzGerald was born at No 19, Lower Mount Street in Dublin on 3 August 1851 to the Reverend William FitzGerald and his wife Anne Francis Stoney. Professor of Moral Philosophy in Trinity and vicar of St. Anne's, Dawson Street, at the time of his son's birth, William FitzGerald was consecrated Bishop of Cork in 1857 and translated to Killaloe in 1862. George returned to Dublin and entered Trinity as a student at the age of 16. He became a Fellow of Trinity in 1877 and spent the rest of his career at the College.

Along with Oliver Lodge, Oliver Heaviside, and Heinrich Hertz, FitzGerald was a leading figure among the group of "Maxwellians" who revised, extended, clarified, and confirmed James Clerk Maxwell's theory of the electromagnetic field in the late 1870s and 1880s.

In 1883, following from Maxwell's equations, he suggested a device for producing rapidly oscillating electric current, to generate electromagnetic waves, a phenomenon first shown experimentally by Heinrich Hertz in 1888.

However, FitzGerald is better known for his conjecture in 1889 that if all moving objects were foreshortened in the direction of their motion, it would account for the curious result of the Michelson-Morley experiment. FitzGerald based this idea in part on the way electromagnetic forces were known to be affected by motion; in particular, he drew on equations that had been derived a short time before by his friend Oliver Heaviside. The Dutch physicist Hendrik Lorentz hit on a very similar idea in 1892 and developed it more fully in connection with his theory of electrons. The so-called FitzGerald-Lorentz contraction or Lorentz-FitzGerald contraction hypothesis later became an important part of Albert Einstein's special theory of relativity, published in 1905.

Long a sufferer from digestive problems, George Francis FitzGerald succumbed to a perforated ulcer at home on 21 February

1901. FitzGerald was the nephew of George Johnstone Stoney, the Irish physicist who invented the term "electron".

GUSTAF DALEN

Nils Gustaf Dalen (November 30, 1869 – December 9, 1937) was a Swedish Nobel Laureate and industrialist, the founder of the AGA company and inventor of the AGA cooker and the Dalen light. In 1912 he was awarded the Nobel Prize in Physics for his automatic valves designed to be used in combination with gas accumulators in lighthouses and light-buoys.

Biography

Dalen was born in Stenstorp, in present day Falkoping municipality, Sweden.

He managed the family farm, which he expanded to include a market garden, a seed merchants and a dairy.

In 1892 he invented a milk-fat tester to check milk quality of the milk delivered. Gustaf de Laval was so impressed by self-taught Dalen and that he encouraged him to start studying.

He was admitted to the Chalmers University of Technology where he earned his Master's degree and a Doctorate on leaving in 1896.

Dalen married Elma Persson in 1901, they had two daughters and two sons, Gunnar and Anders.

Inventor and Industrialist

Initially Dalen worked with acetylene (IUPAC: ethyne), an extremely explosive hydrocarbon gas. Dalen invented Agamassan (Aga), a substrate used to absorb the gas allowing safe storage and hence commercial exploitation. In 1906 he became Chief Engineer at the Gas Accumulator Company (manufacturer and distributor of acetylene).

Acetylene produced an ultra-bright white-light and immediately superseded the duller-flamed LPG as the fuel of choice in lighthouse illuminations. This light also caused Dalen to go blind when an experiment involving acetylene exploded. Dalen exploited the new fuel, developing the Dalen light which itself incorporated a further invention, the sun valve. This solar switch controlled the light during the hours of darkness ensuring that the buoys burnt less fuel and would only operate at night. This inevitably prolonged their service life to beyond a year.

The 'Dalen Flasher' was a device that, except for a small pilot light, only consumed gas during the flash stage. This reduced gas consumption by more than 80%. In 1909 he ascended to the position of Managing Director of the renamed company Svenska Aktiebolaget Gasaccumulator (AGA). AGA developed lighthouses using Dalen's products.

To a rugged coastal area like Scandinavia, his mass-produced long-life minimal maintenance buoys were a significant boon to safety and livelihood. Internationally, AGA Lighthouses were built covering the entire Panama Canal. Early in 1912, Dalen was blinded in an acetylene explosion. Later the same year he was awarded the Nobel Prize for physics. Dalen was too ill to attend the presentation. His brother, ophthalmologist Professor Albin Dalen, of the Caroline Institute stood in his place.

The presentation speech praised the quality of sacrificing personal safety in scientific experimentation, a compliment that compared Dalen with Nobel himself.

In 1922 he invented the AGA cooker, and despite his blindness, Dalen remained in control of AGA until 1937. He made over a 100 patents during his lifetime.

GEOFFREY CHEW

Geoffrey Chew (born 1924) is an American theoretical physicist. Professor of Physics, UC Berkeley, since 1957, Emeritus since 1991. PhD in theoretical particle physics, 1944-1946, from University of Chicago. Physics faculty member at the University of Illinois, 1950-56. Member, National Academy of Sciences and American Academy of Arts and Science. Hughes Prize of the American Physics Society for bootstrap theory of strong interactions, 1962. Lawrence Prize, 1969.

Chew was a student of Enrico Fermi, and his students include David Gross and John H. Schwarz. He was known as a leader of the S-matrix approach to the strong interaction and the associated bootstrap principle, a theory whose popularity peaked in the 1960s when he led an influential theory group at UC Berkeley. S-matrix theorists sought to understand the strong interaction by using the analytic properties of the scattering matrix to calculate the interactions of bound-states without assuming that there is a point-particle field theory underneath. The S-matrix approach did not provide a local space-time description, and although it was not immediately appreciated by the practitioners, it was a natural framework in which to produce a quantum theory of gravity.

Chew's central contribution to the programme came in 1960. Along with collaborator Steven Frautschi, they noted that the mesons fall into families where the square of the mass is linearly proportional to the spin, with the same constant of proportionality for each of the families. Since bound states in quantum mechanics naturally fall into families of this sort, their conclusion, quickly accepted, was that none of the strongly interacting particles were elementary. The conservative point of view was that the bound states were made up of elementary particles, but Chew's more far reaching vision was that there would be a new type of theory which describes the interactions of bound-states which have no point-like constituents at all. This approach was sometimes called **nuclear democracy**, since it avoided singling out certain particles as elementary.

Although the S-matrix approach to the strong interactions was largely abandoned by the particle physics community in the 1970s in favour of quantum chromodynamics, a consistent theory for the scattering of bound-states on straight-line trajectories was eventually constructed and is nowadays known as string theory. Within string theory, Edward Witten reinterpreted S-matrix theory as a flat-space statement of the holographic principle.

GERD BINNIG

Gerd Binnig (born July 20, 1947) is a German physicist, and a Nobel laureate.

He was born in Frankfurt am Main and played in the ruins of the city during his childhood. His family lived partly in Frankfurt and partly in Offenbach, and he attended school in both cities. At the age of 10, he decided to become a physicist, but he soon wondered whether he had made the right choice. He concentrated more on music, playing in a band. He also started playing the violin at 15 and played in his school orchestra.

In 1969, he married Lore Wagler, a psychologist, and they have a daughter born in Switzerland and a son born in California. His hobbies are reading, swimming and golf.

In 1978, he accepted an offer from IBM to join their Zurich research group. There, he met Heinrich Rohrer, with whom he shared the Nobel Prize in Physics in 1986 for their design of the scanning tunneling microscope (STM).

The team included Christoph Gerber and Edmund Weibel, and they were soon recognized with a number of prizes: the German Physics Prize, the Otto Klung Prize, the Hewlett Packard Prize, the King Faisal Prize, and ultimately, the Nobel Prize.

In 1994 Professor Gerd Binnig founded Definiens which turned in the year 2000 into a commercial enterprise. Today, companies and institutions around the world use Definiens' technology to maximize the value of images and thereby enabling better decisions. Definiens currently focuses on applications for Life Sciences and Earth Sciences. In Life Sciences, Definiens' technology is used to accelerate the drug discovery, development, and diagnostics processes. In Earth Sciences, Definiens' technology enables satellite and aerial image classification and analysis with greater speed, accuracy and insight.

GIUSEPPE MERCALLI

Giuseppe Mercalli (May 21, 1850-March 19, 1914) was an Italian volcanologist.

Biography

Born in Milan, Mercalli was ordained a Roman Catholic priest and soon became a professor of the Natural Sciences at the seminary of Milan. He was removed from the professorship when he was suspected of liberalism for openly supporting a national monument to honour the great philosopher-priest Antonio Rosmini-Serbati.

Subsequently the Italian government appointed him a professor at Domodossola, followed by a post at Reggio di Calabria and finally a post at the Naples University. He was also director of the Vesuvius Observatory until the time of his death. Among his pupils was Giuseppe Moscati.

He is best remembered today for his Mercalli scale for measuring earthquakes which is still used today.

The Mercalli scale, unlike the more famous Richter scale, doesn't measure the actual energy released by an earthquake but how much effect an earthquake had on a given area, making it poorly suited for measuring earthquakes in sparsely populated areas, but ideal for comparing damage done by various tremors. The Mercalli scale gives a rating from I to XII, where I is felt only by a very few and XII has near total damage, few or no masonry structures remain standing, and objects are thrown into the air.

GEOFFREY HATTERSLEY-SMITH

Geoffrey Francis Hattersley-Smith (1923-) is an English born geologist and glaciologist. He attended Winchester College in Hampshire and graduated from New College, Oxford.

From 1948-1950 he was the base leader for the Falkland Islands Dependencies Survey (now the British Antarctic Survey) on King George Island.

In 1951 he became a staff member with the Canadian Defence Research Board (DRB) (now part of the Department of National Defence. With the DRB he was part of several expeditions to places such as the Saint Elias Mountains in the Yukon and Cornwallis Island, Northwest Territories (now Nunavut). From 1953-1954 he led the joint Canada-United States expedition to Ellesmere Island In 1956 he received a Doctor of Philosophy from Oxford for his work on Ellesmeres glaciers.

In 1957 he began 16 years of research on Ellesmere Island. As part of the International Geophysical Year (1957-1958) he went to Lake Hazen and until 1973 worked either there or at Ward Hunt Island. In 1963 he set up a camp and conducted field research at Tanquary Fiord. The teams that he led named over 50 features on Ellesmere Island, such as Barbeau Peak and Turnabout River.

He was elected to the Royal Society of Canada in 1970 and in 1973 he retired as head of the DRB's Geotechnical Section and returned to England.

After returning to England he re-joined the British Antarctic Survey and was the secretary of the Antarctic Place-names Committee for the Foreign and Commonwealth Office in London. In 1984 the Advisory Committee on Antarctic Names named Cape Hattersley-Smith after him.

In 1990 Hattersley-Smith retired to Kent.

GEORGE MERCER DAWSON

George Mercer Dawson (August 1, 1849 – March 2, 1901) was a Canadian scientist and surveyor. He was born in Pictou, Nova Scotia, the son of Sir John William Dawson. By age 11, he was afflicted with tuberculosis of the spine (Pott's disease) that resulted in a deformed back and stunted his growth. However, his physical limitations did not deter Dawson from becoming one of Canada's greatest scientists.

Tutors and his father provided his educational needs during his slow recovery from the illness. Dawson later attended the High School of Montreal and McGill University (part-time) before moving to London to study geology and palaeontology at the Royal School of Mines (now part of Imperial College London) beginning in 1869. Dawson graduated after three years with the highest marks in his class. Dawson received an LL.D. from Queen's University in 1890 and then from McGill University in 1891. Dawson began his career in the 1870s as a professor of chemistry at Morrin College in Quebec City. He then performed extensive surveys of Western Canada in the 19th century beginning with the International Boundary Survey from 1872 to 1876. The result was a 387-page report called *Geology and Resources of the Region in the Vicinity of the 49th parallel from the Lake of the Woods to the Rocky Mountains, with Lists of Plants and Animals Collected, and Notes on the Fossils from the Killadeer Badlands currently part of Grasslands National Park.* This report established Dawson as a respected scientist.

During 1883 and 1884, Dawson travelled through the Canadian Rockies where he was tasked by the Canadian government to map out major mountains and mountain passes as well as significant rivers. Some of the many peaks he discovered were Mount Assiniboine 3,618 metres (11,870 ft) and Mount Temple 3,543 metres (11,620 ft). As a result of his field research, a map of his work was published in 1886 covering the Canadian Rockies from the US border to Red Deer Valley and Kicking Horse Pass.

In 1887, he led an expedition into the Yukon, developing some of the first maps of what later became the separate territory. His report was republished ten years later to satisfy the public's interest in the region as a result of the Klondike Gold Rush. Dawson City was named after him. Dawson Creek, British Columbia is also named in his honour.

Dawson became a staff member of the Geological Survey of Canada in 1875, progressed to assistant director in 1883 and finally to director in 1895. Dawson died unexpectedly in Ottawa after a one day bout with acute bronchitis. He was interred in the family plot in the Mount Royal Cemetery in Montreal.

GEORGE V. CHILINGAR

George V. Chilingarian (he uses both Chilingar and Chilingarian as his last name) is a Professor of Civil and Petroleum Engineering at the University of Southern California (USC). He is one of the best-known petroleum geologists in the world and the founder of several prestigious journals in the oil and gas industry. Chilingar has published 61 books and hundreds of articles on geology, petroleum engineering and environmental engineering. He serves as president of the U.S. branch of the Russian Academy of Sciences and 17 of his books have been translated into Russian. In recognition of these contributions, the Russian Academy of Sciences has honoured him as a Knight of Arts and Sciences.

He received his bachelor's and master's degrees in petroleum engineering and a Ph.D. in geology (with a minor in petroleum engineering), all at USC.

His greatest contribution to the petroleum industry may be a means of identifying oil-rich rock by analyzing the ratio of calcium to magnesium in core samples. This method was used in discovering one of Iran's largest oil fields, which was then named after Chilingar. He also played a key role in the development of Thailand's offshore oil reserves. Chilingar saw natural gas bubbles in the Gulf of Siam and redirected exploratory efforts, thus saving the nascent Thai oil industry.

In 2001, King Fahd of Saudi Arabia acknowledged Chilingar's significant contributions to the success of Saudi Aramco as well as the discovery and extraction of oil reserves around the world. The Saudi consul general in Los Angeles, Ambassador Mohammed A. Al-Salloum, presented the award, a globe signifying the worldwide reach and importance of the petroleum industry and Saudi Aramco.

He served as senior petroleum engineering adviser to the United Nations from 1967 to 1969, and then again from 1978 to 1987. He was also an energy policy adviser to California Governor Ronald Reagan in 1973.

GEORG AGRICOLA

Georgius Agricola (March 24, 1494 – November 21, 1555) was a German scholar and scientist. Known as "the father of mineralogy", he was born at Glauchau in Saxony. His real name was

Georg Bauer; *Agricola* is the Latinised version of his name, *Bauer* meaning *peasant*. He is best known for his book De Re Metallica.

Life and Work

Gifted with a precocious intellect, Georg early threw himself into the pursuit of the "new learning," with such effect that at the age of twenty he was appointed Rector extraordinarius of Greek at the so-called Great School of Zwickau, and made his appearance as a writer on philology. After two years he gave up his appointment in order to pursue his studies at Leipzig, where, as rector, he received the support of the professor of classics, Peter Mosellanus (1493-1524), a celebrated humanist of the time, with whom he had already been in correspondence. Here he also devoted himself to the study of medicine, physics, and chemistry. After the death of Mosellanus he went to Italy from 1524 to 1526, where he took his doctor's degree.

He returned to Zwickau in 1527, and was chosen as town physician at Joachimsthal, a centre of mining and smelting works, his object being partly "to fill in the gaps in the art of healing," partly to test what had been written about mineralogy by careful observation of ores and the methods of their treatment.

His thorough grounding in philology and philosophy had accustomed him to systematic thinking, and this enabled him to construct out of his studies and observations of minerals a logical system which he began to publish in 1528. Agricola's dialogue *Bermannus, sive de re metallica dialogus*, (1530) the first attempt to reduce to scientific order the knowledge won by practical work, brought Agricola into notice; it contained an approving letter from Erasmus at the beginning of the book.

In 1530 Prince Maurice of Saxony appointed him historiographer with an annual allowance, and he migrated to Chemnitz, the centre of the mining industry, in order to widen the range of his observations. The citizens showed their appreciation of his learning by appointing him town physician in 1533. In that year, he published a book about Greek and Roman weights and measures, *De Mensuis et Ponderibus*.

He was also elected burgomaster of Chemnitz. His popularity was, however, short-lived. Chemnitz was a violent centre of the Protestant movement, while Agricola never wavered in his allegiance to the old religion; and he was forced to resign his office. He now lived apart from the contentious movements of the time, devoting himself wholly to learning. His chief interest was still in mineralogy; but he occupied himself also with medical, mathematical, theological and historical subjects, his chief historical work being the *Dominatores Saxonici a prima origine ad hanc aetatem*, published at Freiberg. In 1544 he published the *De ortu et causis subterraneorum*, in which he laid the first foundations of a physical geology, and criticized the theories of the ancients. In 1545 followed the *De natura eorum quae effluunt e terra*; in 1546 the *De veteribus et novis metallis*, a comprehensive account of the discovery and occurrence of minerals and also more commonly known as De Natura Fossilium; in 1548 the *De animantibus subterraneis*; and in the two following years a number of smaller works on the metals.

GLAYDE WHITNEY

Glayde D. Whitney (1939–8 January 2002) was a behavioural geneticist and psychology professor at Florida State University. Beyond his work into the genetics of sensory system function in mice, in his later life he supported race and intelligence research and eugenics, and for these views was frequently accused of supporting scientific racism.

Biography

Whitney was born in Montana and grew up in Minnesota. He earned his bachelor's degree from University of Minnesota, as well as his doctorate from there in 1966. He then enlisted in the United States Air Force and served until 1969. He then worked as a postdoctoral fellow at the Institute for Behavioural Genetics with the University of Colorado, under Gerry McClearn and John DeFries. In 1970, Whitney was hired by the Florida State University to represent behavioural genetics in the psychobiology programme, where he would stay until his death. He considered himself to be "a Hubert Humphrey liberal."

Work in Behavioural Genetics

Whitney was the author of over 60 papers on the genetics of taste sensitivity in inbred mice. Support for some of this work came from a prestigious Claude Pepper Award for Research Excellence from the National Institute on Deafness and Other Communication Disorders (NIDCD) and in 1994, Glayde received the Manheimer Lectureship Award from the Monell Chemical Senses Centre, which recognizes career achievements of individuals in the chemosensory sciences. At the height of his genetics career he was the president of the Behaviour Genetics Association (BGA).

GEORGE DAVIS SNELL

George Davis Snell (December 19, 1903 – June 6, 1996) was an American mouse geneticist and basic transplant immunologist.

Work

George Snell shared the 1980 Nobel Prize in Physiology or Medicine with Baruj Benacerraf and Jean Dausset for their discoveries concerning "genetically determined structures on the cell surface that regulate immunological reactions". Snell specifically "discovered the genetic factors that determine the possibilities of transplanting tissue from one individual to another. It was Snell who introduced the concept of H antigens." Snell's work in mice led to the discovery of HLA, the major histocompatibility complex, in humans (and all vertebrates) that is analogous to the H-2 complex in mice. Recognition of these key genes was prerequisite to successful tissue and organ transplantation.

Life

George Snell was born in Bradford, Massachusetts, the youngest of three schildren. His father (who was born in Minnesota), worked as a secretary for the local YMCA; he invented a device for winding induction coils for motorboat engines. Snell was educated in the Brookline, Massachusetts schools and then enrolled at Dartmouth College in Hanover, New Hampshire where he continued his passion for mathematics and science, focusing on genetics. He received his Bachelor's degree from Dartmouth in 1926.

On the recommendation of John Gerould, his genetics professor at Dartmouth, Snell did graduate work at Harvard University with William E. Castle, the first American biologist to look for Mendelian inheritance in mammals. Snell earned his PhD from Harvard in 1930. His doctoral thesis was on genetic linkage in mice.

Snell then spent two years as a postdoctoral fellow at the University of Texas with H.J. Muller, who pioneered radiation genetics (and was also to win a Nobel Prize). Not surprisingly, Snell studied the genetic effects of x-rays on mice with Muller.

This experience "served to convince me that research was my real love," Snell wrote in his autobiography. " If it were to be research, mouse genetics was the clear choice and the Jackson Laboratory, founded in 1929 by Dr. Clarence Cook Little, one of Castle's earlier students, almost the inevitable selection as a place to work." The Jackson Laboratory was (and still is) the world's mecca for mouse genetics.

In 1935 Snell joined the staff of the Jackson Lab in Bar Harbor on beautiful Mt. Desert Island by the coast of Maine and he remained there for the entire balance of his long career. In Bar Harbor, he met and married Rhoda Carson. Together they had three sons, Thomas, Roy, and Peter. In his leisure time, Snell enjoyed skiing, a passion he developed during his years at Dartmouth, as well as tennis.

In 1988, he authored a substantial book, *Search for a Rational Ethic*, on the nature of ethics and the rules by which we live. It includes an evolution-based ethic founded on biological realities that he believed to be applicable to all human beings.

Snell died in Bar Harbor, Maine on June 6, 1996.

GOPALASAMUDRAM NARAYANA IYER RAMACHANDRAN

Gopalasamudram Narayana Iyer Ramachandran (8 October 1922-7 April 2001) is widely acknowledged as one of the most important Indian scientists of the 20th century, best known for his work that led to his creation of the Ramachandran plot for understanding peptide structure. He also made other major contributions in biology and physics.

Birth and Education

Ramachandran was born in the town of Ernakulam, Kerala, India. He joined Indian Institute of Science, Bangalore in 1942 in the Electrical Engineering Department. Quickly realizing his interest in physics, he switched to Department of Physics to complete his master's and doctoral thesis under the supervision of Nobel laureate Sir C. V. Raman.

In 1942 he received a master's degree in physics from Madras University and received D.Sc. in 1947. Here he mostly studied crystal physics and crystal optics. During his studies he created an X-ray focusing mirror for the X-ray Microscope. The resulting field of crystal topography is used extensively in studies involving crystal growth and solid-state reactivity. Ramachandran then spent two years (1947–1949) at the Cavendish Laboratory in Cambridge, where he earned his Ph.D. for 'studies on X-ray diffuse scattering and its application to determination of elastic constants'.

Research

After completing his Ph.D, returned to Indian Institute of Science, Bangalore, India in 1949 as an assistant professor of physics. In 1952 he moved to Madras University as a professor and head, Department of Physics where he continued his work on crystal physics. But his interest shifted to the structure of biological macromolecules. Using X-ray diffraction Ramachandran along with Gopinath Kartha proposed and published the triple helical structure of collagen in 1954.

Wanting to tackle problems at a more fundamental level, Ramachandran decided to use this information to examine the various polypeptide conformations then known and also to develop a good 'yardstick' that could be used for examining and assessing any structure in general, but peptides in particular. The result which emerged from these calculations in 1962,-now commonly known as the Ramachandran plot-was published in the Journal of Molecular Biology in 1963 and has become an essential tool in the field of protein conformation. When it was first calculated, crystal structures had barely been obtained for any protein. From the mid 1960s onward Ramachandran studied many topics relating to the conformation of peptides including types of a-turns, conformation of prolyl residues, cis-peptide units, occurrence and need for non-planarity of the peptides, NMR coupling constants, peptides containing L and D residues and many others.

Ramachandran can be credited for bringing together into the one field of molecular biophysics the then disparate fields of X-ray crystallography, peptide synthesis, NMR and other optical studies, and physico-chemical experimentation.

In 1970 he founded the Molecular Biophysics Unit at the Indian Institute of Science which was later known as the Centre of Advanced Study in Biophysics and Crystallography.

Ramachandran and A.V. Lakshminarayana developed convolution-backprojection algorithms which greatly improved the quality and practicality of results obtainable by x-ray tomography. Compared to previously used methods, their algorithms considerably reduced computer processing time for image reconstruction, as well as providing more numerically accurate images. As a result, commercial manufacturers of x-ray tomographic scanners started building systems capable of reconstructing high resolution images that were almost photographically perfect. In 1971, they published their research in a paper ("Three dimensional reconstructions from radiographs and electron micrographs: Application of convolution instead of Fourier Transforms," Proc. Nat. Acad. Sci., vol. 68, pp. 2236-2240, 1971).

Notable awards that Ramachandran received include the Shanti Swarup Bhatnagar Award for Physics in India and the Fellowship of the Royal Society of London. In 1999 the International Union of Crystallography honoured him with the Ewald Prize for his 'outstanding contributions to crystallography'. In short, though Ramachandran did not receive the Nobel Prize, he will certainly be remembered for his contributions to science which were surely above a Nobel.

Later Years

During the last few years of his life he suffered a stroke and was affected by Parkinson's disease. Ramachandran died in 2001 at the age of 78.

GEORGE R. PRICE

George R. Price (1922–January 6, 1975) was an American population geneticist. Originally a physical chemist and later a science journalist, he moved to London in 1967, where he worked in theoretical biology at the Galton Laboratory, making three important contributions: first, rederiving W.D. Hamilton's work on kin selection with a new Price equation; second, introducing (with John Maynard Smith) the concept of the evolutionarily stable strategy (ESS), a central concept in game theory; and third, formalising Fisher's fundamental theorem of natural selection. A troubled man, Price converted to Christianity from atheism, and after giving all his possessions to the poor, committed suicide.

Early Life

Price was born in 1922, the younger brother of Edison. His father, an electrician, died when he was four. His mother was a former opera singer, and the family struggled through the Great Depression.

Having attended public school in New York, Price graduated with a degree in chemistry from University of Chicago in 1943 and received his doctorate in the subject from the same institution in

1946, having worked on the Manhattan Project. In 1947 he married Julia Madigan, but their relationship was contentious because George was a militant atheist whilst his wife was a practicing Roman Catholic. They divorced in 1955, having had two daughters, Annamarie and Kathleen.

Early Career

Between 1946 and 1948, Price was an instructor in chemistry at Harvard University and consultant to Argonne National Laboratory. Later, he worked as a research associate in medicine at the University of Minnesota, working on, amongst other things, fluorescence microscopy and liver perfusion. In 1955 and 1956, he published two papers in the journal *Science* critisicing the apparently pseudoscientific claims of extra-sensory perception.

Continuing with science journalism, he tried to write a book entitled *No Easy Way* about the United States' Cold War with the Soviet Union and the People's Republic of China but complained that "the world kept changing faster than I could write about it", and so the book was never finished.

From 1961 to 1967, Price was employed by IBM as a consultant on graphic data processing. In 1966 he was treated for thyroid cancer, but the operation to remove the tumour left his shoulder partially paralysed and reliant on thyroxine medication. With the money from his medical insurance, he moved to the United Kingdom to start a new life in November 1967.

G. H. HARDY

Godfrey Harold Hardy (February 7, 1877 Cranleigh, Surrey, England – December 1, 1947 Cambridge, Cambridgeshire, England) was a prominent English mathematician, known for his achievements in number theory and mathematical analysis.

Non-mathematicians usually know him for *A Mathematician's Apology*, his essay from 1940 on the aesthetics of mathematics. The apology is often considered one of the best insights into the mind of a working mathematician written for the layman.

His relationship as mentor, from 1914 onwards, of the Indian mathematician Srinivasa Ramanujan has become celebrated. Hardy almost immediately recognized Ramanujan's extraordinary albeit untutored brilliance, and Hardy and Ramanujan became close collaborators. In an interview by Paul Erdos, when Hardy was asked what his greatest contribution to mathematics was, Hardy unhesitatingly replied that it was the discovery of Ramanujan. He called their collaboration "the one romantic incident in my life."

Life

G.H. Hardy was born 7 February 1877, in Cranleigh, Surrey, England, into a teaching family. His father was Bursar and Art Master at Cranleigh School; his mother had been a senior mistress at Lincoln Training College for teachers. Both parents were mathematically inclined.

Hardy's own natural affinity for mathematics was perceptible at a young age. When just two years old, he wrote numbers up to millions, and when taken to church he amused himself by factorizing the numbers of the hymns.

After schooling at Cranleigh, Hardy was awarded a scholarship to Winchester College for his mathematical work. In 1896 he entered Trinity College, Cambridge. After only two years of preparation he was fourth in the Mathematics Tripos examination. Years later, Hardy sought to abolish the Tripos system, as he felt that it was becoming more an end in itself than a means to an end. While at university, Hardy joined the Cambridge Apostles, an elite, intellectual secret society.

As the most important influence Hardy cites the self-study of *Cours d'analyse de l'Ecole Polytechnique* by the French mathematician Camille Jordan, through which he became acquainted with the more precise mathematics tradition in continental Europe. In 1900 he passed part II of the tripos and was awarded a fellowship. In 1903 he earned his M.A., which was the highest academic degree at English universities at that time. From 1906 onward he held the position of a lecturer, who had to teach six hours per week leaving him plenty of time for research. In 1919 he left Cambridge to take the Savilian Chair of Geometry at Oxford in the aftermath of the Bertrand Russell affair during World War I. He returned to Cambridge in 1931, where he was Sadleirian Professor until 1942.

The Indian Clerk (2007) is a novel by David Leavitt based on Hardy's life at Cambridge, including his discovery of and relationship with Srinivasa Ramanujan.

GABRIEL DOVER

Gabriel A. Dover (Gabby Dover) is a British geneticist. He is best known for coining the term molecular drive in 1982 to describe a putative third evolutionary force operating distinctly from natural selection and genetic drift. More generally, his research has been on the evolution of genes and genomes, particularly the complex processes that occur in multigene families such as ribosomal RNA genes. His recent work has focused on development in flies, in particular the co-evolution between the developmental regulatory elements involved in morphogenesis. His BSc is from the University of Leeds, and his PhD from the University of Cambridge. The majority of his career was spent at the Department of Genetics at the University of Cambridge. In 1992, Dover became a Professor of Genetics at the University of Leicester. He is currently a Research Fellow of the Leverhulme Trust.

Dover co-edited the textbook *Genome Evolution* (Academic Press, 1982) with Richard Flavell. He has also written a popular book on evolution, *Dear Mr Darwin: Letters on the Evolution of Life and Human Nature* (Weidenfeld & Nicolson, 2000), framed as an exchange of letters with Charles Darwin from beyond the grave. The book seeks to refute the selfish gene theory promulgated by Richard Dawkins.

GEORGE WELLS BEADLE

George Wells Beadle (October 22, 1903 – June 9, 1989) was an American scientist in the field of genetics, and Nobel Prize in Physiology or Medicine Nobel laureate who with Edward Lawrie Tatum discovered the role of genes in regulating biochemical events within cells. Beadle and Tatum's key experiments involved exposing the bread mold *Neurospora crassa* to x-rays, causing mutations. In a series of experiments, they showed that these mutations caused changes in specific enzymes involved in metabolic pathways. These experiments led them to propose a direct link between genes and enzymatic reactions, known as the "one gene, one enzyme" hypothesis.

Biography

Beadle was born in Wahoo, Nebraska. He received his Bachelor of Science degree in agronomy from the University of Nebraska's College of Agriculture in 1926 where he was a member of FarmHouse fraternity. At the recommendation of his advisor, Franklin D. Keim, he then entered graduate school in agronomy at Cornell University, intending to study ecology. He soon switched his focus to genetics and cytology, pursuing research on maize (corn) genetics under Rollins Adams Emerson—including some collaboration with Barbara McClintock. He received his Ph.D. from Cornell in 1931.

For post-doctoral work, Beadle joined Thomas Hunt Morgan's "fly lab" at the California Institute of Technology, where he worked with Alfred Sturtevant and others on *Drosophila* genetics. There, working with Boris Ephrussi, he helped develop a technique for transplanting foreign cells in fly larvae (creating a third eye in flies' abdomens); this technique was used to demonstrate that some mutations affecting eye colour involved genes that controlled specific metabolic steps in the production of eye pigment. In an effort to precisely characterize the reactions and substances involved, he recruited biochemist Edward Tatum to work on the pigment problem as well. They eventually isolated and identified the pigment precursor found in the "*vermilion*" mutant, but did so shortly after an independent German group. Over the course of his *Drosophila* work, Beadle was a professor at Harvard University, then Stanford University.

With Tatum, Beadle switched his focus to a model organism more suited to biochemical genetics: *Neurospora*. By constructing mutant strains that required specific nutritional elements (amino acids or vitamins), they established that individual gene mutations were responsible for individual steps in the metabolism and synthesis of vital nutrients. This led, in 1941, to propose the "one gene-one enzyme hypothesis," the idea that a gene specifies a single enzyme, rather than a complex set of characteristics (as was generally assumed).

In 1946, with the support of Linus Pauling, Beadle was recruited to head the newly reorganized biology division of Caltech; the department was one of the prototypes of what would become known as *molecular biology*. During the early Cold War, Beadle was outspoken in his defense of colleagues under investigation for suspected Communist ties, and also worked on defining and publicizing the potential dangers of nuclear weapons-related radiation. In 1958, Beadle and Tatum were awarded the Nobel Prize in Physiology and Medicine for their work on biochemical genetics. Beadle went on to serve as president of the University of Chicago from 1961-1968, helping—through fund-raising and recruitment—to re-establish its reputation as a top research university. He published a book, *The Language of Life*, in 1966.

Following his retirement as university president, Beadle returned to research, now on the evolutionary relationship between corn and teosinte. He continued research until the late 1970s, when Alzheimer's disease made continued intellectual work impossible. George Beadle died in 1989; his second wife Muriel Barnett Beadle died in 1994. He had one son, David (b. 1931), with his first wife Marion Hill Beadle.

GUIDO BARBUJANI

Guido Barbujani (born January 31, 1955) is an Italian population geneticist, evolutionist and literary author born in Adria, who has been working at the State University of New York at Stony Brook (NY), at the Padua and Bologna Universities, and is now a professor at the University of Ferrara since 1996.

Works

A population geneticist by training, has been working on several aspects of human genetic variation. In collaboration with Robert R.

Sokal, he pioneered the statistical comparison of patterns of genetic and linguistic variation, showing that language differences may contribute to reproductive isolation, and hence promote genetic divergence between populations.

His analyses of geographic patterns of genetic variation in Europe support Luca Cavalli-Sforza's Neolithic demic diffusion model, *i.e.* the idea that farming spread in the Neolithic mainly because farmers did, and not by cultural transmission. Two implications of this finding are that most Europeans' ancestors did not live in Europe, but in the Near East, up to Neolithic times, and that in their Westward expansion the early farmers carried with them their genes, their technologies, and possibly their languages too.

His studies of the amount of DNA differentiation among human populations, and of its spatial distribution, led to the conclusion that traditional human racial classification fails to account for most of the existing patterns of genetic variation. Rather, it seems that genetic variation is largely uncorrelated across genes, which, if confirmed, would explain why no consensus was ever reached on a catalog of human biological races. This activity has also resulted in publications for the general public.

His recent DNA studies focus on genetic characterization of ancient human populations, such as Paleolithic anatomically-modern humans of Cro-Magnoid morphology, the Etruscans and the Neolithic (nuragic) Sardinians.

Barbujani is the author of three novels.

GEOFFREY WILKINSON

Sir Geoffrey Wilkinson (14 July 1921 – 26 September 1996) was an English chemist.

Biography

Wilkinsonwas born in the village of Springside, near Todmorden in Yorkshire. His father, also a Geoffrey, was a master house painter and decorator; his mother worked in a local cotton mill. One of his uncles, an organist and choirmaster, had married into a family that owned a small chemical company making Epsom and Glauber's salts for the pharmaceutical industry. This is where he first developed an interest in chemistry. He was educated at the local council primary school and, after winning a County Scholarship in 1932, went to Todmorden Secondary School. There, he had the same physics teacher as Sir John Cockcroft, who received a Nobel Prize for "splitting the atom". Wilkinson's catalyst $RhCl(PPh_3)_3$

In 1939 he obtained a Royal Scholarship for study at Imperial College, London, from where he graduated in 1941. In 1942 Professor Friedrich Adolf Paneth was recruiting young chemists for the nuclear energy project. Wilkinson joined and was sent out to Canada, where he stayed in Montreal and later Chalk River Laboratories until he could leave in 1946. For the next four years he worked with Professor Glenn T. Seaborg at Berkeley, California, mostly on nuclear taxonomy. He then became a Research Associate at the Massachusetts Institute of Technology and began to return to his first interest as a student-transition metal complexes of ligands such as carbon monoxide and olefins.

He was then at the Harvard University from September 1951 until he returned to England in December 1955, with a sabbatical break of nine months in Copenhagen. At Harvard, he still did some nuclear work on excitation functions for protons in cobalt, but had already begun to work on olefin complexes. In June 1955 he was appointed to the chair of Inorganic Chemistry at Imperial College in the University of London, and from then on worked almost entirely on the complexes of transition metals. He was married, with two daughters.

GUNTER WIRTHS

Gunter Wirths was a German chemist who was an authority on uranium production, especially reactor-grade. He worked at *Auergesellschaft* in the production of uranium for the *Heereswaffenamt* and its *Uranverein* project. In 1945, he was sent the Soviet Union to work on the Russian atomic bomb project. When he was released from the Soviet Union, he settled in West Germany, and worked at the Degussa company.

Career

Wirths was a colleague of Nikolaus Riehl, who was the director of the scientific headquarters of *Auergesellschaft*. *Auergesellschaft* had a substantial amount of "waste" uranium from which it had extracted radium. After reading a paper in 1939 by Siegfried Flugge, on the technical use of nuclear energy from uranium, Riehl recognized a business opportunity for the company, and, in July of that year, went to the *Heereswaffenamt* (HWA, Army Ordnance Office) to discuss the production of uranium. The HWA was interested and Riehl committed corporate resources to the task. The HWA eventually provided an order for the production of uranium oxide, which took place in the Auergesellschaft plant in Oranienburg, north of Berlin. It was this that got Wirths involved with the production of uranium metal, which *Auergesellschaft* did for the *Uranverein* project of the *Heereswaffenamt*.

GEORGE M. WHITESIDES

George M. Whitesides (b. August 3, 1939, Louisville, Kentucky) is an American chemist and professor of chemistry at Harvard University. He is best known for his work in the areas of NMR spectroscopy, organometallic chemistry, molecular self-assembly, soft lithography, microfabrication, microfluidics, and nanotechnology. Whitesides is also known for his "outline system" for writing scientific papers. As of March 2008, he has the highest Hirsch index rating of all living chemists.

Education and Academic Career

Whitesides attended secondary school at Phillips Andover and graduated in 1957. He received his A.B. degree from Harvard College in 1960 and earned a Ph.D. in chemistry from the California Institute of Technology in 1964. Under the tutelage of John D. Roberts, Whitesides' graduate work focused on the use of NMR spectroscopy in organic chemistry. Among other research endeavors, he studied spin-spin coupling in a variety of organic compounds and the structure of Grignard reagents in solution.

Research at MIT

Whitesides began his independent career as an assistant professor at the Massachusetts Institute of Technology in 1963 and remained there until 1982. While at MIT, he played a pivotal role in the development of the Corey-House-Posner-Whitesides reaction, which now bears his name.

Research at Harvard

In 1982, Whitesides moved his laboratory to the Department of Chemistry at Harvard University, his alma mater. He has served tenures as chairman of the Chemistry Department (1986-89) and associate Dean of the Faculty of Arts and Sciences (1989-92).

Current Research

Whitesides is currently the Woodford L. and Ann A. Flowers University Professor at Harvard, one of only 21 University Professorships at the institution. He maintains an active research group of over 35 graduate and postdoctoral students with a four-person office support staff and lab space covering more than 6, 000 square feet. According to the biography on his Web site, Whitesides' current research interests include "physical and organic chemistry, materials science, biophysics, complexity, surface science, microfluidics, self-assembly, micro-and nanotechnology, science for developing economies, origin of life, and cell-surface biochemistry." The single primary objective of his lab is "to fundamentally change the paradigms of science."

GLENN T. SEABORG

Glenn Theodore Seaborg (Swedish: *Glenn Teodor Sjoberg*) (April 19, 1912 – February 25, 1999) won the 1951 Nobel Prize in Chemistry for "discoveries in the chemistry of the transuranium elements, " contributed to the discovery and isolation of ten elements, developed the actinide concept and was the first to propose the actinide series which led to the current arrangement of the Periodic Table of the Elements.

He spent most of his career as an educator and research scientist at the University of California, Berkeley where he became the second Chancellor in its history and served as a University Professor. Seaborg advised ten presidents from Truman to Clinton on nuclear policy and was the chairman of the United States Atomic Energy Commission from 1961 to 1971 where he pushed for commercial nuclear energy and peaceful applications of nuclear science. Throughout his career, Seaborg worked for arms control. He was signator to the Franck Report and contributed to the achievement of the Limited Test Ban Treaty, the Nuclear Non-Proliferation Treaty, and the Comprehensive Test Ban Treaty. Seaborg was a well-known advocate for science education and federal funding for pure research. He was a key contributor to the report "A Nation at Risk" as a member of President Reagan's National Commission on Excellence in Education and was the principal author of the Seaborg Report on academic science issued in the closing days of the Eisenhower administration.

Seaborg was the principal or co-discoverer of ten elements: plutonium, americium, curium, berkelium, californium, einsteinium, fermium, mendelevium, nobelium and element 106, which was named seaborgium in his honour while he was still living. He also developed more than 100 atomic isotopes, and is credited with important contributions to the separation of the isotope of uranium used in the atomic bomb at Hiroshima. Early in his career, Seaborg was a pioneer in nuclear medicine and developed numerous isotopes of elements with important applications in the diagnosis and treatment of diseases, most notably iodine-131, which is used in the treatment of thyroid disease. In addition to his theoretical work in the development of the *actinide concept* which placed the actinide series beneath the lanthanide series on the periodic table, Seaborg proposed the placement of super-heavy elements in the transactinide and superactinide series. After sharing the 1951 Nobel Prize in Chemistry with Edwin McMillan, he received approximately 50 honorary doctorates and numerous other awards and honors. The list of things named after Seaborg ranges from his atomic element to an asteroid. Seaborg was a prolific author, penning more than 50 books and 500 journal articles, often in collaboration with others. He received so many awards and honors that he was once listed in the Guinness Book of World Records as the person with the longest entry in *Who's Who in America.*

Biography

Of Swedish ancestry, Seaborg was born in Ishpeming, Michigan, the son of Herman Theodore (Ted) and Selma Olivia Erickson Seaborg. He had one sister, Jeanette. When Glenn Seaborg was a boy, the family moved to the Seaborg Home in a subdivision called Home Gardens, that was later annexed to the City of South Gate, California, a suburb of Los Angeles. He kept a daily journal from 1927 until he suffered a stroke in 1998. As a youth, Seaborg was both a devoted sports fan and an avid movie buff. His mother encouraged him to become a book-keeper as she felt his literary interests were impractical. He did not take an interest in science until his junior year when he was inspired by Dwight Logan Reid, a chemistry and physics teacher at David Starr Jordan High School in Watts. He graduated from Jordan in 1929 at the top of his class and received a bachelor's degree in chemistry at the University of California, Los Angeles in 1934. While at UCLA, he was invited by his German professor to meet Albert Einstein, an experience that had a profound impact on Seaborg and served as a model of graciousness for his encounters with aspiring students in later years. Seaborg worked his way through school as a stevedore (longshoreman), fruit packer and laboratory assistant.

GEORGE ANDREW OLAH

George Andrew Olah (born May 22, 1927 in Budapest, as **Olah Gyorgy**) is a Hungarian-born American chemist. He was significant in stabilizing and in studying carbocations via superacids. He won a Nobel Prize in Chemistry in 1994. Soon after, he was awarded the Priestley Medal, the highest honour granted by the American Chemical Society.

Life

Olah studied, then taught, at what is now Budapest University of Technology and Economics. As a result of the 1956 Hungarian Revolution, he and his family moved briefly to England and then to Canada where he joined Dow Chemical in Sarnia, Ontario, with another Hungarian chemist, Stephen J. Kuhn. Olah's pioneering work on carbocations started during his eight years with Dow. In 1965 he returned to academia at Case Western Reserve University and then to University of Southern California in 1977. In 1971, Olah became a naturalized citizen of the United States.

Olah is currently a distinguished professor at the University of Southern California and the director of the Loker Hydrocarbon Research Institute. In 2005, Olah wrote an essay promoting the methanol economy.

GIULIO NATTA

Giulio Natta (February 26, 1903, Imperia-Bergamo, 2 May 1979) was an Italian chemist, who won a Nobel Prize in Chemistry in 1963 with Karl Ziegler for work on high polymers. He was born in Imperia, Italy, on February 26, 1903. He graduated in Chemical Engineering at the Politecnico di Milano in 1924. In 1927 he passed the exams for becoming a professor there. In 1933 he became a full professor and the director of the Institute of General Chemistry of Pavia University, where he stayed until 1935. In that year he was appointed full professor in physical chemistry at the University of Rome. From 1936 to 1938 he moved as a full professor and director of the Institute of Industrial Chemistry at the Politecnico di Torino. In 1938 he took the head of the Department of chemical engineering at Politecnico di Milano university, in a somehow criticized manner, when his predecessor Mario Giacomo Levi was forced to step down as a consequence of racial laws against Jews being introduced in fascist Italy.

His work at the Politecnico led to the improvement of earlier work by Ziegler and to the development of the Ziegler-Natta catalyst. He won a Nobel Prize in Chemistry in 1963 with Karl Ziegler for work on high polymers.

He was diagnosed with Parkinson's disease in 1956. His condition became severe enough in 1963, that his son had to help him in Stockholm during the Noble Prize Award Ceremony and a colleague had to give the lecture. Prof. Natta died on May 2, 1979.

Natta is buried in the cemetery of Bergamo.

ROBERT SAPOLSKY

Robert Maurice Sapolsky (born 1957) is the John A. and Cynthia Fry Gunn Professor of Biological Sciences, and Professor of Neurology and Neurological Sciences at Stanford University.

Education

Robert Sapolsky received his B.A. in biological anthropology *summa cum laude* from Harvard University and subsequently attended Rockefeller University where he received his Ph.D. in Neuroendocrinology, working in the lab of Bruce McEwen, a world-renowned endocrinologist. He is currently a professor at Stanford University, holding joint appointments in several departments, including Biological Sciences, Neurology & Neurological Sciences, and Neurosurgery.

Career

Sapolsky, a neuroendocrinologist, has focused his research on issues of stress and neuron degeneration, as well as on the possibilities of gene therapy strategies for help in protecting susceptible neurons from disease. Currently, he is working on gene transfer techniques to strengthen neurons against the disabling effects of glucocorticoids. Sapolsky also spends time annually in Kenya studying a population of wild baboons in order to identify the sources of stress of their environment, and the relationship between personality and patterns of stress-related disease in these animals. More specifically, Sapolsky studies the cortisol levels between the Alpha male and female and the subordinates to determine stress level. He is the author of Why Zebras Don't Get Ulcers: An Updated Guide to Stress, Stress-Related Diseases and Coping (1994), which explores the effects of prolonged stress and its contribution to damaging physical and mental afflictions. His other books include, The Trouble with Testosterone: And Other Essays on the Biology of the Human Predicament (1997), Junk Food Monkeys (1997), A Primate's Memoir (2002) and Monkeyluv: And Other Essays on Our Lives as Animals (2005).

ROBERT RIDGWAY

Robert Ridgway (July 2, 1850– March 25, 1929) was an American ornithologist.

Born in Mount Carmel, Illinois, Ridgway was a protege of zoologist Spencer Fullerton Baird, who, on becoming the secretary of the Smithsonian Institution, appointed Ridgway the first full-time curator of birds at the U.S. National Museum.

He served from 1880 until his death in 1929. Ridgway also published one of the first and most important colour system for bird identification, with his 1886 book *A Nomenclature of Colours for Naturalists* (Boston: Little, Brown & Co.). In 1912 he self-published a larger work on colour nomenclature, *Colour Standards and Colour Nomenclature*, financed using money from his friend and colleague Jose Castulo Zeledon of Costa Rica. Ornithologists all over the world continue to cite Ridgway's colour studies and books.

In the Spring of 1867, at the age of 16, Ridgway was hired as the naturalist on Clarence King's Survey of the 40th Parallel. In an undertaking that lasted nearly two years, Ridgway collected many bird specimens and served as a key member on one of the four great surveys of the American West. Upon his return to the Smithsonian, he was taken on in an informal basis until he was formally named as the Curator of Ornithology. Although Ridgway had nothing more than a high school education, he was articulate and literate, and served as the Smithsonian's mouthpiece and representative for many years in the study of birds. Friends and colleagues described him as almost painfully shy, and he generally shirked publicity and the limelight.

In 1875 he married Julia Evelyn Parker. They had one son, Audubon Whelock Ridgway, who died of pneumonia in 1901 while working at the Field Museum in Chicago. Ridgway was the joint author (with Thomas Mayo Brewer and Spencer Fullerton Baird) of *History of North American Birds* (Boston, 1875-1884; Land Birds, 3 vols., Water Birds, 2 vols). He also authored several other books and monographs, and had a total of more than 450 articles and publications to his credit.

In 1899, he joined E. H. Harriman on his famous Harriman Alaska Expedition of the Alaska coastline, where he was accompanied by John Muir and a number of other naturalists and scientists, for an extended study of Alaska's coastline flora and fauna. Robert Ridgway's brother, John Livzey Ridgway (1859–1947) was an illustrator. Birds named for Ridgway include the Buff-collared Nightjar, *Caprimulgus ridgwayi*, Ridgway's Hawk, *Buteo ridgwayi*, the Aztec Thrush *Ridgwayia pinicola*, and the Caribbean subspecies of the Osprey, *Pandion haliaetus ridgwayi.*

RONALD PLASTERK

Ronald Hans Anton Plasterk (born on April 12, 1957 in The Hague) is a Dutch biologist, columnist, and politician. Plasterk became known as a highly cited and prize-winning molecular geneticist, which he combined since 1995 with a position as columnist in several national media. Since 2007 he is the Minister of Education, Culture and Science in the fourth Balkenende cabinet for the Labour Party.

Scientific Career

Plasterk attended the Sint Janscollege in The Hague, where he graduated in 1975, specializing in sciences. After graduation he studied biology at the Leiden University and economics at the University of Amsterdam. During this period he wrote for the student newspaper. In 1981 he graduated for his doctoral exam in biology, roughly equivalent of a Master of Science, cum laude in 1981. He also graduated for his propedeuse in economics in the same year. Between 1981 and 1984 he worked a PhD-student at Leiden University. In 1984 he was promoted to doctor in Mathematics and the Natural Sciences at Leiden University on basis of his thesis "Inversion of the G segment of bacteriophage Mu: analysis of a genetic switch". His study focused on transposon sequences in DNA. As a PhD-student Plasterk also was a member of the Leiden city council for the Labour Party.

Between 1985 and 1986 he worked as post-doc at the California Institute of Technology in Pasadena. Here he studied the transposon sequences in DNA in the parasite Borrelia hermsii. Between 1986 and 1987 he worked as a post-doc at the MRC Laboratory of Molecular Biology at Cambridge, where he worked with John E. Sulston. He studied the caenorhabditis elegans, a nematode that is used as a model organism.

In 1987 he returned to the Netherlands where he became group leader and member of the board of the Netherlands Cancer Institute in Amsterdam. In 1989 he became director of the research school oncology of the institute, which he remained until 2000. Between 1993 and 1997 he occupied the endowned chair in molecular microbiology at the Free University of Amsterdam. Between 1997 and 2000 he was professor of molecular genetics at the University of Amsterdam. In February 2000 he became director of the Netherlands Institute for Developmental Biology, also known as the Hubrecht Laboratory, which falls directly under the Royal Netherlands Academy of Arts and Sciences (KNAW). He combined this with a position as professor in developmental genetics at Utrecht University since May 2000. He retained this positions until February 2007.

Since 2001 Plasterk is a member of the KNAW. Before entering in politics he also was a member of the Health Council, which advises the Minister of Health, Welfare and Sport, a member of the board of the Wellcome Trust, member of the Committee on Biotechnology and Animals and of the European Molecular Biology Organization.

Plasterk's research was in the area of genetics and functional genomics. His study focused on mechanism and regulation of DNA transposition, and on the mechanism of RNAi and miRNAs. This includes for instance the functions of RNAi as a natural defense against the uncontrolled duplication of transposons, the regulation and mechanism of DNA transposition, and the mechanism of RNAi and miRNAs.

ROGER MORSE

Roger A. Morse, Ph.D. (July 5, 1927-May 12, 2000) was a bee biologist who taught many beekeepers both the rudiments and the finer practices, through his research and publications. During his long career, three new parasites of the honeybee, acarine mite, varroa mite and African small hive beetle were introduced to the USA. These, along with the Africanized honeybee and pesticide kills were all important beekeeping issues. Morse was extensively involved in research on each of these and provided guidance to the beekeeping industry.

Education and Career

Morse was born in Saugerties, New York, served in the U. S. Army from 1944 to 1947. He received his bachelor's degree from Cornell University in 1950, his masters in 1953 and his doctorate in 1955, and did postgraduate work with the State Plant Board in Gainesville, Florida After a brief stint as assistant professor at the University of Massachusetts, he returned to Cornell University where he remained until retirement. Dr. Morse lectured a very popular course, Beekeeping, an introductory course, so any Cornellian could take this as an elective. During the 1970s many Cornell students were informed and entertained by his superb relating of the honey bee and its close relationship with human endeavours. He was made chairman of the entomology department in 1986. In 1989 he was made a fellow of the Entomological Society of America, and had been a member of the American Association for the Advancement of Science since 1975. He also served as visiting professor at the University of Helsinki, Finland, the University of Sao Paulo, Brazil, and the University of the Philippines, Los Banos.

RAMON MARGALEF

Ramon Margalef i Lopez (Barcelona 1919-2004) was Emeritus Professor of Ecology at the Faculty of Biology of the University of Barcelona. Margalef, unquestionably one of the most important scientists that Spain has produced, worked at the Institute of Applied Biology (1946-1951), and at the Fisheries Research Institute, which he directed during 1966-1967. He created the Department of Ecology of the University of Barcelona, from where he trained a huge number of ecologists, limnologists and oceanographers. In 1967 he became Spain's first professor of ecology.

In the late 1950s, with the translation into English of his inaugural lecture as a member of the Barcelona Royal Academy of Arts and Sciences "Information Theory in Ecology", he gained a worldwide audience. Another groundbreaking article, "On certain unifying principles in ecology", published in American Naturalist in 1963, and his book "Perspectives in Ecological Theory" (1968), based on his guest lectures at the University of Chicago, consolidated him as one of the leading thinkers of modern ecology.

Some of his most important work includes the application of Information Theory to ecological studies and the creation of mathematical models for the study of populations. Among his books, the most relevant are: Natural Communities (1962), Perspectives In Ecological Theory (1968), Ecology (1974), The Biosphere (1980), Limnology (1983) and Theory of Ecological Systems (1991). He received many scientific awards, including the first edition of the Huntsman Award (the «Nobel» in oceanography), the Naumann-Thienemann for Limnology, the Ramon—Cajal Award, and the Gold Medal of the Generalitat de Catalunya (Catalan Government).

RICHARD LEWONTIN

Richard Charles "Dick" Lewontin (born March 29, 1929) is an American evolutionary biologist, geneticist and social commentator. A leader in developing the mathematical basis of population genetics and evolutionary theory, he pioneered the notion of using techniques from molecular biology such as gel electrophoresis to apply to questions of genetic variation and evolution.

In a pair of 1966 papers co-authored with J.L. Hubby in the journal *Genetics*, Lewontin helped set the stage for the modern field of molecular evolution.

In 1979, he and Stephen Jay Gould introduced the term "spandrel" to evolutionary theory. A spandrel is something that evolves as the necessary result of another trait, which in turn evolved under selection pressure. More generally, he opposed what he saw as the genetic determinism of sociobiology and evolutionary psychology.

Biography

Lewontin was born in New York City to Jewish parents. Lewontin attended Forest Hills High School and the Ecole Libre des Hautes Etudes in New York. In 1951, he obtained a bachelors degree in biology from Harvard University. In 1952, he received a master's degree in mathematical statistics followed by a doctorate in zoology in 1954, both from Columbia University where he was a student of Theodosius Dobzhansky. Lewontin held faculty positions at North Carolina State University, the University of Rochester, and the University of Chicago.

In 1973 Lewontin served as Alexander Agassiz Professor of Zoology and Professor of Biology at Harvard until 1998, and as of 2003 was the Alexander Agassiz Research Professor at Harvard. Lewontin has worked with and had great influence on many philosophers of biology, including William C. Wimsatt, Elliott Sober, Philip Kitcher, Elisabeth Lloyd, Peter Godfrey-Smith, and Robert Brandon, often inviting them to work in his lab.

Work in Population Genetics

Lewontin has worked in both theoretical and experimental population genetics. A hallmark of his work has been an interest in new technology. He was the first person to do a computer simulation of the behavior of a single locus (previous simulation work having been of models with multiple loci). In 1960 he and Ken-Ichi Kojima were the first population geneticists to give the equations for change of haplotype frequencies with interacting natural selection at two loci. This set off a wave of theoretical work on two-locus selection in the 1960s and 1970s. Their paper gave a theoretical derivation of the equilibria expected, and also investigated the dynamics of the model by computer iteration. Lewontin later introduced the D' measure of linkage disequilibrium. (An achievement that he would be less happy to claim is that he introduced the name "linkage disequilibrium" itself, one about which many population geneticists have been unenthusiastic).

In 1966, he and Jack Hubby published a paper that revolutionized population genetics. They used protein gel electrophoresis to survey dozens of loci in *Drosophila pseudoobscura*, and reported that a large fraction of the loci were polymorphic, and that at the average locus there was about a 15% chance that the individual was heterozygous. (Harry Harris reported similar results for humans at about the same time). Previous work with gel electrophoresis had been reports of variation in single loci and did not give any sense of how common variation was.

Lewontin and Hubby's paper also discussed the possible explanation of the high levels of variability by either balancing selection or neutral mutation. Although they did not commit themselves to advocating neutrality, this was the first clear statement of the neutral theory for levels of variability within species. Lewontin and Hubby's paper had great impact—the discovery of high levels of molecular variability gave population geneticists ample material to work on, and gave them access to variation at single loci. The possible theoretical explanations of this rampant polymorphism became the focus of most population genetics work thereafter. Martin Kreitman was later to do a pioneering survey of population-level variability in DNA sequences while a Ph.D. student in Lewontin's lab.

Work on Human Genetic Diversity

In a landmark paper, Richard Lewontin identified that most of the variation (80-85%) within human populations is found within local geographic groups and differences attributable to traditional "race" groups are a minor part of human genetic variability (1-15%). In a 2003 paper, A.W.F. Edwards criticized Lewontin's conclusion, that because the probability of racial misclassification of an individual based on variation in a single genetic locus is approximately 30%, race is an invalid taxonomic construct, terming it Lewontin's Fallacy.

RENE-PRIMEVERE LESSON

Rene Primevere Lesson (March 20, 1794-April 28, 1849) was a French surgeon and naturalist.

Lesson was born at Rochefort, and at the age of sixteen he entered the Naval Medical School there. He served in the French Navy during the Napoleonic Wars; in 1811 he was third surgeon on the frigate *Saal*, and in 1813 second surgeon on the *Regulus*.

In 1816 Lesson changed his classification to pharmacist and served as pharmacist and botanist on Duperrey's round-the-world voyage of *La Coquille* (1822-1825), and was also responsible for collecting natural history specimens with his fellow surgeon Prosper Garnot and officer Dumont d'Urville. Lesson was the first naturalist to see live birds of paradise in the Moluccas and New Guinea.

On returning to Paris, he spent seven years preparing the vertebrate zoological section of the official account of the expedition, *Voyage au tour du monde sur La Coquille* (1826-39). During this time he also produced *Manuel d'Ornithologie* (1828), *Traite d'Ornithologie* (1831), *Centurie Zoologique* (1830-32) and *Illustrations de Zoologie* (1832-35).. He also produced several monographs on hummingbirds and one book on birds of paradise. In 1832 he became Deputy Chief

Pharmacist and later (1839) Chief Pharmacist for the Navy at Rochefort. He received the Legion d'Honneur in 1847.

His experience as a ship's surgeon resulted in his two-volume *Manuel d'Histoire Naturelle Medicale et de Pharmacologie* (1833), intended as a handbook for all naval surgeons.

Rene-Primevere Lesson is sometimes confused with his brother Pierre-Adolphe who was also a doctor and sailed with d'Urville in 1826.

ROBERT KOCH

Heinrich Hermann Robert Koch (December 11, 1843 – May 27, 1910) was a German physician. He became famous for isolating *Bacillus anthracis* (1877), the tuberculosis bacillus (1882) and the vibrio cholera (1883) and for his development of Koch's postulates.

He was awarded the Nobel Prize in Physiology or Medicine for his tuberculosis findings in 1905. He is considered one of the founders of microbiology—he inspired such major figures as Paul Ehrlich and Gerhard Domagk.

Biography

Robert Koch was born in Clausthal, Germany as the son of a mining official. He studied medicine under Friedrich Gustav Jakob Henle at the University of Gottingen and graduated in 1866. He then served in the Franco-Prussian War and later became district medical officer in Wollstein (Wolsztyn), Prussian Poland. Working with very limited resources, he became one of the founders of bacteriology, the other major figure being Louis Pasteur.

After Casimir Davaine showed the direct transmission of the anthrax bacillus between cows, Koch studied anthrax more closely. He invented methods to purify the bacillus from blood samples and grow pure cultures. He found that, while it could not survive outside a host for long, anthrax built persisting endospores that could last a long time.

These endospores, embedded in soil, were the cause of unexplained "spontaneous" outbreaks of anthrax. Koch published his findings in 1876, and was rewarded with a job at the Imperial Health Office in Berlin in 1880. In 1881, he urged the sterilization of surgical instruments using heat.

In Berlin, he improved the methods he used in Wollstein, including staining and purification techniques, and bacterial growth media, including agar plates (thanks to the advice of Angelina and Walther Hesse) and the Petri dish, named after its inventor, his assistant Julius Richard Petri. These devices are still used today. With these techniques, he was able to discover the bacterium causing tuberculosis (*Mycobacterium tuberculosis*) in 1882 (he announced the discovery on March 24). Tuberculosis was the cause of one in seven deaths in the mid-19th century.

In 1883, Koch worked with a French research team in Alexandria, Egypt, studying cholera. Koch identified the vibrio bacterium that caused cholera, though he never managed to prove it in experiments. The bacterium had been previously isolated by Italian anatomist Filippo Pacini in 1854, but his work had been ignored due to the predominance of the miasma theory of disease. Koch was unaware of Pacini's work and made an independent discovery, and his greater preeminence allowed the discovery to be widely spread for the benefit of others. In 1965, however, the bacterium was formally renamed *Vibrio cholera Pacini 1854*.

In 1885, he became professor of hygiene at the University of Berlin, and later, in 1891, director of the newly formed Institute of Infectious Diseases, a position which he resigned from in 1904. He started travelling around the world, studying diseases in South Africa, India, and Java.

Probably as important as his work on tuberculosis, for which he was awarded a Nobel Prize (1905), are *Koch's postulates*, which say that *to establish that an organism is the cause of a disease, it must be:*

- found in all cases of the disease examined
- prepared and maintained in a pure culture

- capable of producing the original infection, even after several generations in culture
- retrievable from an inoculated animal and cultured again.

After Koch's success the quality of his own research declined (especially with the fiasco over his ineffective TB cure "tuberculin"), although his pupils found the organisms responsible for diphtheria, typhoid, pneumonia, gonorrhoea, cerebrospinal meningitis, leprosy, bubonic plague, tetanus, and syphilis, among others, by using his methods.

Koch died on from a heart-attack in Baden-Baden, aged 66.

ROBERT HOOKE

Robert Hooke, (18 July 1635 – 3 March 1703) was an English natural philosopher and polymath who played an important role in the scientific revolution, through both experimental and theoretical work.

Hooke is known principally for his law of elasticity (Hooke's Law). He is also remembered for his work as "the father of microscopy" — it was Hooke who coined the term "cell" to describe the basic unit of life — he also assisted Robert Boyle and built the vacuum pumps used in Boyle's gas law experiments. Hooke was an important architect of his time, and a chief surveyor to the City of London after the Great Fire, built some of the earliest Gregorian telescopes, observed the rotations of Mars and Jupiter, and was an early proponent of the theory of evolution through his observations of microscopic fossils. He investigated the phenomenon of refraction, deducing the wave theory of light, and was the first to suggest that matter expands when heated and that air is made of small particles separated by relatively large distances. He also deduced from experiments that gravity follows an inverse square law, and that such a relation governs the motions of the planets, an idea which was subsequently developed by Newton. Much of Hooke's work was conducted in his capacity as curator of experiments of the Royal Society, a post he held from 1662.

Hooke was, by all accounts, a remarkably industrious man, and was at one time simultaneously the curator of the Royal Society and a member of its council, Gresham Professor of Geometry and Chief Surveyor to the City of London.

Hooke's reputation was largely forgotten during the eighteenth century, and this is popularly attributed to a dispute with Isaac Newton over credit for his work on gravitation; Newton, as President of the Royal Society, did much to obscure Hooke, including, it is said, destroying (or failing to preserve) the only known portrait of the man. Hooke's reputation was revived during the twentieth century through studies of Robert Gunther and Margaret 'Espinasse, and after a long period of relative obscurity he is now recognised as one of the most important scientists of his age.

Biography

Much of what is known of Hooke's early life comes from an autobiography that he commenced in 1696, but did not complete. This was referenced by Richard Waller in his introduction to the *The Posthumous Works of Robert Hooke, M.D. S.R.S.*, printed in 1705. The work of Waller, along with John Ward's *Lives of the Gresham Professors* and John Aubrey's *Brief Lives*, form the major near-contemporaneous biographical accounts of Hooke.

Early Life

Robert Hooke was born in 1635 in Freshwater on the Isle of Wight to John Hooke and Cecily Gyles. Robert was the last of four children, two sons and two daughters, and there was an age difference of seven years between him and the next youngest. Their father ecclesiastically served the Church of England, specifically as the curate of Freshwater's Church of All Saints; his three brothers were also ministers. Robert Hooke was expected to succeed in his education and join the Church.

John Hooke also was in charge of a local school, and so was able to teach Robert, at least partly at home perhaps due to the boy's frail health. He was a Royalist and almost certainly one of a groups who went to pay their respects to Charles II when he escaped to the Isle of Wight. Robert, too, grew up to be a staunch monarchist.

As a youth, Robert Hooke was fascinated by observation, mechanical works, and drawing, interests that would be pursued in various ways throughout his life. He dismantled a brass clock and built a wooden replica that, by all accounts, worked "well enough", and he learned to draw, making his own materials from coal, chalk and ruddle.

On his father's death in 1648, Robert was left a sum of one hundred pounds that enabled him to buy an apprenticeship; with his poor health throughout his life but evident mechanical facility his father had it in mind that he might become a watchmaker or limner, though Hooke was also interested in painting. Hooke was an apt student, so although he went to London to take up an apprenticeship, and studied briefly with Samuel Cowper and Peter Lely, he was soon able to enter Westminster School in London, under Dr. Busby, where he lodged his hundred pounds. Hooke quickly mastered Latin and Greek, made some study of Hebrew, and mastered Euclid's *Elements*. Here, too, he embarked on his life-long study of mechanics.

ROBERT GALLO

Robert Charles Gallo (born March 23, 1937) is a U.S. biomedical researcher. He is best known for his role in identifying the Human Immunodeficiency Virus (HIV) as the infectious agent responsible for the Acquired Immune Deficiency Syndrome (AIDS).

Gallo is the director of the Institute of Human Virology, at the University of Maryland School of Medicine in Baltimore, Maryland. He and two longtime scientific collaborators, Robert R. Redfield and William A. Blattner, co-founded the institute in 1996 after intense recruitment by the State of Maryland and the City of Baltimore. In 2005, co founded Profectus BioSciences, Inc., which develops and commercializes technologies to reduce the morbidity and mortality caused by human viral diseases, including the human immunodeficiency virus (HIV). It is situated in Baltimore, Maryland and he is chairman of its Scientific Advisory Board.

Background

Gallo was born in Waterbury, Connecticut to a working-class family of Italian immigrants. He earned a B.S. degree in Biology in 1959 from Providence College and received an M.D. from Jefferson Medical College in Philadelphia, Pennsylvania in 1963. After completing his medical residency and internship at the University of Chicago, he became a researcher at the National Cancer Institute. Gallo states that his choice of profession was influenced by the early death of his sister from leukemia, a disease to which he initially dedicated much of his research.

Retrovirus Work

After listening to a talk by biologist David Baltimore, Gallo became interested in the study of retroviruses. In 1974 he identified the first retrovirus in humans: the "human T-cell leukemia virus," or HTLV.

HIV/AIDS Research and Subsequent Controversy

In 1984, Gallo and his collaborators published a series of four papers in the research journal *Science* arguing that HIV, a retrovirus that had recently been identified in AIDS patients by Luc Montagnier and his collaborators at the Pasteur Institute in Paris, France, was the cause of AIDS. However, the striking similarity between the first two human immunodeficiency virus type 1 (HIV-1) isolates Lai/LAV (formerly LAV, isolated at the Pasteur Institute) and Lai/IIIB (formerly HTLV-IIIB, reported to be isolated from a pooled culture at the Laboratory of Tumour Cell Biology (LTCB) of the National Cancer Institute), suggested contamination in Gallo's lab and provoked controversy in light of the high level of variability found among subsequent HIV-1 isolates.

Since then, there has been considerable and sometimes acrimonious controversy over the priority for the discovery of HIV, including accusations that Gallo's lab improperly used a sample of HIV produced at the Institut Pasteur. In November 1990, the Office of Scientific Integrity at the National Institutes of Health commissioned a group at Roche to analyze archival samples established at the Pasteur Institute and the Laboratory of Tumour Cell Biology (LTCB) of the National Cancer Institute between 1983 and 1985. Retrospective analyses showed that contamination of a culture derived from patient BRU by one from patient LAI was responsible for the provenance of HIV-1 Lai/LAV; the contaminated culture (M2T-/B) was sent to LTCB in September 1983.

Chang et al. (1993) examined archival specimens and reported in *Nature* the detection of six novel HIV-1 sequences in the cultures used to establish the pool: none was closely related to HIV-1 Lai/IIIB. A sample derived from patient LAI contained variants of both HIV-1 Lai/IIIB and HIV-1 Lai/LAV, and a sequence identical to a variant of HIV-1 Lai/IIIB was detected in the contaminated M2T-/B culture. They concluded that the pool, and probably another LTCB culture, MoV, were contaminated between October 1983 and early 1984 by variants of HIV-1 Lai from the M2T-/B culture. Contamination of this kind is common in labs handling viruses, and must be carefully guarded against. In this case, the origin of the HIV-1 Lai/IIIB isolate also was patient LAI.

Today it is generally agreed that Montagnier's group first identified HIV, although Gallo's group is credited with much of the science that made the discovery possible, and to demonstrating that it causes AIDS. Gallo's group also was the first to grow the virus in an immortalized cell line, leading to the development of blood tests for HIV and the ability to screen donated blood for this virus. Also, Gallo insisted the work of Montagnier had relied on a technique previously developed by Gallo for growing T cells in the laboratory by supplementing interleukin-2.

The two scientists continued be at the centre of a bitter dispute between the United States and France over royalties from the blood test patent until 1987, when they agreed to share credit for the discovery of HIV. In the November 29, 2002, issue of *Science*, Gallo and Montagnier published a series of articles, one of which was co-written by both scientists, in which they acknowledged the pivotal roles that each had played in the discovery of HIV.

In 1995, Gallo published his discovery that chemokines, a class of naturally occurring compounds, can block HIV and halt the progression of AIDS. This was heralded by *Science* magazine as one of the top scientific breakthroughs within the same year of his publication.

The role chemokines play in controlling the progression of HIV infection has influenced thinking on how AIDS works against the human immune system and led to a class of drugs used to treat HIV, the chemokine antagonists or entry inhibitors.

Gallo's team at the Institute of Human Virology maintain an ongoing programme of scientific research and clinical care and treatment for people living with HIV/AIDS, treating more that 4,000 patients in Baltimore and nearly 100,000 patients at institute-supported clinics in Africa and the Caribbean. In July 2007, Gallo and his team were awarded a $15 million grant from the Bill and Melinda Gates Foundation for research into a preventive vaccine for HIV/AIDS.

ROSALIND FRANKLIN

Rosalind Elsie Franklin (25 July 1920 Notting Hill, London – 16 April 1958 Chelsea, London) was an English biophysicist and X-ray crystallographer who made very important contributions to the understanding of the fine structures of DNA, viruses, coal and graphite. Franklin is best known for her work on the X-ray diffraction images of DNA which were an important influence on Crick and Watson's 1953 hypothesis regarding the structure of DNA. When her work was published it also presented critical evidence in support of their hypothesis. Later she led pioneering work on the tobacco mosaic and polio viruses. She died in 1958 of complications arising from cancer of the ovary.

Background

Franklin was born in Notting Hill, London into an affluent and influential British-Jewish family. Her father was Ellis Arthur Franklin (1894-1964), a London merchant banker and her mother was Muriel Frances Waley (1894-1976); she was the elder daughter and second of the family of five children.

Her uncle was Herbert Samuel (later Viscount Samuel) who was Home Secretary in 1916 and the first practicing Jew to serve in the British Cabinet. He was also the first High Commissioner (effectively governor) for the British Mandate of Palestine.

Her aunt Helen Carolin Franklin was married to Norman de Mattos Bentwich, who was Attorney General in the British Mandate of Palestine. She was active in trade union organization and women's suffrage, and was later a member of the London County Council.

Franklin was educated at St. Paul's Girls' School where she excelled in Latin and sport. Her family were actively involved with a Working Men's College, where Ellis Franklin, her father, taught electricity, magnetism and the history of the Great War in the evenings and later became vice principal. Later they helped settle Jewish refugees from Europe who had escaped the Nazis.

University Education

In the summer of 1938 Franklin went to Newnham College, Cambridge. She passed her finals in 1941, but was only awarded a degree titular, as women were not entitled to degrees (BA Cantab.) from Cambridge at the time. In 1945 Rosalind Franklin received her PhD from Cambridge University.

British Coal Utilisation Research Association

She worked for Ronald Norish between 1941 and 1942. Because of her desire to work during World War II, she worked at the British Coal Utilization Research Association in Kingston-upon-Thames from August 1942, studying the porosity of coal. Her work helped spark the idea of high-strength carbon fibres and was the basis of her doctoral degree-"The physical chemistry of solid organic colloids with special reference to coal and related materials" that she earned in 1945.

Laboratoire Central des Services Chimiques de l'Etat

After the war ended Franklin accepted an offer to work in Paris with Jacques Mering. She learned x-ray diffraction techniques during her three years at the *Laboratoire central des services chimiques de l'Etat.* She seemed to have been very happy there and earned an international reputation based on her published research on the structure of coal. In 1950 she sought work in England and in June 1950 she was appointed to a position at King's College London.

King's College London

In January 1951, Franklin started working as a research associate at King's College London in the Medical Research Council's (MRC) Biophysics Unit, directed by John Randall. Although originally she was to have worked on x-ray diffraction of proteins in solution, her work was redirected to DNA fibres before she started working at King's. Maurice Wilkins and Raymond Gosling had been carrying out x-ray diffraction analysis of DNA in the Unit since 1950.

Franklin, working with her student Raymond Gosling started to apply her expertise in x-ray diffraction techniques to the structure of DNA. They discovered that there were two forms of DNA: at high humidity (when wet) the DNA fibre became long and thin, when it was dried it became short and fat. These were termed DNA 'B' and 'A' respectively. The work on DNA was subsequently divided, Franklin taking the A form to study and Wilkins the 'B' form. The x-ray diffraction pictures taken by Franklin at this time have been called, by J. D. Bernal, "amongst the most beautiful x-ray photographs of any substance ever taken".

By the end of 1951 it was generally accepted in King's that the B form of DNA was a helix, but Franklin in particular was unconvinced that the A form of DNA was helical in structure. As a practical joke Franklin and Gosling produced a death notice regretting the loss of helical crystalline DNA (A-DNA). During 1952 Rosalind Franklin and Raymond Gosling worked at applying the Patterson function to the x-ray pictures of DNA they had produced, this was a long and labour-intensive approach but would give an insight into the structure of the molecule.

In February 1953 Francis Crick and James D. Watson of the Cavendish Laboratory in Cambridge University had started to build a model of the B form of DNA using similar data to that available to the team at King's. Model building had been applied successfully in the elucidation of the structure of the alpha helix by Linus Pauling in 1951, but Rosalind Franklin was opposed to building theoretical models, taking the view that building a model was only to be undertaken after the structure was known. Watson and Crick then indirectly obtained a pre-publication version of Franklin's DNA X-ray diffraction data (possibly without her knowledge), and a pre-publication manuscript by Pauling and Corey, giving them critical insights into the DNA structure. Francis Crick and James Watson then published their model in *Nature* on 25 April 1953 in an article describing the double-helical structure of DNA with a small footnote to Franklin's data. Articles by Wilkins and Franklin illuminating their x-ray diffraction data published in the same issue of *Nature* supported the Crick and Watson model for the B form of DNA. Franklin eventually left King's College London in March 1953 to move to Birkbeck College in a move that had been planned for some time. Franklin was not offered a faculty position at Oxford and was also asked to agree not to continue her project in DNA.

ROBERT FORTUNE

Robert Fortune (September 16, 1812-April 13, 1880), was a Scottish botanist and traveller best known for introducing tea plants from China to India.

Travels and Botanical Introductions to Europe

Fortune was born in Kelloe, Berwickshire. He was employed in the botanical garden in Edinburgh, and later in the Royal

Horticultural Society's garden at Chiswick, and following the Treaty of Nanking in 1842 was sent out by the Society to collect plants in China.

His travels resulted in the introduction to Europe of many beautiful flowers; but another three-year-long journey, undertaken in 1848 on behalf of the British East India Company, had much more important consequences, resulting in the successful introduction of 20,000 tea plants to Darjeeling of India. His personal endeavour created the tea industries of India and Ceylon and ended China's natural monopoly of tea. He was the first European to discover that varieties of teas such as black tea and green tea were produced from the same plant.

In subsequent journeys he visited Formosa and Japan, and described the culture of the silkworm and the manufacture of rice. He introduced many trees, shrubs and flowers to the West, including the cumquat, a climbing double yellow rose ('Fortune's Double Yellow' (syn. Gold of Ophir) which proved a failure in England's climate) and many varieties of tree peonies, azaleas and chrysanthemums. A climbing white rose that he brought back from China in 1850, believed to be a natural cross between *Rosa laevigata* and *R. banksiae*, was dubbed *R. fortuniana* (syn. *R. fortuneana*) in his honour. This rose, too, proved a failure in England, though it serves as a valuable rootstock in Australia and the southern regions of the United States.

The incidents of his travels were related in a succession of interesting books. He died in London.

The standard author abbreviation **Fortune** is used to indicate this individual as the author when citing a botanical name.

RONALD FISHER

Sir Ronald Aylmer Fisher, (17 February 1890 – 29 July 1962) was an English statistician, evolutionary biologist, and geneticist. He was described by Anders Hald as "a genius who almost single-handedly created the foundations for modern statistical science" and

Richard Dawkins described him as "the greatest of Darwin's successors".

Early Life

Fisher was born in East Finchley in London, England, to George and Katie Fisher. His father was a successful fine arts dealer. He had a happy childhood, being doted on by three older sisters, an older brother, and his mother, who died when Fisher was 14. His father lost his business in several ill-considered transactions only 18 months later.

Although Fisher had very poor eyesight, he was a precocious student, winning the Neeld Medal (a competitive essay in Mathematics) at Harrow School at the age of 16. Because of his poor eyesight, he was tutored in mathematics without the aid of paper and pen, which developed his ability to visualize problems in geometrical terms, as opposed to using algebraic manipulations. He was legendary in being abie to produce mathematical results without setting down the intermediate steps. He also developed a strong interest in biology, and, especially, evolution.

In 1909 he won a scholarship to Gonville and Caius College, Cambridge. There he formed many friendships and became enthralled with the heady intellectual atmosphere. At Cambridge, Fisher learned of the newly rediscovered theory of Mendelian genetics; he saw biometry—and its growing corpus of statistical methods—as a potential way to reconcile the discontinuous nature of Mendelian inheritance with continuous variation and gradual evolution. However, his foremost concern was eugenics, which he saw as a pressing social as well as scientific issue that encompassed both genetics and statistics. In 1911 he was involved in forming the Cambridge University Eugenics Society with such luminaries as John Maynard Keynes, R. C. Punnett and Horace Darwin (Charles Darwin's son). The group was active, and held monthly meetings, often featuring addresses by leaders of mainstream eugenics organizations, such as the Eugenics Education Society of London, founded by Charles Darwin's half-cousin, Francis Galton in 1909.

After graduating in 1913, Fisher was eager to join the army in anticipation of Great Britain's entry into World War I; however, he failed the medical examinations (repeatedly) because of his eyesight. Over the next six years, he worked as a statistician for the City of London. For his war work, he took up teaching physics and mathematics at a series of public schools, including Bradfield College in Berkshire, as well as aboard H.M. Training Ship *Worcester*. Major Leonard Darwin (another of Charles Darwin's sons) and an unconventional and vivacious friend he called Gudruna were almost his only contacts with his Cambridge circle. They sustained him through this difficult period. A bright spot in his life was that Gudruna matched him to her sister Eileen Guinness; they married in 1917 when she was only 17. With the sisters' help, he set up a subsistence farming operation on the Bradfield estate, where they had a large garden and raised animals, learning to make do on very little. They lived through the war without ever using their food coupons. During this period, Fisher started writing book reviews for the *Eugenic Review* and gradually increased his interest in genetic and statistical work. He volunteered to undertake all such reviews for the journal, and was hired to a part-time position by Major Darwin. He published several articles on biometry during this period, including the ground-breaking "The Correlation Between Relatives on the Supposition of Mendelian Inheritance", written in 1916 and published in 1918. This paper laid the foundation for what came to be known as biometrical genetics, and introduced the very important methodology of the analysis of variance, which was a considerable advance over the correlation methods used previously. The paper showed very convincingly that the inheritance of traits measurable by real values, the values of continuous variables, is consistent with Mendelian principles.

With the end of the war he went looking for a new job, and was offered one at the famed Galton Laboratory by Karl Pearson. Because he saw the developing rivalry with Pearson as a professional obstacle, however, he accepted instead a temporary job as a statistician with a small agricultural station in the country in 1919.

RENATO DULBECCO

Renato Dulbecco (born February 22, 1914) is an Italian virologist who won a 1975 Nobel Prize in Physiology or Medicine for his work on reverse transcriptase. In 1973 he was awarded the Louisa Gross Horwitz Prize from Columbia University together with Theodore Puck and Harry Eagle.

Early Life

He was born in Catanzaro (Southern Italy) to a Calabrese mother and a Ligurian father. He graduated from high school at 16, then moved to the University of Turin. Despite a strong interest for mathematics and physics, he decided to study medicine. At only 22, he graduated in morbid anatomy and pathology under the supervision of professor Giuseppe Levi. During these years he met Salvador Luria and Rita Levi-Montalcini, whose friendship and encouragement would later bring him to the United States. In 1936 he was called up for military service as a medical officer, and later (1938) discharged. In 1940 Italy entered World War II and Dulbecco was recalled and sent to the front in France and Russia, where he was wounded. After hospitalization and the collapse of Fascism, he joined the resistance against the German occupation.

Scientific Career

After the war he resumed his work at Levi's laboratory, but soon he moved, together with Levi-Montalcini, to the USA, where, in Bloomington, Indiana, he worked with Salvador Luria on bacteriophages. In the summer of 1949 he moved to Caltech, joining Max Delbruck's group. There he started his studies about animal oncoviruses. In the late 1950s, he took Howard Temin as a student, with whom, and together with David Baltimore, he would later share the 1975 Nobel Prize in Physiology or Medicine for "their discoveries concerning the interaction between tumour viruses and the genetic material of the cell." Temin and Baltimore arrived at the discovery of reverse transcriptase simultaneously and independently from each other; although Dulbecco did not take direct part in either of their experiments, he had taught the two methods they used to make the discovery.

Throughout this time he also worked with Marguerite Vogt. In 1962, he moved to the Salk Institute and then in 1972 to The Imperial Cancer Research Fund (now named the Cancer Research UK London Research Institute). In 1986 he was among the scientists who launched the Human Genome Project. In 1993 he moved back to Italy, where he is currently president of the Institute of Biomedical Technologies at C.N.R. (National Council of Research) in Milan. He also retains his position on the faculty of Salk Institute for Biological Studies.

REMBERT DODOENS

Rembert Dodoens (Mechelen June 29, 1517 – Leyden March 10, 1585) was a Flemish physician and botanist, also known under his Latinized name **Rembertus Dodonaeus**.

In 1530 he started his studies of medicine, cosmography and geography at the University of Leuven, where he graduated in 1535. He established himself as a physician in Mechelen in 1538. He married Kathelijne De Bruyn(e) in 1539. He had a short stay in Basel (1542-1546). He turned down a chair at the University of Leuven in 1557. He equally turned down an offer to become court physician of emperor Philip II of Spain. He became the court physician of the Austrian emperor Rudolph II in Vienna (1575-1578). He then became professor in medicine at the University of Leiden in 1582.

Dodoens' herbal *Cruydeboeck* with 715 images (1554) was influenced by that of Leonhart Fuchs. He divided the plant kingdom in six groups. It treated in detail especially the medicinal herbs, which made this work, in the eyes of many, a pharmacopoeia.

It was translated first into French in 1557 by Charles de L'Ecluse (*Histoire des Plantes*), into English (via L'Ecluse) in 1578 by Henry Lyte (*A new herbal, or historie of plants*), and later into Latin in 1583. In his times, it was the most translated book after the Bible. It became a work of worldwide renown, used as a reference book for two centuries. Dodoens's last book, *Stirpium historiae pemptades sex* (1583) was the Latin translation of his *Cruydeboeck*. It was used as a source by John Gerard for his *Herball*.

Dodoens is commemorated in the plant genus *Dodonaea*, which was named after him by Carolus Linnaeus. **Dodoens** indicates Rembert Dodoens when citing a botanical name.

RICHARD DAWKINS

Clinton Richard Dawkins, (born March 26, 1941) is a British ethologist, evolutionary biologist and popular science writer. He holds the Charles Simonyi Chair for the Public Understanding of Science at the University of Oxford and is a professorial fellow of New College, Oxford.

Dawkins came to prominence with his 1976 book *The Selfish Gene*, which popularised the gene-centred view of evolution and introduced the term *meme*. In 1982, he made a widely cited contribution to evolutionary biology with the theory, presented in his book *The Extended Phenotype*, that the phenotypic effects of a gene are not necessarily limited to an organism's body, but can stretch far into the environment, including the bodies of other organisms.

In addition to his biological work, Dawkins is well known for his views on atheism, evolution, creationism and religion. He is a prominent critic of creationism and intelligent design.

In his 1986 book *The Blind Watchmaker*, he argued against the watchmaker analogy, an argument for the existence of a supernatural creator based upon the observed complexity of living organisms, and instead described evolutionary processes as being analogous to a *blind* watchmaker. He has since written several popular science books, and has made regular appearances on television and radio programmes, predominantly discussing the aforementioned topics.

Dawkins is an atheist, secular humanist, sceptic, scientific rationalist, and supporter of the Brights movement. He has widely been referred to in the media as "Darwin's Rottweiler", by analogy with English biologist T. H. Huxley, who was known as "Darwin's

Bulldog" for his advocacy of natural selection. In his 2006 book *The God Delusion*, Dawkins contends that a supernatural creator almost certainly does not exist and that religious faith qualifies as a delusion " as a fixed false belief.

As of November 2007, the English language version had sold more than 1.5 million copies and had been translated into 31 other languages, making it his most popular book to date.

Biography

Richard Dawkins was born on March 26, 1941, in Nairobi, Colony of Kenya, British Empire.. His father, Clinton John Dawkins, was a soldier who moved to Kenya from England during the Second World War to join the Allied Forces, returning to England in 1949 when Richard was eight. Both of his parents were interested in natural sciences, and they answered Dawkins' questions in scientific terms.

Dawkins describes his childhood as "a normal Anglican upbringing", but reveals that he began doubting the existence of God when he was about nine years old. He later reconverted because he was persuaded by the argument from design, an argument for the existence of God or a creator based on perceived evidence of order, purpose, design or direction " or some combination of these " in nature. However, he began to feel that the customs of the Church of England were absurd, and had more to do with dictating morals than with God. Later, when he better understood the process of evolution, his religious position again changed, because he felt that natural selection could account for the complexity of life in purely material terms, rendering a supernatural designer unnecessary.

Dawkins attended Oundle School from 1954 to 1959. He studied zoology at Balliol College, Oxford, where he was tutored by Nobel Prize-winning ethologist Nikolaas Tinbergen, graduating with a second class degree in 1962. He continued as a research student under Tinbergen's supervision at the University of Oxford, receiving his M.A. and D.Phil. degrees in 1966, while staying as a research assistant for another year. Tinbergen was a pioneer in the study of animal behaviour, particularly the questions of instinct, learning and choice. Dawkins' research in this period concerned models of animal decision making.

From 1967 to 1969, Dawkins was an assistant professor of zoology at the University of California, Berkeley. During this period, the students and faculty at UC Berkeley were largely opposed to the ongoing Vietnam War, and Dawkins became heavily involved in the anti-war demonstrations and activities. He returned to the University of Oxford in 1970 taking a position as a lecturer, and " in 1990 " a reader, in zoology. In 1995, he was appointed Simonyi Professor for the Public Understanding of Science at the University of Oxford, a position that had been endowed by Charles Simonyi with the express intention that the holder "be expected to make important contributions to the public understanding of some scientific field". Since 1970, he has been a fellow of New College, Oxford.

In the 1970s Dawkins turned to explaining the life sciences to a popular audience, beginning with his well-known and influential, 1976 book, *The Selfish Gene.*

Dawkins has delivered a number of inaugural and other notable lectures, including the Henry Sidgwick Memorial Lecture (1989), first Erasmus Darwin Memorial Lecture (1990), Michael Faraday Lecture (1991), T.H. Huxley Memorial Lecture (1992), Irvine Memorial Lecture (1997), Sheldon Doyle Lecture (1999), Tinbergen Lecture (2004) and Tanner Lectures (2003). In 1991, he gave the Royal Institution Christmas Lectures for Children (released on DVD in 2007 as *Growing Up in the Universe*). He has also served as editor of a number of prominent journals, and has acted as editorial advisor to *Encarta Encyclopedia* and the *Encyclopedia of Evolution.* He is a senior editor of the Council for Secular Humanism's *Free Inquiry* magazine, for which he also writes a column. He has been a member of the editorial board of *Skeptic* magazine since its foundation.

He has sat on numerous judging panels for awards as diverse as the Royal Society's Faraday Award and the British Academy Television Awards, and has been president of the Biological Sciences section of the British Association for the Advancement of Science. In 2004, Balliol College, Oxford instituted the Dawkins Prize, awarded for "outstanding research into the ecology and behaviour of animals whose welfare and survival may be endangered by human activities".

In September 2008, Dawkins is due to retire from his post as Simonyi Professor for the Public Understanding of Science, due to reaching the university's mandatory retirement age.

In 1967, Dawkins married fellow ethologist Marian Stamp, and they divorced in 1984. Later that year, Dawkins married Eve Barham " with whom he had a daughter, Juliet Emma Dawkins " but they too divorced, and Barham died of cancer in early 1999. In 1992, he married actress Lalla Ward. Dawkins had met her through their mutual friend Douglas Adams, who had previously worked with Ward on the BBC science-fiction television programme *Doctor Who* (in 2008 Dawkins made a cameo appearance as himself in the Doctor Who episode *The Stolen Earth*). Ward has illustrated over half of Dawkins' books and co-narrated the audio versions of two of his books, *The Ancestor's Tale* and *The God Delusion.*

Evolutionary Biology

In his scientific works, Dawkins is best known for his popularisation of the gene-centred view of evolution. This view is most clearly set out in his books *The Selfish Gene* (1976), where he notes that "all life evolves by the differential survival of replicating entities", and *The Extended Phenotype* (1982), in which he describes natural selection as "the process whereby replicators out-propagate each other". In his role as an ethologist, interested in animal behaviour and its relation to natural selection, he advocates the idea that the gene is the principal unit of selection in evolution.

Dawkins has consistently been sceptical about non-adaptive processes in evolution (such as spandrels, described by Gould and Lewontin) and about selection at levels "above" that of the gene. He is particularly sceptical about the practical possibility or importance of group selection as a basis for understanding altruism.

This behaviour appears at first to be an evolutionary paradox, since helping others costs precious resources and decreases one's own fitness. Previously, many had interpreted this as an aspect of group selection: individuals were doing what was best for the survival of the population or species as a whole, and not specifically for themselves. British evolutionary biologist W. D. Hamilton had used the gene-centred view to explain altruism in terms of inclusive fitness and kin selection " that individuals behave altruistically toward their close relatives, who share many of their own genes. Similarly, Robert Trivers, thinking in terms of the gene-centred model, developed the theory of reciprocal altruism, whereby one organism provides a benefit to another in the expectation of future reciprocation. Dawkins popularised these ideas in *The Selfish Gene*, and developed them in his own work.

Critics of Dawkins' approach suggest that taking the gene as the unit of *selection* " of a single event in which an individual either succeeds or fails to reproduce " is misleading, but that the gene could be better described as a unit of *evolution* " of the long-term changes in allele frequencies in a population. In *The Selfish Gene*, Dawkins explains that he is using George C. Williams' definition of the gene as "that which segregates and recombines with appreciable frequency". Another common objection is that genes cannot survive alone, but must cooperate to build an individual, and therefore cannot be an independent "unit". In *The Extended Phenotype*, Dawkins suggests that because of genetic recombination and sexual reproduction, from an individual gene's viewpoint all other genes are part of the environment to which it is adapted.

Advocates for higher levels of selection such as Richard Lewontin, David Sloan Wilson, and Elliot Sober suggest that there are many phenomena (including altruism) that gene-based selection cannot satisfactorily explain. The philosopher Mary Midgley, whom Dawkins has intermittently debated since the late 1970s, has criticised gene selection, memetics and sociobiology as being excessively reductionist.

In a set of controversies over the mechanisms and interpretation of evolution (the so-called "Darwin Wars"), one faction was often named after Dawkins and its rival after American biologist Stephen Jay Gould, reflecting the pre-eminence of each as a populariser of pertinent ideas. In particular, Dawkins and Gould have been prominent commentators in the controversy over sociobiology and evolutionary psychology, with Dawkins generally approving and Gould generally critical. A typical example of Dawkins' position was his scathing review of *Not in Our Genes* by Steven Rose, Leon J. Kamin and Richard C. Lewontin. Two other thinkers on the subject often considered to be in the same camp as Dawkins are Steven Pinker and Daniel Dennett; Dennett has promoted a gene-centred view of evolution and defended reductionism in biology. Despite their academic disagreements, Dawkins and Gould did not have a hostile personal relationship, and Dawkins dedicated a large portion of his 2003 book *A Devil's Chaplain* posthumously to Gould, who had died the previous year.

Dawkins' next book, which will marshal empirical evidence supporting the theory of evolution, is scheduled to be published in the United States by Free Press on November 24, 2009, the 150th anniversary of the publication of Charles Darwin's seminal *On the Origin of Species.*

SIMON STEVIN

Simon Stevin (1548/49 – 1620) was a Flemish mathematician and engineer. He was active in a great many areas of science and engineering, both theoretical and practical. He also translated various mathematical terms into Dutch, making it one of the few European languages in which the word for mathematics, *wiskunde*, was not derived from Greek (via Latin).

Biography

Stevin was born in Bruges, Flanders (now Belgium) in the year 1548 by Antheunis Stevin and Cathelyne van der Poort. Very little has been recorded about his life. Even the exact date of birth and the date and place of his death (The Hague or Leiden) are uncertain. It is known that he left a widow with two children; and one or two hints scattered throughout his works inform us that he began life as a merchant's clerk in Antwerp, that he travelled in Poland, Denmark and other parts of northern Europe. After his travels, he became advisor and teacher of Prince Maurice of Nassau, who asked his advice on many occasions, and made him a public officer—at first director of the so-called "waterstaet" (the government authority for public works), and later quartermaster-general. In Bruges there is a Simon Stevin Square which contains his statue by Eugen Simonis, which includes his inclined plane diagram.

Discoveries and Inventions

His claims to fame are varied. His contemporaries were most struck by his invention of a so-called land yacht, a carriage with sails, of which a little model had been preserved in Scheveningen until 1802. The carriage itself had been lost long before. Around the year 1600 Stevin, with Prince Maurice of Orange and twenty-six others, made use of it on the beach between Scheveningen and Petten. The carriage was propelled solely by the force of wind, and acquired a speed which exceeded that of horses.

Philosophy of Science

Stevin had developed a theory about a bygone age of wisdom, for which even Hugo Grotius gave him great credit. Stevin's goal was to bring about a second age of wisdom, in which mankind would have recovered all of its earlier knowledge. He had deduced that the language spoken in this age would have had to be Dutch, because, as he had showed empirically, in that language, more concepts could be indicated with monosyllabic words than in any of the (European) languages he had compared it with. This was one of the reasons why he wrote all of his works in Dutch and left translations to others. The other reason was that he wanted his works to be practically useful to people who had not mastered the common scientific language of the time, Latin.

SERGE RUDAZ

Serge Rudaz (born August 19, 1954, pronounced "Ru-DAH") is a Canadian theoretical physicist and Professor of Physics at the University of Minnesota. He previously served as the Director of Undergraduate Studies of the University of Minnesota's Physics Department, and is now the Director of Undergraduate Honours at the University of Minnesota. Rudaz received his Ph.D. in 1979 from Cornell University and his undergraduate degree from McGill University.

Teaching

Rudaz is a veteran instructor of physics. He finds it critical that students understand how more complex phenomena can be explained by the basic laws of physics. In introductory level courses, he emphasizes particularly Newton's second law, but he has noted that in more advanced topics and particularly in quantum physics, "It's not just F=ma!" Such an understanding of basic principles, he says, will prevent students from viewing physics as "an ad hoc collection of recipes."

Rudaz is the recipient of the 1998 IT Best Instructor Award and the 1992 Outstanding Instructor Award, both from the IT Student Board of the University of Minnesota. On April 3rd, 2006, he was awarded the George W. Taylor/IT Alumni Society Award for Distinguished Teaching.

In the spring of 2007, Rudaz was named as the director of the University of Minnesota's new campus-wide Honours programme, slated to begin operation during the fall of 2008.

SIMON NEWCOMB

Simon Newcomb (March 12, 1835 – July 11, 1909) was a Canadian-American astronomer and mathematician. Though he had little conventional schooling, he made important contributions to timekeeping as well as writing on economics, statistics and authoring a science fiction novel.

The Life of Newcomb

Newcomb was born in the town of Wallace, Nova Scotia. His parents were Emily Prince, the daughter of a New Brunswick magistrate, and itinerant school teacher John Burton Newcomb. John moved around teaching in different parts of Canada, particularly in different villages in Nova Scotia and Prince Edward Island. Newcomb seems to have had little conventional schooling other than from his father and from a short apprenticeship to Dr Foshay, a charlatan herbalist, in New Brunswick in 1851. Nevertheless, his father provided him with an excellent foundation for his future studies. Newcomb's apprenticeship with Dr. Forshay occurred when he was but 16 years old.

They entered an agreement that Newcomb would serve a five year apprenticeship during which time Foshay would train him in using herbs to treat illnesses. For two years he was an apprentice but became increasingly unhappy and disillusioned with his apprenticeship and about Foshay's unscientific approach, realising that the man was a charlatan. He made the decision to walk out on Foshay and break their agreement. He walked the 120 miles to port of Calais in Maine where he met the captain of a ship who agreed to take him to Salem, Massachusetts so that he could join his father. In about 1854, he joined his father in Salem (John Newcomb had moved earlier to the United States), and the two journeyed together to Maryland.

After arriving in Maryland, Newcomb taught for two years from 1854 to 1856; for the first year in a country school in Massey's Cross Roads, Kent County, then for a year at a school not far south in Sudlersville. In his spare time he studied a variety of subjects such as political economy and religion, but his deepest studies were made in mathematics and astronomy. In particular he read Newton's *Principia* at this time. In 1856 he took up a position as a private tutor close to Washington and he often travelled to that city to study mathematics in the libraries there. He was able to borrow a copy of Bowditch's translation of Laplace's *Traite de mecanique celeste* from the library of the Smithsonian Institution but found that the mathematics which the book contained was rather beyond his current knowledge.

Newcomb studied mathematics and physics privately and supported himself with some school-teaching before becoming a human computer (a functionary in charge of calculations) at the Nautical Almanac Office in Cambridge, Massachusetts in 1857. At around the same time, he enrolled at the Lawrence Scientific School of Harvard University, graduating BS in 1858.

SETH NEDDERMEYER

Seth Henry Neddermeyer (16 September 1907, Richmond, Michigan-29 January 1988, Seattle, Washington) was an American physicist who worked in the Manhattan Project. He had been Carl D. Anderson's student at Caltech. In 1937, he helped discover muons using cloud chamber measurements of cosmic rays.

Manhattan Project Work

While at Los Alamos, Neddermeyer was an early advocate for development of an implosion technique for assembling a critical mass in an atomic bomb. While implosion was previously suggested by Richard Tolman as early as 1942, and discussed in the introductory lectures given to Los Alamos scientists by Robert Serber, Neddermeyer was one of the first to urge its full development. Unable to find much initial enthusiasm for the concept amongst his fellow Los Alamos scientists, Neddermeyer presented the first substantial technical analysis of implosion in late April 1943. Though many remained unimpressed, Robert Oppenheimer appointed Neddermeyer the head of a new group to test implosion. Neddermeyer embarked on an intensive series of experiments testing cylindrical implosions.

Nevertheless, seemingly irresolvable problems with shockwave uniformity brought progress on implosion to a crawl. At the urging of James Conant, Oppenheimer, brought in George Kistiakowsky (who had a specialized knowledge in the precision use of explosives) to help jumpstart flagging programme in January 1944. In mid-June

1944 Kistiakowsky's report to Oppenheimer about the dysfunctionality within the implosion team led to the ouster of Neddermeyer and his replacement by Kistiakowsky. Neddermeyer was said to have been much embittered by this event.

Accordingly, it was left to others like Kistiakowsky (who contributed a background in military ordnance and explosives), Robert Christy (who contributed the insight that a subcritical sphere of plutonium could be imploded to a critical mass), John von Neumann (who contributed the breakthrough mathematical model for using shaped charges to create a truly spherical implosion), and Edward Teller (whose knowledge of the compressibility of metals lead to the use of density change to achieve criticality rather than mere, same-density, "assembly"), to complete the work. The implosion method championed by Neddermeyer was used in the first atom bomb exploded (Trinity test), the Fat Man bomb dropped on Nagasaki, and almost all modern weapons.

In 1982, he was awarded with the Enrico Fermi award.

STANISLAV MIKHEYEV

Stanislav Pavlovich Mikeyev is a Russian physicist best known as one of the discoverers of the MSW effect.

Research, Education and Achievements

Stanislav Mikheyev graduated from Faculty of Physics of the Moscow State University in 1965. He then became a researcher at Lebedev Physical Institute. Since 1970 he has been a researcher at the Institute for Nuclear Research of the USSR Academy of Sciences (Russian Academy of Sciences since 1991). He has worked on Baksan Underground Scintillator Telescope for a long time. He has been the leader of two experiments carried out on Baksan Telescope: observation of upward-going muons and searches for superheavy magnetic monopoles. He earned his Ph.D. in physics from the Institute for Nuclear Research in 1983.

In 1985 Mikheyev and A. Smirnov considered the propagation of oscillating neutrinos in matter with varying density and suggested an explanation for the solar neutrino problem (the MSW effect). From 1991 to 1998 Mikheyev worked on the MACRO detector. His current activities are related to the Baksan Neutrino Observatory, the Baikal Neutrino Telescope and the T2K experiment.

In 2006, Mikheyev, Smirnov and Wolfenstein were awarded the Bruno Pontecorvo Prize. Recently these three scientists have been awarded the 2008 J. J. Sakurai Prize as well.

SAMUEL ABRAHAM GOUDSMIT

Samuel Abraham Goudsmit (born July 11, 1902 Den Haag, The Netherlands, died December 4, 1978 in Reno, Nevada) was a Dutch-American physicist famous for jointly proposing the concept of electron spin with George Eugene Uhlenbeck. He studied physics at the University of Leiden under Paul Ehrenfest, where he obtained his PhD in 1927. After receiving his PhD, Goudsmit served as a Professor at the University of Michigan between 1927 and 1946. In 1930 he co-authored a text with Linus Pauling titled *The Structure of Line Spectra.*

He was also the scientific head of the Alsos mission of the Manhattan Project, which was designed to assess the progress of the Nazi atomic bomb project. In the book *Alsos* published in 1947, Goudsmit concluded that the Germans did not get close to creating a weapon, which he attributed to the inability of science to function under a totalitarian state (the development of atomic weapons by at least two other totalitarian states has been seen to go against this conclusion, although it needs to be said that later atomic weapons were developed with the knowledge of their possibility, and also sometimes with stolen technology).

His other conclusion, that the German scientists simply did not understand how to make an atomic bomb, has been disputed by later historians (see Heisenberg), but his assessment of the lack of progress in the German programme — if not his conclusions as to *why* it was that way — has generally held up over time. After the war he was briefly a professor at Northwestern University and from 1948-1970 was a senior scientist at the Brookhaven National Laboratory, chairing the Physics Department 1952-1960. He meanwhile became well known as the Editor-in-chief of the leading physics journal Physical Review, published by the American Physical Society. On his retirement as editor in 1974, Goudsmit moved to the faculty of the University of Nevada in Reno.

He also made some scholarly contributions to egyptology published in Expedition, Summer 1972, pp. 13-16 ; American Journal of Archaeology 78, 1974 p. 78; and Journal of Near Eastern Studies 40, 1981 pp.43-46. The Samuel A. Goudsmit Collection of Egyptian Antiquities resides at the Kelsey Museum of Archaeology, The University of Michigan, Ann Arbor, MI..

STEVEN CHU

Steven Chu (b. February 28, 1948, St. Louis, Missouri) is an American experimental physicist. He is known for his research in laser cooling and trapping of atoms, which won him the Nobel Prize in Physics in 1997. His current research is concerned primarily with the study of biological systems at the single molecule level. He is currently Professor of Physics and Molecular and Cellular Biology of University of California, Berkeley and the director of the Lawrence Berkeley National Laboratory. As global warming warnings grow more dire, Chu is currently pushing his scientists at Lawrence Berkeley National Laboratory and industry to develop technologies to reverse climate change. Chief in Chu's campaign is an unprecedented research pact reached between UC Berkeley, oil industry giant BP, the Lawrence Berkeley Lab and the University of Illinois.

Nearly US$400 million in new lab space will expand energy-related molecular work centred at Lawrence Berkeley that involves a cast of partners around the world; a US$160 million Energy Biosciences Institute to be built in three years and funded by BP will include Chu's separate solar energy programme.

Education and Career

Steven Chu received his bachelor's degree in 1970 from the University of Rochester, and his doctorate **degree from University** of California, Berkeley in 1976. He remained at Berkeley as a Postdoc for two years before joining Bell Labs where he and his several co-workers carried out his Nobel-winning laser cooling work. None of his co-workers, however, were recognized with the Nobel Prize. He left Bell Labs and became a professor of Physics in Stanford University in 1987. Steven Chu has served as the chair of the Physics Department in Stanford University from 1990-1993 and 1999-2001. He was appointed as the director of Lawrence Berkeley National Laboratory in 2004.

Chu, with three other professors, was involved with the Bio-X programme in Stanford that is intended to bring together scientists from physics, chemistry, biology and engineering background under one roof, the James H. Clark Centre. He also played an important role for the funding of Kavli Institute at Stanford.

SUBRAHMANYAN CHANDRASEKHAR

Padma Vibhushan Subrahmanyan Chandrasekhar, FRS (October 19, 1910– August 21, 1995) was an Indian born American astrophysicist, and Nobel laureate in physics along with William Alfred Fowler for their work in the theoretical structure and evolution of stars.

Chandrasekhar served on the University of Chicago faculty from 1937 until his death in 1995 at the age of 84. He became a naturalized citizen of the United States in 1953.

Biography

Chandrasekhar was born in Punjab Lahore, British India (Present day Pakistan), into an Iyer family, the third of ten children to Sita Balakrishnan, and Subrahmanya Ayyar, a senior officer in the Indian Audits and Accounts Department. Subrahmanya Ayyar was posted in Lahore as the Deputy Auditor General of the Northwestern Railways at the time of Chandrasekhar's birth.

Chandra's father was also an accomplished Carnatic music violinist who had authored several books on musicology. His mother was devoted to intellectual pursuits and had translated Henrik Ibsen's

A Doll's House into Tamil. She is credited with arousing Chandra's intellectual curiosity early on. Chandra's father's brother, physicist C. V. Raman is also a Nobel laureate in physics.

Chandra was tutored at home initially through middle school and later attended the Hindu High School, Triplicane, Madras, British India during the years 1922-25. Subsequently, he studied at Presidency College from 1925 to 1930, obtaining his bachelor's degree, B.Sc. (Hon.), in physics in June 1930. In July 1930, Chandrasekhar was awarded a Government of India scholarship to pursue graduate studies at the University of Cambridge, where he was admitted to Trinity College and became a research student of Professor R. H. Fowler. On the advice of Prof. P. A. M. Dirac, as part of his graduate studies, Chandra spent a year at the *Institut for Teoretisk Fysik* in Copenhagen, where he met Prof. Niels Bohr. In the summer of 1933, Chandrasekhar was awarded his Ph.D. degree at Cambridge, and the following October, he was elected to a Prize Fellowship at Trinity College for the period 1933-37. During this time, he made acquaintances with Sir Arthur Eddington and Professor E. A. Milne.

In September 1936, Chandrasekhar married Lalitha Doraiswamy, who he had met as a fellow student at Presidency College, Madras, and who was a year junior to him. In his Nobel autobiography, Chandrasekhar wrote, "Lalitha's patient understanding, support, and encouragement have been the central facts of my life."

Career

The following year in January 1937, Chandrasekhar was recruited to the University of Chicago faculty as Assistant Professor by Dr. Otto Struve and President Robert Maynard Hutchins. He was to remain at the university for his entire career, becoming Morton D. Hull Distinguished Service Professor of Theoretical Astrophysics in 1952 and attaining emeritus status in 1985.

During World War II, Chandrasekhar worked at the Ballistic Research Laboratories at the Aberdeen Proving Ground in Maryland. While there, he worked on problems of ballistics; for example, two reports from 1943 were titled, *On the decay of plane shock waves* and

The normal reflection of a blast wave. Chandrasekhar developed a style of working continuously in one specific area of physics for a number of years; consequently, his working life can be divided into distinct periods. He studied stellar structure, including the theory of white dwarfs, during the years 1929 to 1939, and subsequently focused on stellar dynamics from 1939 to 1943. Next, he concentrated on the theory of radiative transfer and the quantum theory of the negative ion of hydrogen from 1943 to 1950.

This was followed by sustained work on hydrodynamic and hydromagnetic stability from 1950 to 1961. In the 1960s, he studied the equilibrium and the stability of ellipsoidal figures of equilibrium, but also general relativity. During the period, 1971 to 1983 he studied the mathematical theory of black holes, and, finally, during the late 80s, he worked on the theory of colliding gravitational waves.

During the years 1990 to 1995, Chandrasekhar worked on a project which was devoted to explaining the detailed geometric arguments in Sir Isaac Newton's *Philosophiae Naturalis Principia Mathematica* using the language and methods of ordinary calculus. The effort resulted in the book *Newton's Principia for the Common Reader*, published in 1995. Chandrasekhar was an honorary member of the International Academy of Science.

Subrahmanyan Chandrasekhar died of heart failure in Chicago in 1995, and was survived by his wife, Lalitha Chandrasekhar. In the *Biographical Memoirs of the Fellows of the Royal Society of London*, R. J. Tayler wrote: "Chandrasekhar was a classical applied mathematician whose research was primarily applied in astronomy and whose like will probably never be seen again."

SAMUEL KING ALLISON

Samuel King Allison (November 13, 1900 – September 15, 1965) was an American physicist, most notable for his role in the Manhattan Project — where among other things he read the countdown for the detonation of the "Trinity" test — and his postwar work in the "scientists' movement".

Biography

Samuel K. Allison was born in Chicago, Illinois, and attended the University of Chicago for his undergraduate degree as well as for his PhD (in chemistry, though his thesis was related to experimental physics). From 1923 until 1925 he was a research fellow at Harvard University and from 1925 until 1926 he was a research fellow at the Carnegie Institution From 1926 until 1928 he taught physics at University of California, Berkeley, after which he returned to the University of Chicago, where he studied the Compton effect and the dynamical theory of x-ray diffraction. He developed a high resolution x-ray spectrometer with a graduate student, John H. Williams. In the late 1930s, he studied with John Cockcroft at the Cavendish Laboratory, learning about linear accelerators, and after returning to Chicago he built one. He authored a textbook on x-rays with Arthur Compton which became widely used.

During World War II, Allison was a consultant to the National Defense Research Committee and the Uranium (S-1) Committee, the early investigations into the feasibility of an atomic bomb which would later become the Manhattan Project. He worked at the Chicago Metallurgical Laboratory and was its director from 1943 until 1944. He then went to work at the secret Los Alamos laboratory in New Mexico. Notably, he was the one who read the countdown over the loudspeakers for the "Trinity" test in 1945.

After the war, Allison became director of the Enrico Fermi Institute of Nuclear Studies from 1946 until 1957, and again from 1963 until 1965. He was active in the "scientist's movement" for the control of atomic weapons, and was a founder of the *Bulletin of the Atomic Scientists*. He was a strong opponent of secrecy in science, and was once quoted as saying:

We are determined to return to free research as before the war. If secrecy is imposed on scientific research in physics, we will find all first-rate scientists working on subjects as innocuous as the colours of butterfly wings.

Allison died in 1965 while attending the Plasma Physics and Controlled Nuclear Fusion Research Conference in Culham, England of complications following an aortic aneurism. His papers are kept at the American Institute of Physics.

SHEN KUO

Shen Kuo or **Shen Kua** (1031–1095), style name **Cunzhong** and pseudonym **Mengqi Weng**, was a polymathic Chinese scientist and statesman of the Song Dynasty (960–1279). Excelling in many fields of study and statecraft, he was a mathematician, astronomer, meteorologist, geologist, zoologist, botanist, pharmacologist, agronomist, archaeologist, ethnographer, cartographer, encyclopedist, general, diplomat, hydraulic engineer, inventor, academy chancellor, finance minister, governmental state inspector, poet, and musician. He was the head official for the Bureau of Astronomy in the Song court, as well as an Assistant Minister of Imperial Hospitality. At court his political allegiance was to the Reformist faction known as the New Policies Group, headed by Chancellor Wang Anshi (1021–1086).

In his *Dream Pool Essays* of 1088, Shen was the first to describe the magnetic needle compass, which would be used for navigation (first described in Europe by Alexander Neckam in 1187). Shen discovered the concept of true north in terms of magnetic declination towards the north pole, with experimentation of suspended magnetic needles and "the improved meridian determined by Shen's [astronomical] measurement of the distance between the polestar and true north". This was the decisive step in human history to make compasses more useful for navigation, and may have been a concept unknown in Europe for another four hundred years.

Alongside his colleague Wei Pu, Shen accurately mapped the orbital paths of the moon and the planets, in an intensive five-year project that rivaled the later work of the Danish astronomer Tycho Brahe (1546–1601). To aid his work in astronomy, Shen Kuo made improved designs of the armillary sphere, gnomon, sighting tube, and invented a new type of inflow water clock. Shen Kuo devised a geological hypothesis for land formation (geomorphology), based upon findings of inland marine fossils, knowledge of soil erosion, and the deposition of silt. He also proposed a hypothesis of gradual climate change, after observing ancient petrified bamboos that were preserved underground in a dry northern habitat that would not support bamboo growth in his time. He was the first literary figure in China to mention the use of the drydock to repair boats suspended out of water, and also wrote of the effectiveness of the relatively new invention of the canal pound lock. Although Ibn al-Haytham (965–1039) was the first to describe camera obscura, Shen was the first in China to do so, several decades later. Shen wrote extensively about movable type printing invented by Bi Sheng (990–1051), and because of his written works the legacy of Bi Sheng and the modern understanding of the earliest movable type has been handed down to later generations. Shen was the first in world history to create a raised-relief map. His description of an ancient crossbow mechanism which he himself unearthed proved to be Jacob's staff, a surveying tool which wasn't known in Europe until described by Levi ben Gerson in 1321.

Shen Kuo wrote several other books besides the *Dream Pool Essays*, yet much of the writing in his other books has not survived. Some of Shen's poetry was preserved in posthumous written works. Although much of his focus was on technical and scientific issues, he had an interest in divination and the supernatural, the latter including his vivid description of unidentified flying objects from eyewitness testimony. He also wrote commentary on ancient Daoist and Confucian texts.

Life

Shen Kuo was born in Qiantang (modern-day Hangzhou) in the year 1031. His father Shen Zhou (978–1052) was a somewhat lower-class gentry figure serving in official posts on the provincial level; his mother was from a family of equal status in Suzhou, with her maiden name being Xu (1s). Shen Kuo received his initial childhood education from his mother, which was a common practice in China during this period. She was very educated herself, teaching Kuo and his brother Pi the military doctrines of her own elder brother Xu Tang (1sm; 975–1016). Since Shen was unable to boast of a prominent familial clan history like many of his elite peers born in the north, he was forced to rely on his wit and stern determination to achieve in his studies to enter the challenging and sophisticated life of an exam-drafted state bureaucrat.

From about 1040, Shen's family moved around Sichuan province and finally to the international seaport at Xiamen, where Shen's father accepted minor provincial posts in each new location. Shen Zhou also served several years in the prestigious capital judiciary, the equivalent of a federal supreme court. Shen Kuo took notice of the various towns and rural features of China as his family travelled, while he became interested during his youth in the diverse topography of the land. He also observed the intriguing aspects of his father's engagement in administrative governance and the managerial problems involved; these experiences had a deep impact on him as he later became a government official. Since he often became ill as a child, Shen Kuo also developed a natural curiosity about medicine and pharmaceutics.

Shen Zhou died in the late winter of 1051 (or early 1052), when his son Shen Kuo was 21 years old. Shen Kuo grieved for his father, and following Confucian ethics, remained inactive in a state of mourning for three years until 1054 (or early 1055). As of 1054, Shen began serving in minor local governmental posts. However, his natural abilities to plan, organize, and design were proven early in life; one example is his design and supervision of the hydraulic drainage of an embankment system, which converted some one hundred thousand acres (400 km^2) of swampland into prime farmland. Shen Kuo noted that the success of the silt fertilization method relied upon the effective operation of sluice gates of irrigation canals.

SUE HENDRICKSON

Sue Hendrickson (b. December 2, 1949) is an American paleontologist. She was born in Chicago, Illinois, and later moved to Munster, Indiana where she grew up.

Hendrickson is best known for her discovery of the remains of a *Tyrannosaurus rex* in South Dakota on August 12, 1990. Her discovery was the largest specimen of a *T. rex* found and one of the most complete skeletons. This skeleton is now known as 'Sue' in honour of her discovery. It is on display at the Field Museum in Chicago, Illinois. She has also found other important fossils and artifacts around the world.

In 1992, she joined a team of marine archaeologists headed by Franck Goddio. With them, she took part in many diving expeditions, the most notable of which were the Royal Quarters of Cleopatra, and Napoleon Bonaparte's lost fleet from the Battle of the Nile.

In 2000, *Glamour* Magazine honoured her in their "Glamour Woman of the Year Awards."

In 2003 she published an autobiography entitled *Hunt for the Past: My Life as an Explorer.*

In 2008, she was on the Dare to Explore chapter of *National Geographic Kids.*

She now lives on the island of Guanaja, off the coast of Honduras.

SIR JAMES HALL, 4TH BARONET

Sir James Hall of Dunglass, 4th Baronet (January 17, 1761-June 23, 1832) was a geologist and geophysicist, born at Dunglass, Haddingtonshire, to Sir John Hall, 3rd Baronet (d. 1776), by his spouse, Magdalen (d. 1763) daughter of Sir Robert Pringle, 3rd Baronet, of Stichill, Roxburghshire. Sir James was also Member of Parliament for St. Michael's borough (Mitchell, Cornwall) 1807-1812. Hall studied at Cambridge University and the University of Edinburgh. Early in his career, Hall studied chemistry under Joseph Black and natural history under John Walker (naturalist). During the 1780s he travelled to France and met Lavoisier. He returned to Scotland to promote the new French chemical nomenclature.

He was particularly taken by James Hutton's *Theory of the Earth* during the 1780s and 1790s, and published several papers on the chemical composition of strata. He carried out research on granite that showed that it was possible for molten rock to form conformities.

His results were published in the *Transactions* of the Royal Society of Edinburgh and were well received by those like John Playfair who wanted to use Hutton's theory to promote a more mathematical approach to geology. Hall travelled extensively in Europe to examine geological formations of the Alps and Mount Etna, and noted the similarity of lava flows in Italy to locations in Scotland.

Sir James Hall was President of the Royal Society of Edinburgh, and author of various works on architecture and the sciences. He married Helen (d. 1837), daughter of Dunbar Hamilton later Douglas (d. 1799), Earl of Selkirk and sister of the 5th Earl of Selkirk. They had issue: three sons and three daughters. Sir James Hall died at Edinburgh, Scotland. He was succeeded by his son and heir, Sir John Hall, 5th Baronet, F.R.S.

Another son, Basil Hall, was a noted traveller and writer; his daughter Eliza was mother of Houston Stewart Chamberlain.

A daughter Magdalene Hall (1793-1822) married 1stly 1815 Colonel Sir William Howe DeLancey and secondly Captain Henry Harvey; she was author of *A Week at Waterloo* (first privately published) and died in childbirth with her third child. By DeLancey, her first husband, Magdalene had no issue.

SIMON CONWAY MORRIS

Simon Conway Morris is a British paleontologist. He was born in 1951 and brought up in London, England. He made his reputation with a very detailed and careful study of the Burgess Shale fossils, an exploit celebrated in Stephen Jay Gould's *Wonderful Life*, though Conway Morris' own book on the subject, *The Crucible of Creation*, is somewhat critical of Gould's presentation and interpretation.

Conway Morris is a former student of Harry Blackmore Whittington. He is Professor of Evolutionary Palaeobiology in the Department of Earth Sciences at the University of Cambridge. He is renowned for his insights into early evolution, and his studies of paleobiology. He gave the Royal Institution Christmas Lectures in 1996. He was elected a Fellow of the Royal Society aged 39, was awarded the Walcott Medal of the National Academy of Sciences in 1987, and the Lyell Medal of the Geological Society of London in 1998.

Work

He is based in the Department of Earth Sciences at the University of Cambridge and is best known for his work on the Cambrian "explosion", especially in terms of his study of the famous Burgess Shale fossil fauna and similar deposits in China and Greenland. In addition to working in these countries he has undertaken research in Australia, Canada, Mongolia and the United States. His studies on the Burgess Shale-type faunas, as well as the early evolution of skeletons, has encompassed a wide variety of groups, ranging from ctenophores to the earliest vertebrates.

His thinking on the significance of the Burgess Shale has evolved, and his current interest in evolutionary convergence and its wider significance— the topic of his 2007 Gifford Lectures – was in part spurred by Steven Jay Gould's arguments for the importance of contingency in the history of life.

Burgess Shale

His views on the Burgess Shale are reported in numerous technical papers, and more generally in The Crucible of Creation (Oxford University Press, 1998). In recent years he has been investigating the phenomenon of evolutionary convergence, the main thesis of which is put forward in Life's Solution: Inevitable Humans in a Lonely Universe (Cambridge University Press, 2003).

He is now involved on a major project to investigate both the scientific ramifications of convergence and also to establish a web-site (Map of Life) that aims to provide an easily accessible introduction to the thousands of known examples of convergence. This work is funded by the John Templeton Foundation.

Evolution, Science and Religion

He is known as an effective communicator in the public understanding of science, and has done extensive radio and television work. The latter includes the Royal Institution Christmas Lectures, delivered in 1996. A Christian, he is also actively involved in various science and religion debates, including arguments against Intelligent design on the one hand and Materialism on the other. In 2005 he gave the Second Boyle Lecture. He is an increasingly active participant in discussions relating to science and religion. He is active in the Faraday Institute for Science and Religion and has lectured there on "Evolution and fine-tuning in Biology". He gave the University of Edinburgh's prestigious Gifford Lectures for 2007 in a series titled "Darwin's Compass: How Evolution Discovers the Song of Creation".

SAMUEL WARREN CAREY

Samuel Warren Carey (November 1, 1911 in Campbelltown; † March 20, 2002 in Hobart) was an Australian geologist who was an early advocate of the theory of continental drift. His work on plate tectonics reconstructions led him to develop the theory of the expanding earth.

Biography

Carey was born in New South Wales and grew up on a farm three miles from Campbelltown. The family was to move to the town centre, saving the young Carey the walk to school. An interest in physics and chemistry during high school was to lead to selection of both subjects when he attended the University of Sydney in 1929. Mathematics was required and he was encouraged to study Geology as his fourth subject, a department still under the influence of retired Professor Edgeworth David. He started a student Geology club as he became attracted to the subjects mixture of laboratory and field work; David gave the inaugural speech.

Along with classmates Alan Voisey and Dorothy York, he was to earn high distinctions at the University. He also joined the Sydney University Regiment. His Masters and Honours degree were based on four papers on the Werris Creek area. He received his MSc in 1934. It was at this time that Carey read the 1924 translation of Wegener's *The Origin of Continents and Oceans*, the book largely responsible for introducing the concept of continental drift to English-speaking academics. He was to become a key figure in advancing this concept and plate tectonic models that followed.

Carey served in World War II as a Lieutenant in the special forces unit Z Force, developing a bold plan using small teams to mine ships in an enemy harbour. This operation (Scorpion) became obsolete but Carey secretly tested his plan by infilrating Townsville harbour, placing dummy limpet mines on American ships.

After the war, Carey was a highly regarded contributor to geology and his many contributions to the emerging theories and proposals were often in advance of the accepted view. Maps and data produced from his field work in New Guinea were sought after by engineers and fellows. He backed the moving of continents proposed by Alfred Wegener and had decided on the mechanism for this when it became the accepted view. Carey's expanding earth bears many resemblances to the current model, including supercontinents dividing and going adrift, zones of new crust being generated in deep oceanic ridges, and other phenomenae of a still active crust. His theory gave the 'mechanism' for this as an expanding earth; whereas the new theory of plate tectonics accounted for it with subduction.

Despite the eventual acceptance of the plate expansion and subduction paradigm over Carey's theory, he is widely regarded as making substantial contributions to the field of tectonics and considerable influence in the initial acceptance of continental drift over a static model. In 1946, he became the founding professor of geology at the University of Tasmania. He retired from this position 30 years later in 1976.

In the Australia Day Honours list of 1977, Carey was awarded the Officer of the Order of Australia for his services to the field of geology.

He, and a small number of other researchers, continued to support and investigate expanding earth models.

SELWYN G. BLAYLOCK

Selwyn Gwillym Blaylock (1879-November 19, 1945) was a part of starting the mining industry in western Canada. He was president of Cominco, recipient of several international awards for his work in metallurgy, and was the President of the Canadian Institute of Mining, Metallurgy and Petroleum in 1934-35. For his work he was inducted into the Canadian Mining Hall of Fame.

Early Life

He was born in Paspebiac, Quebec. Blaylock attended Bishop's College School in Lennoxville, Quebec. In 1899, he obtained a B.Sc. from McGill University.

Career

After grduating, he moved west and obtained work as a surveyor for the Canadian Smelting Works in Trail, British Columbia. Two years later, he became the company's chief chemist, but soon moved to Nelson, British Columbia to become general supintendent of the Hall Mines Smelter, then general superintendent of the St. Eugene mines. In 1908, Blaylock joined the Consolidated Mining and Smelting Company (Cominco). In 1919, he became Cominco's general manager. In 1922 a director, vice-president in 1927, managing director in 1938 and president in 1939.

Blaylock died in Trail, six months after his retirement. He was buried at Danville, Quebec.

STEWART BLUSSON

Dr. Stewart Lynn "Stu" Blusson OC (born 1939) is a multimillionaire and philanthropist. He co-discovered billion-dollar Ekati Diamond Mine, 300 kilometres from Yellowknife, Northwest Territories, Canada. He is President of Archon Minerals Ltd. In 2002, Blusson donated key start-up funds necessary for Quest

University Canada in Squamish, British Columbia. In 2006, Blusson donated $10 million for the Archon X PRIZE to develop a quick and inexpensive way to sequence the human genome. Blusson had a net worth of $660 million CDN in 2006.

Early Life

Blusson was born in Vancouver, BC. He completed an undergraduate degree at the University of British Columbia (1960) and a doctorate in geology at the University of California, Berkeley (1964).

Career

After school, he joined the federal Geological Survey of Canada, leading regional geological mapping and research programmes in the central Yukon and parts of British Columbia. During that time he survived a serious helicopter crash and a Grizzly bear attack. In 1969, Chuck Fipke, a geologist, needed to be rescued from the side of a mountain where he had been stranded for close to a week. Blusson was the helicopter pilot that saved him. From this first encounter, Fipke and Blusson became friends and prospecting partners. In 1980, Blusson married his wife, Marilyn.

He left the Geological Survey in 1979 to explore the modes of formation of mineral deposits from Mexico to the Arctic. He discovered a number of important occurrences of gold, copper and other metals. In 1981, he and Fipke began searching for diamonds in the Northwest Territories, concentrating their search on indicator minerals commonly associated with kimberlite, a host rock for diamond. They found kimberlitic indicator minerals near Lac de Gras in the Northwest Territories in 1985, and their first kimberlite at Pointe Lake in 1991. In 1998, Ekati opened, a joint venture between BHP Diamonds Inc. (51%), Dia Met Minerals (29%), Fipke (10%), and Blusson (10%). Blusson's net worth in 2002 was estimated to be $295 million (US).

In 2004, he was appointed as an Officer of the Order of Canada and was presented with the Logan Medal, Geological Association of Canada's highest honour.

SPENCER WELLS

Spencer Wells (born April 6, 1969 in Georgia, United States) is a geneticist and anthropologist, and an Explorer-in-Residence at the National Geographic Society. He leads The Genographic Project.

Work

Wells did his Ph.D. work under Richard Lewontin, and later did postdoctoral research with Luigi Luca Cavalli-Sforza and Sir Walter Bodmer. His work, which has helped to establish the critical role played by Central Asia in the peopling of the world, has been published in journals such as *Science*, *American Journal of Human Genetics*, and the *Proceedings of the National Academy of Sciences.*

He wrote the book *The Journey of Man: A Genetic Odyssey* (2002), which explains how genetic data has been used to trace human migrations over the past 50,000 years, when modern humans first migrated outside of Africa. According to Wells, one group took a southern route and populated southern India and southeast Asia, then Australia.

The other group, accounting for 90% of the world's non-African population (some 5 billion people as of late 2006), took a northern route, eventually peopling most of Eurasia (largely displacing the aboriginals in southern India, Sri Lanka and Southeast Asia in the process), North Africa and the Americas.

Wells also wrote and presented the PBS/National Geographic documentary of the same name. By analyzing DNA from people in all regions of the world, Wells has concluded that all humans alive today are descended from a single man who lived in Africa around 60,000-90,000 years ago, a man also known as Y-chromosomal Adam.

Since 2005, Wells has headed The Genographic Project, undertaken by the National Geographic Society, IBM and the Waitt Family Foundation, which will add to our knowledge of human history by analyzing DNA samples from around the world, thereby creating a picture of how our ancestors populated the planet.

Personal

Wells lives in Washington, D.C. with his wife, documentary filmmaker Pamela Caragol Wells. He has two daughters, Margot and Sasha, from his first marriage.

SEVERO OCHOA

Severo Ochoa de Albornoz (September 24, 1905 – November 1, 1993) was a Spanish-American biochemist, and the recipient of the 1959 Nobel Prize in Physiology or Medicine.

Life

Severo Ochoa was born in Luarca (Asturias), Spain. His father was Severo Manuel Ochoa, a lawyer and businessman, and his mother, Carmen de Albornoz. His father died when Ochoa was seven and he and his mother moved to Malaga, where he attended school through high school. His interest in biology was stimulated by the publications of the Spanish neurologist and Nobel awardee Santiago Ramon y Cajal. In 1923, he went to the University of Madrid Medical School, where he hoped to work with Cajal, but Cajal retired. In 1929, he obtained his MD degree with honours. In 1931, Ochoa married Carmen Garcia Cobian, but they had no children.

From then until 1938, he held many positions and worked with many people at many places. For example, Otto Meyerhof appointed him Guest Research Assistant at the Kaiser Wilhelm Institute for Medical Research in Heidelberg for one year.

From 1938 until 1941 he was Demonstrator and Nuffield Research Assistant at the University of Oxford. He then went to America, where he again held many positions at many universities. In 1942 he was appointed Research Associate in Medicine at the New York University School of Medicine and there subsequently became Assistant Professor of Biochemistry (1945), Professor of Pharmacology (1946), Professor of Biochemistry (1954), and Chairman of the Department of Biochemistry.

In 1956, he became an American citizen. In 1959, Ochoa was awarded the Nobel Prize for Physiology or Medicine for his work on the synthesis of RNA.

Ochoa continued research on protein synthesis and replication of RNA viruses until 1985, when he returned to Spain and gave advice to Spanish science policy authorities and scientists. Ochoa was also a recipient of U.S. National Medal of Science in 1979. Ochoa died in Madrid, and a new research centre that was planned in the 1970s, was finally built and named after Ochoa. The asteroid 117435 Severochoa is also named in his honour.

Severo Ochoa died in Madrid, Spain on November 1, 1993.

SUSAN LINDQUIST

Susan Lindquist (born 5 June 1949) is a well-known molecular biologist studying (among other things) the biology of protein folding, heat-shock proteins, and prions. Lindquist is a member and former Director of the Whitehead Institute.

Lindquist's Science

Lindquist is best known for her research that provided strong evidence for a new paradigm in genetics based upon the inheritance of proteins with new, self-perpetuating shapes rather than new DNA sequences. This research provided a biochemical framework for understanding other mysteries in biology, such as Alzheimer's disease and Creutzfeldt-Jakob disease. She is considered an expert in protein folding which, as explained by Lindquist in the following excerpt, is an ancient, fundamental problem in biology:

"What do "mad cows", people with neurodegenerative diseases, and an unusual type of inheritance in yeast have in common? They are all experiencing the consequences of misfolded proteins.... In humans the consequences can be deadly, leading to such devastating illnesses as Alzheimer's Disease. In one case, the misfolded protein is not only deadly to the unfortunate individual in which it has appeared, but it can apparently be passed from one individual to another under special circumstances-producing infectious neurodegenerative diseases such as mad-cow disease in cattle and Creutzfeld-Jacob Disease in humans."—from "From Mad Cows to 'Psi-chotic' Yeast: A New Paradigm in Genetics," *NAS Distinguished Leaders in Science Lecture Series*, 10 November 1999.

Lindquist worked on the PSI+ element in yeast (a prion) and how it can act as a switch that hides or reveals numerous mutations throughout the genome, thus acting as an evolutionary capacitor. She also proposed that a heat shock protein, hsp90, may act in the same way, normally preventing phenotypic consequences of genetic changes, but showing all changes at once when the HSP system is overloaded.

Recently, Lindquist has made advances in nanotechnology, researching organic fibres capable of self-organizing into structures smaller than manufactured materials. Her group also developed a yeast "living test tube" model to study protein folding transitions in neurodegenerative diseases and to test therapeutic strategies through high-throughput screening. She is a co-founder of FoldRx, a company developing drug therapies for diseases of protein misfolding and amyloidosis. In June 2006, Dr. Lindquist was the inaugural guest on the "Futures in Biotech" podcast on Leo Laporte's TWiT network.

STANLEY FALKOW

Stanley Falkow, PhD, is microbiologist and a professor of microbiology and immunology at Stanford University School of Medicine. He is sometimes referred to as the father of molecular microbial pathogenesis, which is the study of how infectious microbes and host cells interact to cause disease at the molecular level. He formulated molecular Koch's postulates, which have guided the study of the microbial determinants of infectious diseases since the late 1980s.

Education and Early Career

Falkow received his B.S. degree from the University of Maine, graduating cum laude, and went on to earn his Ph.D. from Brown

University. Following the completion of his graduate studies, Dr. Falkow went on to become a staff member at the Walter Reed Army Institute of Research (WRAIR) in the Department of Bacterial Immunology where he was eventually named the assistant chief of the department. Dr. Falkow's early work in the 1960s focused on the genetic mechanisms that enable populations of bacteria to become resistant to antibiotics.

He demonstrated that organisms, such as shigella, can possess gene fragments called plasmids that exist apart from the bacterial chromosome and that they carry specialized information for survival. Under selective pressure from antibiotics, one species of bacteria can pass its plasmids to another unidirectionally rather than by mating, thereby preserving its own specialized survival genes.

In 1966, he joined Georgetown University School of Medicine as a professor of microbiology. He later moved to Seattle to become a member of the faculty of the Department of Microbiology and Immunology at the University of Washington School of Medicine. Here he described how meningitis and gonorrhea organisms acquire plasmids to become resistant to penicillin and other antibiotics.

In the 1970s, Dr. Falkow shifted his focus to the infection process. During this period, he showed that a life-threatening diarrhea prevalent in many developing countries is caused by a sub-type of E. coli. In 1981, he was named chairman of the Department of Medical Microbiology at Stanford University School of Medicine, a position he held until 1985.

SEYMOUR BENZER

Seymour Benzer (October 15, 1921 – November 30, 2007) was an accomplished American physicist, molecular biologist and behavioural geneticist. With a career that started with the molecular biology revolution of the 1950s, Seymour Benzer was to the end very active as a researcher, where he led a productive lab as the James G. Boswell Professor of Neuroscience, Emeritus, at the California Institute of Technology.

Benzer was born in New York City to parents from Poland. As a boy, he had his first experiences in studying biology, catching frogs and dissecting them. For his 13th birthday he received a microscope, "and that opened up the whole world," Benzer recalled in a 1990 interview for an oral history project at Caltech. In 1938 he enrolled at Brooklyn College where he majored in physics.

Molecular Biology

Seymour Benzer started his scientific career as a solid state physicist at Purdue University. After completing his Ph.D, he began his research in biophysics and moved into the area of bacteriophage genetics. After a short stay at Caltech, Benzer returned to Purdue where he developed the rII system, a new genetic technique involving recombination in mutant bacteriophage. Taking advantage of the enormous number of recombinants that could be analyzed in the rII mutant system, Benzer provided the first evidence that the gene is not an indivisible entity, as previously believed. Benzer proved that mutations were distributed in many different parts of a single gene, and the resolving power of his system allowed him to discern mutants that differ at the level of a single nucleotide. Benzer's experiments with the rII system are widely considered among the most elegant experiments in modern genetics, and many believe that Benzer should have been awarded the Nobel Prize for it.

In his molecular biology period, Benzer dissected the fine structure of a single gene, laying down the ground work for decades of mutation analysis and genetic engineering, and setting up a paradigm using the rII phage that would later be used by Francis Crick and James Watson to establish the triplet code of DNA.

Behavioural Genetics

After his work in phage genetics, Benzer turned to the fruit fly *Drosophila* to study the genetic basis of animal behaviour. He then pioneered the field of neurogenetics working with mutants of *Drosophila melanogaster*. Benzer, with student Ron Konopka, discovered the first circadian rhythm mutants in a gene they called "period".

This was the first of several seminal studies of single genes affecting behaviour, studies that have been replicated in other animal models and are now the basis for the booming field of molecular biology of behaviour. In particular, the study of circadian rhythms has now become ubiquitous, and homologs of the original gene have been identified in many organisms.

Benzer was at the forefront of the study of neurodegeneration in fruit flies, modeling human diseases and attempting to suppress them. He also contributed to the field of aging biology, looking for mutants with altered longevity and trying to dissect the mechanisms by which an organism can escape the inevitable functional downfall and its associated diseases.

S. P. L. SORENSEN

Soren Peder Lauritz Sorensen (January 9, 1868-February 12, 1939) was a Danish chemist, famous for the introduction of the concept of pH, a scale for measuring acidity. He was born in Havrebjerg, Denmark. From 1901 to 1938 he was head of the prestigious Carlsberg Laboratory, Copenhagen. While working at the Carlsberg Laboratory he studied the effect of ion concentration on proteins, and because the concentration of hydrogen ions was particularly important, he introduced the pH-scale as a simple way of expressing it in 1909. The article in which he introduced the scale (using the notation p_H), described two new methods for measuring acidity. The first method was based on electrodes, while the second involved comparing the colours of samples and a preselected set of indicators.

He is also known for the Sorensen formol titration.

SUSAN SOLOMON

Susan Solomon (born 1956 in Chicago) is an atmospheric chemist working for the National Oceanic and Atmospheric Administration. Solomon was one of the first to propose chlorofluorocarbons as the cause of the Antarctic ozone hole.

Solomon is a member of the U.S. National Academy of Sciences, the European Academy of Sciences, and the Academy of Sciences of France.

Biography

Solomon began her interest in science as a child watching *The Undersea World of Jacques Cousteau.* In high school she placed third in a national science fair, with a project that measured the percent of oxygen in a gas mixture.

Solomon studied Chemistry at the Illinois Institute of Technology, receiving her B.S. in 1977. She received her Ph.D. in chemistry from the University of California, Berkeley in 1981, where she specialized in atmospheric chemistry.

Marriage

Solomon married Barry Sidwell in 1988.

Work

Solomon is the head of the Chemistry and Climate Processes Group of the National Oceanic and Atmospheric Administration Chemical Sciences Division.

SALIMUZZAMAN SIDDIQUI

Prof Dr. **Salimuzzaman Siddiqui** (19 October 1897-14 April 1994) was a leading Pakistani scientist in natural products chemistry. He is credited for pioneering the isolation of unique chemical compounds from the Neem (*Azadirachta indica*), Rauwolfia, and various other flora.

As the founder director of H.E.J. Research Institute of Chemistry, he revolutionised the research on pharmacology of various domestic plants found in South Asia to extract novel chemical substances of medicinal importance. In addition to his scientific talents, Siddiqui was also a painter, a poet, and a great connoisseur of music. His paintings were exhibited in Germany, India, and Pakistan.

Early Life

Siddiqui was born in Subeha (Barabanki District) near Lucknow on October 19, 1897. He received his early education from Lucknow, both in the Urdu and Persian languages, and soon developed interest in literature, poetry, and calligraphy from his father Sheikh Muhammad Zaman. After completing his matriculation, he joined the Calcutta School of Arts, and became a pupil of Rabindranath Tagore, the founder of the famous Bengal School of painting. He graduated in Philosophy and Persian language, from M.A.O College (that would later become Aligarh University) in 1919. In 1920, Siddiqui proceeded to University College London to read medicine. However, after one year of pre-medical studies, he moved to Frankfurt University in 1921 to read chemistry. In 1924, he married his German classmate, Ethel Wilhelmina Schneeman. He received Doctor of Philosophy under the supervision of Prof Julius Von Bram in 1927. On his return, he established the Ayurvedic and Unani Tibbi Research Institute at the Tibbia College Delhi, under the guidance of Hakim Ajmal Khan. He was appointed its first Director. However, soon after the death of Hakim Ajmal Khan, Siddiqui left the post. In 1940, he joined Indian Council for Scientific and Industrial Research where he worked until 1951 when he migrated to Pakistan on the request of Prime Minister Liaquat Ali Khan.

STUART SCHREIBER

Stuart L. Schreiber (b. February 6, 1956) is a scientist at Harvard University and the Broad Institute of Harvard and MIT. He has been a pioneer in a field of research named chemical biology for over 20 years. His name is closely associated with the increasingly common use of small molecules as probes of biology and medicine. Small molecules are the molecules of life most associated with dynamic information flow; these work in concert with the macromolecules (DNA, RNA, proteins) that are the basis for inherited information flow. During the 1980s and '90s, he provided dramatic advances in biology using this approach, and, in the past ten years, his systematization efforts have made this one of the fastest growing areas of life-science research.

Education and Training

Schreiber obtained a Bachelor of Science degree in Chemistry from the University of Virginia, after which he entered Harvard University as a Graduate Student in Chemistry. He joined the research group of Robert B. Woodward and after Woodward's death continued his studies under the supervision of Yoshito Kishi. In 1980 he joined the faculty of Yale University as an Assistant Professor in Chemistry.

STUART A. RICE

Stuart Alan Rice (born 1932 in New York City) is an American theoretical chemist and physical chemist. He is well-known as a theoretical chemist who also does experimental research. He is currently the Frank P. Hixon Distinguished Service Professor Emeritus at The University of Chicago. He received the National Medal of Science in 1999.

Education and Career

Stuart Rice received his bachelor's degree in 1952 from Brooklyn College, and earned his master's and doctorate from Harvard University in 1954 and 1955, respectively. He remained at Harvard as a Junior Fellow for two years before joining the faculty of The University of Chicago in 1957, where he has remained since.

Professor Rice has served the university in a wide variety of capacities during his forty-eight year tenure. He served as the director of the James Franck Institute (the university's centre for physical chemistry and condensed matter physics) from 1961 to 1967. He was Chairman of the Department of Chemistry from 1971 to 1976 and was Dean of the Physical Sciences Division from 1981 to 1995. In addition to his work at the University, he is currently on the Board of Governors at Tel Aviv University and has served as editor for the journals *Chemical Physics Letters* and *Advances in Chemical Physics*, and co-authored several physical chemistry textbooks with Stephen Berry and John Ross. He currently maintains a full research lab but has retired from teaching classes.

Personal Life

Prof. Rice is also famous on campus for eating lunch almost every weekday at the university's Quadrangle Club restaurant (a faculty club), where he has dined over 9, 000 times. Rice is known to sit at the head of the Chemistry table, not because he is the most senior member of the department, but because he is very tall.

STANLEY MILLER

Stanley Lloyd Miller (March 7, 1930-May 20, 2007) was an American chemist and biologist who is known for his studies into the origin of life, particularly the Miller-Urey experiment which demonstrated that organic compounds can be created by fairly simple physical processes from inorganic substances. The experiment used conditions then thought to provide an approximate representation of those present on the primordial Earth.

Life and Career

Born in Oakland, California, he studied at University of California (obtaining his B.S. in 1951) and then at University of Chicago where he received his Ph.D. in chemistry in 1954. While at Chicago, Miller was a student of Harold Urey. Miller continued his research at California Institute of Technology (1954-1955) and then joined the department of biochemistry at Columbia University, New York where he worked for the next five years. He then returned to California where he was an assistant professor (1960-1962), associate professor (1962-1968), then full professor of chemistry at University of California, San Diego (from 1968).

His work dealt with the origin of life (and he was considered a pioneer in the field of exobiology), the natural occurrence of clathrate hydrates, and general mechanisms of anesthesia. He was a member of the National Academy of Science, and received the Oparin Medal. He was a participant in the pioneering Miller-Urey experiment. In the 1950s, Urey guessed that the early atmosphere of the Earth was probably like the atmosphere now present on Jupiter—*i.e.*, rich in ammonia, methane, and hydrogen. Miller, working in his laboratory at the University of Chicago, demonstrated that when exposed to an energy source such as ultraviolet radiation, these compounds and water can react to produce amino acids essential for the formation of living matter. (Similar ideas had been suggested by Aleksandr Oparin in the 1920s.) Since then there have been objections that the early environment was possibly not as reducing as Miller and Urey assumed and Miller acknowledged this.

In 1828 Friedrich Wohler had showed that it is possible to synthesize urea. As urea is an organic molecule, many at the time thought it could only be made by living organisms. This led to recognition that there is no obvious difference between a physically produced and an organically produced molecule. Miller's experiment went slightly further by showing that basic biomolecules can be formed through simple physical processes, and that it was not impossible for the first stages of abiogenesis to have occurred on the early earth.

SVANTE ARRHENIUS

Svante August Arrhenius (February 19, 1859 – October 2, 1927) was a Swedish scientist, originally a physicist, but often referred to as a chemist, and one of the founders of the science of physical chemistry. The Arrhenius equation, lunar crater Arrhenius and the Arrhenius Labs at Stockholm University are named after him.

Early Years

Arrhenius was born at Vik (also spelled Wik or Wijk), near Uppsala, Sweden, the son of Svante Gustav and Carolina Thunberg Arrhenius. His father had been a land surveyor for Uppsala University, moving up to a supervisory position. At the age of three, Arrhenius taught himself to read without the encouragement of his parents, and by watching his father's addition of numbers in his account books, became an arithmetical prodigy.

In later life, Arrhenius enjoyed using masses of data to discover mathematical relationships and laws. At age 8, he entered the local cathedral school, starting in the fifth grade, distinguishing himself in physics and mathematics, and graduating as the youngest and most able student in 1876.

At the University of Uppsala, he was unsatisfied with the chief instructor of physics and the only faculty member who could have supervised him in chemistry, Per Teodor Cleve, so he left to study at the Physical Institute of the Swedish Academy of Sciences in Stockholm under the physicist Erik Edlund in 1881. His work focused on the conductivities of electrolytes. In 1884, based on this work, he submitted a 150-page dissertation on electrolytic conductivity to Uppsala for the doctorate. It did not impress the professors, like Per Teodor Cleve, and he received the lowest possible passing grade. Later this very work would earn him the Nobel Prize in Chemistry.

There were 56 theses put forth in the 1884 dissertation, and most would still be accepted today unchanged or with minor modifications. The most important idea in the dissertation was his explanation of the fact that neither pure salts nor pure water is a conductor, but solutions of salts in water are.

Arrhenius' explanation was that in forming a solution, the salt dissociates into charged particles (which Michael Faraday had given the name ions many years earlier). Faraday's belief had been that ions were produced in the process of electrolysis; Arrhenius proposed that, even in the absence of an electric current, solutions of salts contained ions. He thus proposed that chemical reactions in solution were reactions between ions. For weak electrolytes this is still believed to be the case, but modifications (by Peter J. W. Debye and Erich Huckel) were found necessary to account for the behaviour of strong electrolytes. The dissertation was not very impressive to the professors at Uppsala, but Arrhenius sent it to a number of scientists in Europe who were developing the new science of physical chemistry, such as Rudolf Clausius, Wilhelm Ostwald, and J. H. van 't Hoff. They were far more impressed, and Ostwald even came to Uppsala to persuade Arrhenius to join his research team. Arrhenius declined, however, as he preferred to stay in Sweden for a while (his father was very ill and would die in 1885) and had received an appointment at Uppsala.

SEWALL WRIGHT

Sewall Green Wright (December 21, 1889 – March 3, 1988) was an American geneticist known for his influential work on evolutionary theory and also for his work on path analysis. With R. A. Fisher and J.B.S. Haldane, he was a founder of theoretical population genetics. He is the discoverer of the inbreeding coefficient and of methods of computing it in pedigrees. He extended this work to populations, computing the amount of inbreeding of members of populations as a result of random genetic drift, and he and Fisher pioneered methods for computing the distribution of gene frequencies among populations as a result of the interaction of natural selection, mutation, migration and genetic drift. The work of Fisher, Wright, and Haldane on theoretical population genetics was a major step in the development of the modern evolutionary synthesis of genetics with evolution. Wright also made major contributions to mammalian genetics and biochemical genetics.

Biography

Sewall Wright was born in Melrose, Massachusetts to Philip Green Wright and Elizabeth Quincy Sewall Wright. The family moved three years later after Philip accepted a teaching job at Lombard College, a Universalist college in Galesburg, Illinois.

He was the youngest of three gifted brothers – the others being the aeronautical engineer Theodore Paul Wright and the political scientist Quincy Wright. From an early age Wright had a love and talent for mathematics and biology. Wright attended Galesburg High School and graduated in 1906. He then enrolled in Lombard College where his father taught, to study mathematics. He was influenced greatly by Professor Wilhelmine Entemann Key, one of the first women to receive a Ph.D. in biology. Wright received his Ph.D. from Harvard University, where he worked with the pioneering mammalian geneticist William Ernest Castle investigating the inheritance of coat colours in mammals. He worked for the U.S. Department of Agriculture until 1925, when he joined the Department of Zoology at the University of Chicago. He remained there until his retirement in 1955, when he moved to the University of Wisconsin-Madison.

He received many honours in his long career, including the National Medal of Science, the Balzan Prize, and the Darwin Medal of the Royal Society. He was a member of the National Academy of Science and a Foreign Member of the Royal Society.

Wright married Louise Lane Williams (1895-1975) in 1921. They had three children: Richard, Robert, and Elizabeth.

Scientific Achievements and Credits

His papers on inbreeding, mating systems, and genetic drift make him a principal founder of theoretical population genetics, along with R. A. Fisher and J. B. S. Haldane. Their theoretical work is the origin of the modern evolutionary synthesis or neodarwinian synthesis. Wright was the inventor/discoverer of the inbreeding coefficient and F-statistics, standard tools in population genetics. He was the chief developer of the mathematical theory of genetic drift, which is sometimes known as the Sewall Wright effect, cumulative stochastic changes in gene frequencies that arise from random births, deaths, and Mendelian segregations in reproduction.

Wright was convinced that the interaction of genetic drift and the other evolutionary forces was important in the process of adaptation. He described the relationship between genotype or phenotype and fitness as fitness surfaces or fitness landscapes. On these landscapes fitness was the height, plotted against horizontal axes representing the allele frequencies or the average phenotypes of the population. Natural selection would lead to a population climbing the nearest peak, while genetic drift would cause random wandering. Wright's explanation for stasis was that organisms come to occupy adaptive peaks. In order to evolve to another, higher peak, the species would first have to pass through a valley of maladaptive intermediate stages. This could happen by genetic drift if the population is small enough. If a species was divided into small populations, some could find higher peaks. If there was some gene flow between the populations, these adaptations could spread to the rest of the species. This was Wright's shifting balance theory of evolution. There has been much skepticism among evolutionary biologists as to whether these rather delicate conditions hold often in natural populations. Wright had a long standing and bitter debate about this with R. A. Fisher, who felt that most populations in nature were too large for these effects of genetic drift to be important.

Wright strongly influenced Jay Lush, who was the most influential figure in introducing quantitative genetics into animal and plant breeding. Wright's statistical method of path analysis, which he invented in 1921 and which was one of the first methods using a graphical model, is still widely used in social science. He was a hugely influential reviewer of manuscripts, as one of the most frequent reviewers for Genetics. Such was his reputation that he was often credited with reviews that he did not write.

He did major work on the genetics of guinea pigs, and many of his students became influential in the development of mammalian genetics. He appreciated as early as 1917 that genes acted by controlling enzymes.

SELMAN WAKSMAN

Selman Abraham Waksman (22 July 1888 – 16 August 1973) was an American biochemist and microbiologist whose research into organic substances—largely into organisms that live in soil—and their decomposition led to the discovery of Streptomycin, and several other antibiotics. A professor of biochemistry and microbiology at Rutgers University for four decades, his work led to the discovery of over twenty antibiotics (a word which he coined) and procedures that have led to the development of many others. The proceeds earned from the licensing of his patents funded a foundation for microbiological research, which established the Waksman Institute of Microbiology located on Rutgers University's Busch Campus in Piscataway, New Jersey (USA). In 1952 he was awarded the Nobel Prize in Physiology or Medicine in recognition for his discovery of "streptomycin" the first antibiotic active against tuberculosis. In 2005 Selman Waksman was designated an ACS National Historical Chemical Landmark in recognition of his significance for isolating more than fifteen antibiotics, including streptomycin, which was the first effective treatment for tuberculosis.

Biography

Selman Waksman was born on 22 July 1888 to Jewish parents in Pryluky, a peasant village near Kiev, in the Russian Empire, now Ukraine. He immigrated to the United States in 1910, shortly after receiving his matriculation diploma from the Fifth Gymnasium in Odessa, Ukraine, and became a naturalised American citizen six years later.

Waksman attended Rutgers College (now Rutgers University), where he was graduated in 1915 with a Bachelor of Science (B.Sc.) in Agriculture. He continued his studies at Rutgers, receiving a Master of Science (M.Sc.) the following year. During his graduate study, he worked under J. G. Lipman at the New Jersey Agricultural Experiment Station at Rutgers performing research in soil bacteriology. Waksman was then appointed as Research Fellow at the University of California, Berkeley from where he was awarded his Doctor of Philosophy (Ph.D.) in Biochemistry in 1918. He later joined the faculty at Rutgers University in the Department of Biochemistry and Microbiology. It was at Rutgers that Waksman discovered several antibiotics, including actinomycin, clavacin, streptothricin, streptomycin, grisein, neomycin, fradicin, candicidin, candidin, and others. Two of these, streptomycin and neomycin, have found extensive application in the treatment of numerous infectious diseases. Streptomycin was the first antibiotic that could be used to cure the disease tuberculosis. Waksman coined the term antibiotics. Many awards and honours were showered on Waksman after 1940, most notably the Nobel Prize in 1952; the Star of the Rising Sun, bestowed on him by the emperor of Japan, and the rank of Commandeur in the French Legion d'honneur.

Selman Waksman died on 16 August 1973 and was interred at the Crowell Cemetery in Woods Hole, Barnstable County, Massachusetts. His tombstone is inscribed simply as *Selman Abraham Waksman: Scientist* and following his dates of birth and death, an apt paraphrase (given his life's work) of a verse from the prophetic Old Testament Book of Isaiah, carved in both Hebrew and English stating "The earth will open and bring forth salvation".

SUSUMU TONEGAWA

Susumu Tonegawa (born September 6, 1939) is a Japanese scientist who won the Nobel Prize for Physiology or Medicine in 1987 for "his discovery of the genetic principle for generation of antibody diversity." Although he won the Nobel Prize for his work in immunology, Tonegawa is a molecular biologist by training. In his later years, he has turned his attention to the molecular and cellular basis of memory formation. Tonegawa is best known for elucidating the genetic mechanism in the adaptive immune system. To achieve the diversity of antibodies needed to protect against any type of antigen, the immune system would require millions of genes coding for different antibodies, if each antibody was encoded by one gene. Instead, as Tonegawa showed in a landmark series of experiments beginning in 1976, genetic material can rearrange itself to form the vast array of available antibodies. Comparing the DNA of B cells (a type of white blood cell) in embryonic and adult mice, he observed that genes in the mature B cells of the adult mice are moved around, recombined, and deleted to form the diversity of the variable region of antibodies. Tonegawa was born in Nagoya, Japan and attended the Hibiya High School in Tokyo.. He received his bachelor's degree from Kyoto University in 1963. He received his doctorate from the University of California, San Diego. He did post-doctoral work at the Salk Institute in San Diego in the laboratory of Renato Dulbecco, then worked at the Basel Institute for Immunology in Basel, Switzerland, where he performed his landmark immunology experiments.

In 1981, he became a professor at the Massachusetts Institute of Technology, and founded and directed the Picower Institute for Learning and Memory at MIT. In 1982, he was awarded the Louisa Gross Horwitz Prize from Columbia University together with Barbara McClintock another Nobel Prize winner in 1983. He is a member of the Scientific Board of Governors at The Scripps Research Institute. In 2006, Tonegawa was accused of discouraging the recruitment of a female junior faculty candidate in the McGovern Institute for Brain Research, another MIT neuroscience unit, by informing her that they would likely become competitors at MIT. In a letter to MIT President Susan Hockfield, 11 tenured female MIT professors requested an investigation of potentially unethical conduct. An investigation by an internal MIT committee submitted a report to the Provost, who with the President wrote letters to the MIT community. The committee found no evidence of gender bias. On November 17, 2006, Tonegawa announced his resignation as director of the Picower Institute for Learning and Memory, effective December 31, 2006.

THANU PADMANABHAN

Thanu Padmanabhan, (born. 10th March 1957, Thiruvananthapuram, Kerala) is an Indian theoretical physicist. He is currently Distinguished Professor at the Inter-University Centre for Astronomy and Astrophysics, (IUCAA) at Pune, India. His principal fields of research are Cosmology and the interface between Gravity and Quantum theory.

Life and Career

Padmanabhan did his schooling in Thiruvananthapuram, Kerala and did his B.Sc (1977) and M.Sc (1979) in Physics from University College, Kerala University, securing Gold Medals for his academic brilliance. He published his first research paper (on general relativity) when he was a B.Sc student, at the age of 20. He joined TIFR, Mumbai for PhD and became a faculty member there in 1980 where he continued till 1992. He moved to IUCAA in 1992 and is currently the Dean of Core Academic Programmes. He has served as visiting faculty at many institutes including the California Institute of Technology, Princeton University and the Pennsylvania State University as well as the Institute of Astronomy, Cambridge. He is married to Dr. Vasanthi Padmanabhan, who has a Ph.D in astrophysics from TIFR, Mumbai.

Research Contributions

Padmanabhan has worked in several contemporary areas of theoretical physics like quantum cosmology, structure formation in the universe, statistical mechanics of gravitating systems, black holes and quantum gravity and has published nearly 200 papers in leading international journals. His current research interest is in understanding the nature of dark energy in the universe and its implications for quantum gravity. He has developed a new, holographic, perspective on Gravity which has the potential of resolving some of the difficult problems in quantum gravity. Apart from his scientific research, Padmanabhan has given many popular science lectures and authored more than a hundred popular science articles published in various national and international journals.

Awards and Distinctions

Padmanabhan has received several national and international awards including the Birla Science Prize (1991), Shanti Swarup Bhatnagar Award (1996), the Millennium Medal (CSIR, 2000), Al-Khwarizmi International Award (2002), Sackler Distinguished Astronomer (Institute of Astronomy, Cambridge), Miegunah Fellowship Award (University of Melbourne, Australia, 2004) and the G.D.Birla Award for Scientific Research (2003). His work has won awards from the Gravity Research Foundation, USA four times, in 1984, 2002, 2003 and 2006. He is an elected Fellow of the three National Academies of Science in India. Some of his research papers have been rated as the most influential paper of the year. He has also been awarded the Padmashri award from the Government of India in the year 2007.

THOMAS CORWIN MENDENHALL

Thomas Corwin Mendenhall (October 4, 1841 – March 23, 1924) was an autodidact US physicist and meteorologist.

Biography

Mendenhall was born in Hanoverton, Ohio to Stephen Mendenhall, a farmer and carriage-maker, and Mary Thomas, and married Susan Allan Marple in 1870. The couple had one child. In 1852 the family moved to Marlboro, Ohio and Mendenhall became principal of the local primary school in 1858. He formalized his teaching qualifications at Southwest Normal School in 1861 with an *Instructor Normalis* qualification.

He taught at a number of high schools, gaining an impressive reputation as a teacher and educator until 1873 when, although lacking conventional academic credentials, he was appointed professor of physics and mechanics at the Ohio Agricultural and Mechanical College. The College ultimately became Ohio State University, Mendenhall being the first member of the original faculty.

In 1878, on the recommendation of Edward S. Morse, he was recruited to help the modernization of Meiji Era Japan as one of the *o-yatoi gaikokujin* (hired foreigners), serving as visiting professor of physics at Tokyo Imperial University. In connection with this appointment he founded a meteorological observatory in which systematic observations were made during his residence in Japan. From measurements using a Kater's pendulum of the force of gravity at the sea level and at the summit of Mount Fuji, Mendenhall deduced a value for the mass of the Earth that agreed closely with that which Francis Baily had obtained in England by another method. He also made a series of elaborate measurements of the wavelengths of the solar spectrum by means of a large spectrometer. He also became interested in earthquakes while in Japan, and was one of the founders of the Seismological Society of Japan. During his time in Japan, he also gave public lectures on various scientific topics to general audiences in temples and in theaters.

Returning to Ohio in 1881, Mendenhall was instrumental in developing the Ohio State Meteorological Service. He devised a system of weather signals for display on railroad trains. This method became general throughout the United States and Canada.

He became professor at the US Signal Corps in 1884, introducing of systematic observations of lightning, and investigating methods for determining ground temperatures. He was the first to establish stations in the United States for the systematic observation of earthquake phenomena.

Resigning in 1886, Mendenhall took up the presidency of the Rose Polytechnic Institute in Terre Haute, Indiana before becoming superintendent of the U.S. Coast and Geodetic Survey in 1889. During his time as superintendent, he issued the Mendenhall Order and oversaw the consequent transition of the United States's weights and measures from the customary system, based on that of England, to the metric system. Mendenhall remained a strong proponent for the official adoption of the metric system all his life. Also, as superintendent of the U.S. Coast and Geodetic Survey, he was also responsible for defining the exact national boundary between the United States (Alaska) and Canada. Mendenhall was president of the Worcester Polytechnic Institute from 1894 until 1901 when he emigrated to Europe. He returned to the United States in 1912. He was appointed to the Board of Trustees of Ohio State University in 1919, and is remembered for his successful efforts to close the College of Homeopathic Medicine and his unsuccessful effort to limit the capacity of Ohio Stadium to 45,000 seats, contending that it would never be able to fill to its design capacity of 63,000 seats. He continued to serve as a trustee until his death at Ravenna, Ohio in 1924.

THEODORE HAROLD MAIMAN

Theodore Harold "Ted" Maiman (July 11, 1927-May 5, 2007) was an American physicist who made the first working laser. Maiman received the Japan Prize in 1987. He was the author of a book titled *The Laser Odyssey*.

Biography

Maiman was born in Los Angeles, California, where in his teens, he earned college money by repairing electrical appliances and radios. He attended the University of Colorado and received a B.S. in engineering physics in 1949 then went on to do graduate work at Stanford University, where he received an M.S. in electrical engineering in 1951 and a Ph.D. in physics in 1955.

Maiman's laser, based on a synthetic ruby crystal grown by Dr. Ralph L. Hutcheson, was first operated on 16 May 1960 at Hughes Research Laboratories in Malibu, California. After a protracted legal battle, some key laser patents were awarded to Gordon Gould. After leaving Hughes, Maiman joined Quantatron where he was in charge of the laser activities. In 1962 Maiman became president of the newly formed Korad Corporation, a wholly owned subsidiary of Union Carbide. Union Carbide bought the laser assets owned by Quantatron. Korad was devoted to the research, development, and manufacture of lasers. All minority owned stock of Korad Corporation was exchanged for Union Carbide stock during the first five years. Not wishing to continue working for Union Carbide, he formed Maiman Associates in 1968.

Due to his work on the laser, he was twice nominated for a Nobel Prize and was given membership in both the National Academies of Science and Engineering. He received the Oliver E. Buckley Prize in 1966. He was the recipient of the 1983/84 Wolf Prize in Physics, and was inducted into the National Inventors Hall of Fame that same year.

Maiman died from systemic mastocytosis on May 5, 2007 in Vancouver, Canada, where he lived with his wife.

TSUNG-DAO LEE

Tsung-Dao Lee (born November 24, 1926) is a Chinese-born American physicist, well known for his work on parity violation, Lee Model, particle physics, relativistic heavy ion (RHIC) physics, nontopological solitons and soliton stars. In 1957, Lee, at age 31, with C. N. Yang received the Nobel Prize in Physics for work on the violation of parity law in weak interaction, which Chien-Shiung Wu experimentally verified. Lee is the second youngest Nobel laureate, and Lee and Yang were the first Chinese Laureates.

Biography

Lee's ancestral hometown is Suzhou, Jiangsu. He was born in Shanghai, China, and received his secondary education in Shanghai and Jiangxi. The first part of his university education (1943-1944) began at Zhejiang University, but was interrupted by the war, so he continued at the National Southwestern Associated University in Kunming the next year (1945).

Lee went to the University of Chicago in 1946 and completed his PhD with Enrico Fermi. He then worked with collaborators on phase transitions in statistical mechanics and polarons in condensed matter physics. In 1953, he became an assistant professor at Columbia University, and worked mainly in particle physics and field theory. Three years later, at age 29, Lee became the university's youngest full professor.

Over the years, Lee has pioneered and developed research ranging from symmetry violations in weak interactions to fields of high energy neutrino physics and RHIC physics. He remains an active member of the Columbia faculty and has held its highest academic rank, University Professor, since 1984. Currently, his interests have turned to the bosonic nature of high Tc superconductivity, the neutrino mapping matrix and new ways to solve Schrodinger equation.

Educational Activities

Soon after the re-establishment of China-American relations with the PRC, Lee and his wife, Hui-Chun Jeannette Chin, were able to go to China, where Lee gave a series of lectures and seminars, and organized the CUSPEA (China-U.S. Physics Examination and Application). In 1998, Lee established the Chun-Tsung Endowment Fund in Beijing in memory of his wife, Hui-Chun Chin, who died 3 years earlier. The Chun-Tsung scholarships are awarded to undergraduates, usually in their 2nd or 3rd year, at five universities, which are Fudan University, Lanzhou university, Suzhou University, Beijing University and Taiwan Tsing Hua University. Students selected for such scholarships are named "Chun-Tsung Scholars".

Personal Life

Chin and Lee were married in 1950 and have two sons: James and Stephen. Lee reads whodunit novels when he does not work on physics. His English given name differs dramatically from the then-existing Chinese Romanizations, such as Wade-Giles and Gwoyeu Romatzyh. Tsung-Dao Lee is also known as T.-D. Lee.

THOMAS EDVARD KROGH

Thomas Edvard *"Tom"* Krogh, (1936 – April 29, 2008) was a geochronologist and a former curator for the Royal Ontario Museum. He revolutionized the technique of radiometric uranium-lead dating with the development of new laboratory procedures and analytical methodologies. His discoveries have yielded an unprecedented level of precision in the dating of Precambrian rocks. Krogh's techniques have become the international defacto standard. The application of these techniques has provided a detailed understanding of the evolution of the Earth's Precambrian shield areas.

Education

Krogh was born in Peterborough, Ontario. Between 1955 and 1959, he studied geological engineering at Queen's University and held several jobs. For the first two summers he worked as a Geological Assistant at Noranda Mines and Triana Explorations, respectively. Between 1957 and 1959, he worked as a Teaching Assistant at the university. In 1958, he supported the Geological Survey of Canada as a Geological Assistant. In 1959, he was a Senior Assistant for the Ontario Department of Mines. Krogh obtained a MSc in geology from the university in 1960. He left Canada to study at the Massachusetts Institute of Technology, where he continued to work whenever he was not studying. His first job was as a Teaching Assistant in Mineralogy, then as a Geologist at Cominco, then as a Research Assistant in Geochronology. In 1964, he obtained his PhD in geochronology.

Career

Between 1964 and 1975, Krogh worked at the Carnegie Institution in Washington, D.C. He was a post-doctoral fellow in isotopic geochemistry until 1964 when he became a Scientific Staff Member. From 1964 to 1970, he specialized in Rubidium–Strontium dating of minerals and rocks. In 1970, he switched to specializing in the Uranium-Lead dating of zircons and other minerals. In 1975, Krogh returned to Canada to work as the Associate Curator/Director of the Royal Ontario Museum's Geochronology Laboratory. In 1976, he became a Professor in the Geology Department of the University of Toronto. In 1978, he shifted to be Graduate Faculty Member with the university. In 1979, he returned to the Royal Ontario Museum to be their Full Curator. He worked on the Lithoprobe project between 1991 and 1996.

Discovery

Krogh's main focus of research has been geochronology, an effort which has long involved the integration of field work (particularly in high-grade gneisses of the Grenville Province) with clean-laboratory isotope dilution techniques. With uranium-lead (U-Pb) dating he developed a simple, yet innovative air-abrasion technique for removing exterior portions of minerals that may have suffered Pb-loss, which, combined with improved magnetic separation methods, greatly improved the accuracy and precision of zircon geochronology. In addition, Krogh's laboratory methods for the dissolution of minerals and the subsequent chemical separation of trace quantities of uranium and lead resulted in a significant reduction of environmental Pb contamination (blank) to ultra-low levels, and permitted increasingly small quantities of mineral grains and sub-grain domains to be analyzed. In the mid-1980's, he was instrumental in producing a synthetic 205Pb isotopic tracer (spike) that was distributed for use in U-Pb geochronology laboratories worldwide. The application of Krogh's novel and innovative techniques has revolutionized U-Pb geochronology and permitted the ages of rocks to be determined with unprecedented accuracy and precision. Most of what is known of the Earth's 4.5 billion-year history has been placed in precise geological sequence using these dating methods.

T. H. CLARK

Thomas Henry Clark, (December 3, 1893 – April 28, 1996) was a Canadian geologist who is considered to have been one of the nation's top scientists of the 20th century. He was a professor who authored over 100 scientific publications. After his death, a mineral was named in his honour.

Clark was born in London, England. He emigrated to the United States and attended Harvard University. In 1917, he graduated with an A.B. The start of World War I interrupted his studies. He enlisted in the U.S. Army Medical Corps (1917-19) and served in France. Clark returned to Harvard after the war and obtained his A.M. (1921) and Ph.D. (1923).

Career

In 1924, Clark moved to Montreal to take an assistant professor position in the Geology Department at McGill University. He began by teaching geology, palaeontology and stratigraphy. In 1926, Clark began a major project to map the geology of the Quebec Appalachian Mountains along the U.S. border in the Eastern Townships. He published a series of papers on the geology and palaeontology of the Townships. These papers established him as a leading geologist in Canada.

In 1927, he married Olive Marguerite Melvenia Prichard, a former student. They had a daughter, Joan. Clark served as Director of McGill's Redpath Museum from 1932 to 1952. He was largely responsible for personally collecting many of the museum's fossils. After ten years, Clark shifted his focus away from the Eastern Townships. He discovered that early maps of Laval were incorrect, so he proposed the production of a completely new map of the Montreal area. He began that project as well as a project to map the St. Lawrence lowlands in 1938. By the late 1960s, Montreal's development and various projects along the St. Lawrence seaway necessitated a revision of Clark's previous geological studies of the area. He was charged with undertaking the field work. This time the work involved capturing information from the many oil and gas and engineering projects, as well as acquiring core samples from excavations for future research.

Over the years, Clark authored more than 100 scientific publications. He co-authored with Colin W. Stearn *The Geological Evolution of North America* (1960), which was a standard text in university-level geology.

THOMAS BARGER

Thomas Barger (1909-1986) was an American geologist, explorer, miner, businessman and former CEO of the Arabian American Oil Company (formerly Aramco now Saudi Aramco).

Biography

Thomas Barger was born in Minneapolis, Minnesota in 1909 to Mary Barger and Michael Thomas Barger.

He grew up in Linton, North Dakota and graduated from the University of North Dakota's College of Engineering in Grand Forks, North Dakota with a degree in mining and metallurgy in 1931. After college he worked as a surveyor and miner in Canada, an engineer, assayer and assistant manager of a silver and radium mine in the Northwest Territories and as an assistant professor of mining at the University of North Dakota.

He accepted a position at the Anaconda Copper Mining Company but the Great Depression and falling copper prices resulted in his being forced to find work elsewhere. In 1937 Barger interviewed with J.O. Nomland, the chief geologist at the Standard Oil Company of California, in San Francisco and accepted a job as a surveyor in Saudi Arabia. He married Kathleen Elizabeth Ray on November 18, 1937 shortly before heading off to Saudi Arabia by himself for what ended up being three years exploring potential oil sites in the Saudi Arabian desert along with fellow American geologists Max Steineke, Jerry Harriss, Ernie Berg and others as well as a group of Bedouin guides headed by Khamis bin Rimthan of the Ajman tribe.

After the men discovered Saudi Arabia's vast fields of oil Barger began a career with Aramco that would last 32 years. He started as a surveyor and geologist then worked as the director of Local Government Relations, was the company representative to the Saudi government and was manager for Concession Affairs.

Fluent in Arabic, Barger was a key element in the company's relationship with the Saudi government and people. He ensured that the goal of the company was to be mutually beneficial, training and employing thousands of Saudis and eventually becoming a Saudi run and owned entity (which it is today). In 1957 Barger became a vice president and assistant to President Norman Hardy. In 1959 Barger became president of Aramco and in 1961 he was appointed the company's Chief Executive Officer. Kathleen and Thomas lived in Dhahran and had six children. Barger retired from the company in 1969.

TRACY SONNEBORN

Tracy Morton Sonneborn (October 19, 1905–January 26, 1981) was an American biologist. His life's study was of the protozoan group *Paramecium.*

Non-Mendelian Inheritance

In the late 1950s he conducted an elegant series of experiments in his endeavours to discover what it is that mediates the synchronised movement of the paramecium's cilia. These minuscule hair-like projections enable the cell to 'swim'. They move together and paddle the cell through the water in which it lives. The paramecium is a single-cell organism, so has nothing remotely resembling a brain. Yet its cilia move together like dancers in a ballet. How is it that their movements are co-ordinated?

Sonneborn surgically removed a small section of cell wall and replaced it rotated by 180 degrees. The cilia in the replaced section continued to 'wave' in the same direction as they had before surgery, *i.e.* now in antiphase to the others. What was remarkable is that both daughters of paramecia on which this operation had been performed also showed the same trait of a reverse phase wave in a similar area of their cell wall, as did, to a lesser extent, the granddaughter cells. It is a mark of his excellence as a scientist that he should have taken the trouble to follow the fate of subsequent generations and so be able to make this observation. It may seem surprising that the clear evidence for non-Mendelian inheritance should have been largely overlooked by the scientific community.

Further research was at that time limited because the available staining techniques to allow electron microscopy denatured the microtubules which 'power' the cilia so their presence in cells could not be seen. It may also be that, as at that time the mechanisms of genetic inheritance in DNA were becoming open to investigation, this example of non-Mendelian inheritance was not of great interest to the scientific community.

THEODORE PUCK

Theodore Puck (born September 24, 1916-died November 6, 2005) was an American geneticist born in Chicago, Illinois. He attended Chicago public schools and obtained his bachelors and masters degree from the University of Chicago.

Puck was an early pioneer of "somatic cell genetics" and single-cell plating (*i.e.* "cloning".) This work allowed the genetics of human and other mammalian cells to be studied in detail. Pucks key work ultimately made modern genetics, such as the human genome and other mammalian genome projects, possible.

Puck made many basic discoveries in several areas. His team which found that humans had 46 chromosomes rather than 48 which had earlier been believed. He developed the CHO cell line from chinese hamster ovarian cells for this work. These cells are still widely utilized in the biopharmaceutical industry. Puck studied X-rays and cellular mutations. He also isolated and studied cellular mutations.

Puck has won a number of honours for his work most notably the Albert Lasker Award for Basic Medical Research in 1958. In 1973 he was awarded the Louisa Gross Horwitz Prize from Columbia University together with Renato Dulbecco and Harry Eagle.

Dulbecco won the Nobel Prize in medicine in 1975. He also founded the Eleanor Roosevelt Institute at the University of Denver where he was an Emeritus Professor. A member of the National Academy of Science since 1960, Puck published more than 200 papers on topics including Alzheimer's Disease and Downs Syndrome, and optimising radiotherapy dosages for the treatment of cancer.

He died following complications from a broken hip.

THEOPHILUS PAINTER

Theophilus Shickel Painter (August 22, 1889 – October 5, 1969) was an American zoologist known for his work in identifying genes in fruit flies (Drosophila). He did so by applying the incredible detail that had just been discovered to be visible in the giant polytene chromosomes in the salivary glands of Drosophila and other Dipteran larvae. Painter joined the faculty at the University of Texas in 1916 and, except for military duty during World War I, stayed there his whole career. He was, in succession, associate professor, professor and distinguished professor of zoology. He served as acting president (1944-1946) and president (1946-1952) of the University of Texas and retired from active teaching in 1966. Painter is also known for his early study of human chromosomes. In 1921 he first gave the number 24 for the count of human meiotic chromosomes. He had tried to count the tangled mass of chromosomes he could see under a microscope in spermatocytes in slices of testicle and arrived at the figure of 24. "I feel confident that this is correct," he said. Others later repeated his experiment in other ways and agreed the number was 24. If there were 24 chromosomes in spermatocytes, there must be an equal number contributed by the female and the human chromosome number must be 48. For over 30 years nobody disputed this 'fact.'

Then in 1955 Joe Hin Tjio, using better techniques, looked at the chromosomes in human somatic cells and plainly saw 46 chromosomes. Together with Albert Levan, Tjio published this revolutionary finding in early 1956, and the human chromosome number was finally revised. The wonder of Painter's work is not that it was in error but that, given the almost indecipherable mass of chromosomes he examined, he came so very close to the correct human chromosome number.

TOM MANIATIS

Tom Maniatis born 8 May 1943 in Denver, Colorado is an American professor of molecular and cellular biology. Maniatis is a graduate of the University of Colorado and one of the founders of modern molecular cloning. At the age of 28 he received a PhD in Molecular Biology from Vanderbilt University, and he received Honourary PhD's from the University of Athens and the Watson School of Cold Spring Harbor Laboratory. Maniatis carried out postdoctoral studies with Professor Mark Ptashne at Harvard University and with Dr. Fred Sanger at the Medical Research Council Laboratory of Molecular Biology in Cambridge England. Maniatis has held faculty positions at Harvard University, The Cold Spring Harbor Laboratory and the California Institute of Technology.

Tom Maniatis has worked at the forefront of the field of molecular and cellular biology throughout his career. Maniatis not only determined the nucleotide sequence of one of lambda's regulatory elements while working in Fred Sanger's lab without the aid of standard procedures for DNA sequencing, he also perfected protocols for identifying and isolating genes. Dr. Maniatis is also credited with being a pioneer in the development of gene cloning technology. In 1982 Maniatis along with Joe Sambrook and Edward Fritsch wrote "Molecular Cloning-A Laboratory Manual", which has had an enormous impact on life sciences. Maniatis has received numerous awards including the 1981 Eli Lilly Research Award in Microbiology and Immunology from the American Society of Microbiology, the 1985 Richard Lounsbery Award for Biology and the 1998 Novartis Drew Award in Biomedical Research, the 2000 AMA Scientific Achievement Award, and the 2001 Pasarow Award in Cancer Research from the Pasarow Foundation. Maniatis was elected to the U.S. National Academy of Sciences in 1985.

Maniatis is also a pioneer in the biotechnology industry, having cofounded Genetics Institute in 1980, ProScript Pharma in 1994, and Acceleron Pharma in 2004. His contributions to biotechnology were recognized by the Jacob Heskel Gabbay Award in Biotechnology and Medicine, Brandeis University, in 1999.

Today Maniatis is the Thomas H. Lee Professor of Molecular and Cellular Biology, where in 1981 he returned from Caltech as chairman of the Department of Biochemistry and Molecular Biology at the Harvard University. Maniatis' current research focuses on the mechanisms of gene regulation in innate immunity and in the brain. Recently, his laboratory has initiated studies of the disease amyotrophic lateral sclerosis (ALS).

Personal

Tom Maniatis family origins are Peloponese. To his Hellenic roots, he attributes his good work ethic. "What I love about Greece," he says, "is the warmth and friendliness of the people and the fact that the cities as well as the countryside are so beautiful."

TAK WAH MAK

Tak Wah Mak, (born 1946 in China) is an award-winning Canadian researcher who has worked in a variety of areas including biochemistry, immunology, and cancer genetics. He first became widely known for his pioneering work in the genetics of immunology.

Born in southern China in 1946 and raised in Hong Kong, Mak studied biochemistry and biophysics at the University of Wisconsin. In the early 1970s, he earned his PhD in biochemistry from the University of Alberta, in Edmonton. After he obtained his degree, Dr. Mak moved to Toronto and became a Canadian citizen.

In 1984, Dr. Mak published his work on the cloning of T-cell receptor genes; as of 2005, that article has been cited nearly 1200 times. Dr. Mak's role in advancing the use of genetically-altered mice in scientific study has led to important breakthroughs in immunology and understanding cancer at the cellular level. The basic research in breast cancer conducted by Dr. Mak has been published in top international scientific journals and he has given several keynote addresses at breast cancer symposia across Canada and the United States. In spite of offers from prestigious institutions around the world, Dr. Mak remained committed to Canada's scientific community. In 1993, Dr. Mak received support to establish the AMGEN Research Institute in Toronto. As of 2005, AMGEN-produced papers have been cited more than 40,000 times.

Dr. Mak holds Honourary Doctoral Degrees from numerous universities in North America and Europe. He is an Officer of the

Order of Canada and has been elected a Foreign Associate of the National Academy of Sciences (USA) as well as a Fellow of the Royal Society of London (UK.) He has won international recognition in the forms of the Emil von Behring Prize, the King Faisal Prize for Medicine, the Gairdner Foundation International Award, the Sloan Prize of the General Motors Cancer Foundation, the Paul Ehrlich Prize and the Novartis Prize in Immunology. In 2004 Mak became the director of the Advanced Medical Discovery Institute and the Campbell Family Institute for Breast Cancer Research. He is also the senior scientist, division of Stem Cell and Developmental Biology, Advanced Medical Discovery Institute/Ontario Cancer Institute. Since 1984, he has been a Professor in the Departments of Medical Biophysics and Immunology at the University of Toronto.

THOMAS J. HUDSON

Thomas James Hudson, M.D., (born June 12, 1961) is a Canadian genome scientist noted for his leading role in the generation of physical maps of the human and mouse genomes and also his role in the International HapMap Project whose goal is to develop a haplotype map of the human genome. As director of the McGill University and Genome Quebec Innovation Centre, which he established, Hudson and his team have made a number of discoveries in human genetics. These include genes mutated in rare diseases and genes involved in complex diseases such as asthma, type II diabetes and inflammatory bowel disease. In July 2006, he was appointed president and scientific director of the Ontario Institute for Cancer Research. He is also editor-in-chief of the journal *Human Genetics*. Thomas Hudson is married and has five children.

New Horizons

In July 2006, Hudson announced that he was leaving Montreal to lead the newly created Ontario Institute for Cancer Research in Toronto, Ontario which will focus on the genomics of cancer. Until his successor is announced, Hudson will remain acting scientific director of the McGill University and Genome Quebec Innovation Centre.

Bibliography

A. J. Ihde: *The Development of Modern Chemistry*, Dover Publications, New York, 1984.

Benson J.: *The Pictorial Field-Book of the Revolution,* New York, Harper, 1859.

Carvill, James: *Famous Names in Engineering*, London; Boston, Butterworths, 1981.

Elasser, W. M.: *The Chief Abstractions of Biology*, New York and Amsterdam, North Holland-Elsevier, 1975.

Fort, Charles: *New Lands*, Boni and Liveright, 1923.

Harold A.: *Decision at the Chesapeake,* New York, C. N. Potter, 1964.

Ireland, Norma Olin: *Index to Scientists of the World, from Ancient to Modern Times: Biographies and Portraits*, Boston, Faxon, 1962.

Janet R. Carroll: *The Atlas of Breeding Birds in New York State,* Ithaca, Cornell University Press, 1988

Kamal Kishore : *Economic History of Moghul India: An Annotated Bibliography, 1526-1875*, Calcutta, Santiniketan, 1991.

Lakomski, G. : *Knowing Educational Administration*, Oxford, Pergamon, 1991.

Marson, Ron: *Magnetism*, Canby, OR, TOPS Learning Systems (Science with simple things series), 1983.

Pelletier, Paul A.: *Prominent Scientists : an Index to Collective Biographies.* 3d ed. New York, Neal-Schuman, 1994.

Schaller, G. B.: *The Serengeti Lion*, Chicago, Ill., University of Chicago Press, 1972.

Waldron, Jeremy: *God, Locke and Equality*, Cambridge Uni, Press, 2002.

Zepp, R. G., Sonntag, Ch.: *The Role of Nonliving Organic Matter in the Earth's Carbon Cycle,* Wiley, Chichester, 1995.

Index